THE BOOKS OF

PHILIPPIANS & COLOSSIANS

JOY AND COMPLETENESS IN CHRIST

AMG *Publishers*

CHATTANOOGA, TENNESSEE

TWENTY-FIRST CENTURY
BIBLICAL COMMENTARY SERIES

THE BOOKS OF
PHILIPPIANS
& COLOSSIANS

JOY AND COMPLETENESS
IN CHRIST

ROBERT
GROMACKI

GENERAL EDITORS

MAL COUCH & ED HINDSON

ISBN 0–89957–815–2

Cover Design by Phillip Rodgers
Interior Design and typesetting by Warren Baker
Edited and Proofread by Warren Baker, Patrick Belville, and Weller
Editorial Services, Chippewa Lake, MI

Printed in the United States of America
08 07 06 05 04 –R– 7 6 5 4 3 2

*With appreciation to these schools that have
spiritually enriched my family and me*

*Baptist Bible College and Seminary
Cedarville University
Dallas Theological Seminary
Grace Theological Seminary
Practical Bible College*

Twenty-First Century Biblical Commentary Series

Mal Couch, Th.D., and Ed Hindson, D.Phil.

The New Testament has guided the Christian Church for over two thousand years. This one testament is made up of twenty-seven books, penned by godly men through the inspiration of the Holy Spirit. It tells us of the life of Jesus Christ, His atoning death for our sins, His miraculous resurrection, His ascension back to heaven, and the promise of His second coming. It also tells the story of the birth and growth of the Church and the people and principles that shaped it in its earliest days. The New Testament concludes with the book of Revelation pointing ahead to the glorious return of Jesus Christ.

Without the New Testament, the message of the Bible would be incomplete. The Old Testament emphasizes the promise of a coming Messiah. It constantly points us ahead to the One who is coming to be the King of Israel and the Savior of the world. But the Old Testament ends with this event still unfulfilled. All of its ceremonies, pictures, types, and prophecies are left awaiting the arrival of the "Lamb of God who takes away the sin of the world!" (John 1:29).

The message of the New Testament represents the timeless truth of God. As each generation seeks to apply that truth to its specific context, an up-to-date commentary needs to be created just for them. The editors and authors of the Twenty-First Century Biblical Commentary Series have endeavored to do just that. This team of scholars represents conservative, evangelical, and dispensational scholarship at its best. The individual authors may differ on minor points of interpretation, but all are convinced that the Old and New Testaments teach a dispensational framework for biblical history. They also hold to a pretribulational and premillennial understanding of biblical prophecy.

The French scholar René Pache reminded each succeeding generation, "If the power of the Holy Spirit is to be made manifest anew among us, it is of primary importance that His message should regain its due place. Then we shall be able to put the enemy to flight by the sword of the Spirit which is the Word of God."

Paul's New Testament letters exhibit common structural and stylistic similarities. Philippians and Colossians are especially unique in their emphasis on practical Christian living. Moises Silva observes, "Philippians and Colossians correspond to each other so closely, both structurally and conceptually, that the relationship deserves special attention." Therefore, their combination in this commentary follows a natural literary pattern.

In commenting on the letter to the Philippians, James Montgomery Boyce writes, "Philippians is at once so simple and so profound that it speaks with power to Christians at all levels of their spiritual maturity and at the same time, calls the attention of many non-believers to all of the essential doctrines of the Christian faith."

Similarly, Herbert Carson points out that Colossians also speaks to believers and unbelievers alike. He writes, "Faced with the spread of false teaching, Paul turns our hearts and minds to the Person and work of Christ with whose glory he himself is so taken up. For this reason the letter has a message for every age, and especially for our own day."

Contents

SECTION 1

Joy in Christ

The Book of Philippians

CHAPTER 1

Background of Philippians

Writer

The contents of the epistle strongly support the traditional view that Paul wrote Philippians. The author calls himself "Paul" (1:1). Not only is Timothy closely associated with Paul in the greeting and in the ministry, but Paul regarded him as his spiritual son (1:1; 2:19–23; cf. 1 Tim. 1:2). The reference to Timothy is significant because he was on Paul's missionary team that originally evangelized Philippi (Acts 16).

The autobiographical background, cited by the author (3:4–6), harmonizes with the details of Paul's life as recorded in the other Pauline letters and in the book of Acts. The historical background for the writing of the letter fits into Paul's known life. He was in prison, probably in Rome (1:7, 13), but he expected to be released and to revisit Philippi (1:25–27; 2:24; cf. 1 Tim. 1:3).

Peter O'Brian writes about the Pauline authorship:

Philippians has generally been accepted as a genuine letter of Paul. The apostle's claim to have been its author has rarely been challenged, and for good reason. The picture the writer draws of himself coincides with that known of Paul from other sources, including Galatians and Acts. So the disclosure of his inner feelings (Phil. 1:18–24), the description of his present situation (1:12–13) and the names of his friends and coworkers (2:19–24), and his references to the gifts sent to him from Philippi and Thessalonica (4:15–16; cf. Acts 17:1–9; 2 Cor. 8:1–5) are consistent with what we know of him from elsewhere.

. . . Further, echoes of Philippians may be heard in the writings of Clement (ca. A.D. 95), Ignatius (ca. A.D. 107), Hermas (ca. A.D. 140), Justin

Martyr (ca. A.D. 165), and others. Apparently there was never any real question in the minds of the Church Fathers about the authorship or canonical authority of Philippians, for a number of them not only quote from the letter but assign it to Paul as well. Philippians also appears in the oldest extant lists of NT writings, the Muratorian Canon (later second century) and the canon of Marcion (d. ca. A.D. 160).[1]

City of Philippi

The city of Philippi was located on a fertile plain about nine miles from the Aegean Sea, northwest of the island of Thasos. Neapolis served as the seaport. In New Testament times it was regarded as "the chief city of that part of Macedonia, and a colony" (Acts 16:12), but Thessalonica was actually the capital of that Roman province.

The city's inhabitants were regarded as legal Roman citizens who had the right to vote and to govern themselves. Because no Jewish synagogue was located there, scholars believe the citizens of Philippi were anti-Semitic. Large numbers of Jews could be found in other Greek cities, such as Thessalonica, Berea, and Corinth.

Originally, the city was a Phoenician mining town because of its proximity to gold mines located in nearby mountains and on the island of Thasos. Later, Philip of Macedon, the father of Alexander the Great, took the city from the empire of Thrace and renamed it after himself.

Subsequently, a crucial battle between the coalition of Octavius and Antony and that of Brutus and Cassius was fought there. The former won, thus ending the Roman republic in 42 B.C. As a Roman colony, the city grew in prominence because it was on the main road from Rome to the province of Asia.

Today the city lies in ruins. The site has been excavated by archaeologists who have uncovered a marketplace, the foundation of a larger arched gateway, and an amphitheater dating back to Roman times.

> The population of Philippi consisted largely of Roman military personnel, either retired legionaries and officers who made it their permanent home or those who were stationed there on duty. Descendants of the original colonists helped to preserve the Roman atmosphere. They guarded their privileges jealously and resented any activity that might evoke official disapproval. The Jewish community in Philippi was too small to support a synagogue but held a weekly prayer meeting outside the city on the river bank. . . . The Roman population would probably possess more wealth than did the native Greeks.[2]

Establishment of the Church

Soon after Paul and Silas started out on Paul's second missionary journey, they recruited Timothy to assist them (Acts 15:36—16:5). Forbidden by the Holy Spirit to preach in Asia and Bithynia, the three came to the coastal city of Troas. Paul there received a vision directing the team to go to Macedonia (Acts 16:9). Luke joined the team, and the four departed for Neapolis in Macedonia the next day. This was the first time Paul brought the gospel to Europe.

The missionaries left Neapolis for Philippi, where they ministered to a group of women on the Sabbath by the river, since there was no synagogue in the city. Lydia, a merchant woman of Thyatira, and her household believed and were baptized (Acts 16:15; cf. 16:40).

The next significant event in Philippi occurred when Paul cast out a demonic spirit from a slave girl. Her enraged masters seized Paul and Silas, dragged them to the city's rulers, and brought a false accusation against them (Acts 16:20-21).[3] Because of the Philippian antagonism toward Jews, the multitude beat them and cast them into prison.

At midnight Paul and Silas prayed, sang, and communicated their faith to the other prisoners. An earthquake shook the prison's foundations, opened the doors, and loosed the chains from the walls. The jailer, fearful that the prisoners under his care had fled, was about to commit suicide when Paul stopped him. Paul then led the jailer and his household to a saving knowledge of Christ.

At his release the next day, Paul revealed that both Silas and he had Roman citizenship and that they had been wrongfully beaten. They then went to Lydia's house, ministered to the believers, and departed for Thessalonica, leaving Luke behind.[4] The young church at Philippi began with an unusual membership of a converted businesswoman, a former demonic soothsayer, a jailer, and perhaps some prisoners.

Close contact between Paul and the Philippian church was maintained after this initial contact. The church sent gifts to Paul on two separate occasions during his ministry in Thessalonica (4:14-16; cf. Acts 17:1-9). Silas was probably sent by Paul from Athens to do some additional work there (Acts 17:15-16; 18:5; 1 Thess. 3:1-6).

During his third missionary journey, Paul went into the province of Macedonia, with an obvious stop at Philippi (Acts 20:1). After three months in Corinth, he revisited Macedonia and Philippi before he left for Jerusalem (Acts 20:2-6). On this final contact, Luke rejoined Paul and accompanied the apostle.[5]

Time and Place of Writing

News of Paul's imprisonment in Rome had come to the Philippian church by some unknown means, and it created a great deal of concern and anxiety. To get firsthand information on Paul's predicament, the church authorized Epaphroditus to go to Rome to confer with Paul and to present him with a monetary gift for his financial needs (4:10, 14–18). When Epaphroditus saw that Paul's material needs were much greater than the size of the Philippian gift, he stayed on in Rome, working to raise more money for Paul (2:25, 30). In so doing, Epaphroditus became very ill and almost died (2:27, 30). Word of his severe sickness somehow reached Philippi and caused a new concern for the church (2:26). When Epaphroditus discovered that the church knew about his illness, he became distressed (2:26).

During the time period covered by the last communications, God had healed Epaphroditus totally, or at least sufficiently, so that he was well enough to return to Philippi (2:27). Paul determined then to send Epaphroditus back to Philippi so that the church might rejoice at his return (2:28). The apostle thus used this occasion to write this epistle and to send it to Philippi by way of Epaphroditus. Paul's confidence in his imminent acquittal and release (1:25; 2:24) probably indicates that it was written near the end of Paul's two years of imprisonment at Rome (A.D. 59—61).

Some have speculated that Paul wrote this letter from a prison in Ephesus rather than in Rome. There are at least four arguments against and criticisms of that viewpoint. First, Paul planned to send Timothy to Philippi, and he did just that from Ephesus (2:19–23; cf. Acts 19:22). But why did Paul not mention Erastus in the epistle if these two sendings of Timothy are identical?

Second, it is possible that there was a praetorian guard[6] stationed at Ephesus (1:13) and that "Caesar's household" referred to the imperial civil servants located there (4:22); but the natural use of those phrases argues for a Roman setting.

Third, Luke is not mentioned in Philippians although he was in Rome with Paul and was listed both in Colossians and Philemon. Since Luke was not with Paul in Ephesus (Acts 19), that city seems to be the more likely place of origin. However, Luke is not mentioned in Ephesians either. And, if Paul did write from Ephesus, why did he not include the names of Gaius and Aristarchus, who were with him in that city (Acts 19:29)?

Fourth, the Ephesian proponents say that too much time would have been involved in the five exchanges of communication; however, it only required a month to travel from Rome to Philippi. These exchanges could have taken place within a six-month period, well within the two-year limits of

Paul's Roman imprisonment. Until more objective evidence is forthcoming, the traditional view that Paul wrote from Rome must stand.

Purposes

Paul learned about the spiritual needs of the church through conversations with Epaphroditus and with those who came to Rome with the report of the church's concern over Epaphroditus's illness. First, Paul wanted to relieve their anxiety over the circumstances of his imprisonment (1:1–30). They thought that the apostle's ministry had been brought to an abrupt stop, but Paul assured them that God was using the episode for the advancement of the gospel.

Paul had several other reasons for writing. There apparently was a growing disunity among the members as evidenced by Paul's appeal to them to manifest humility and unity (2:1–8). Paul also informed the church of a possible imminent visit by Timothy (2:18–24); explained the reasons behind Epaphroditus's sickness and healing (2:25–30); warned against the deceitful tactics and doctrines of the Judaizers (3:1—4:1); admonished Euodia and Syntyche to maintain spiritual and sisterly unity (4:2–3); prescribed truth that would give the members mental and emotional stability to replace their anxiety (4:4–9); expressed thankfulness for their financial assistance (4:10–20); and shared greetings with all of them (4:21–23).

In conclusion, Harrison writes:

> Warning is issued against Judaizing propagandists with whom Paul was well acquainted from long experience (3:2ff.). More gentle is the rebuke of the perfectionists in the ranks of the saints (3:15). Once more the language becomes severe in reference to sensualists and materialists (3:18–29).

> Finally, the apostle writes to encourage his readers in the conduct of Christian life—in suffering (1:27–30), in witness (2:16), in the cultivation of joy and peace (4:4–7) and of high and holy thoughts (4:8)—in fine [Latin, "towards the goal"], to join in imitation of the apostle as he runs the race incident to the upward calling in Christ (3:13–17).[7]

Distinctive Features

The intimate relationship that existed between Paul and the Philippian church can be seen in his frequent use of the first person singular personal pronoun. In these four short chapters, there are over one hundred occurrences of such words as *I*, *me*, and *my*. In fact, the pronoun *I* can be found fifty-two times.

This fact does not mean that Paul lacked humility; rather, it shows the natural person-to-person rapport between him and the people. Thus, of all the epistles written to churches, Philippians is the most personal.

Within the book is a strong emphasis on the word *gospel*, found nine times in various constructions: "participation in the gospel" (1:5); "defense and confirmation of the gospel" (1:7); "greater progress of the gospel" (1:12); "defense of the gospel" (1:16); "conduct yourselves in a manner worthy of the gospel of Christ" (1:27a); "faith of the gospel" (1:27b); "served with me in the furtherance of the gospel" (2:22); in *the cause of* the gospel" (4:3); and "the first preaching of the gospel" (4:15).

This book has a traditional reputation of being the epistle of joy. Various forms of the words *joy* and *rejoice* are found eighteen times. This theme can be seen in the key verse: "Rejoice in the Lord always: again I will say, rejoice!" (4:4).

One of the greatest Christological passages occurs within this book as an example of genuine humility and obedience (2:5–11). It speaks of Christ's eternal deity, incarnation, humiliation, death, resurrection, and exaltation via ascension. Theologians have called it the *kenosis* passage, based on the Greek text underlying the phrase: "But emptied Himself" (2:7). The three Greek words of this phrase (*alla heauton ekenōsen*) are literally translated: "But himself he emptied." The kenosis concept takes its name from a transliteration of the Greek word *ekenōsen*. The question thus raised is: Of what did Christ empty Himself when He became man? Did He empty Himself of His divine attributes? If He did, then he was less than God when He walked on the earth. But He was just as much God when he was in the womb of Mary or when he hung on the cross as He was when He created the universe. Rather, Christ surrendered the independent exercise of His divine attributes when He became incarnate. He had them, but He did not always use them. He learned, hungered, and grew weary; these are characteristics of His human nature. However, He did use His divine attributes at times under the control of the Holy Spirit. He forgave sin, created food, gave life to the dead, and walked on water. The emptying of Himself also involved the veiling of the outward display of His deity and glory in human flesh. No halo was upon His head, nor did a glow radiate from His face. Only on the Mount of Transfiguration was His glory permitted to shine through His flesh (Matt. 17:1–13). He also emptied Himself of the rights of sovereignty in order to become a servant to others.

> St. Paul steps forward to check the growing tendency [of feuds]. This he does with characteristic delicacy, striking not less surely because he strikes for the most part indirectly. He begins by hinting to them that he is no partisan: he offers prayers and thanksgiving for *all*; he hopes well of *all*; he looks upon *all* as companions in grace; his heart yearns after *all* in Christ

Jesus. He entreats them later on, to be "steadfast in one spirit," to "strive together with one mind for the faith of the Gospel." He implores them by all their deepest Christian experiences, by all their truest natural impulses, to "be of one mind," to "do nothing from party-spirit or from vainglory."

He urges the Philippians generally to exhibit to the world a spectacle of *forbearance.* He reminds them of the peace of God, which surpasses all the thoughts of men. He entreats them lastly, by all that is noble and beautiful and good, to hear and to obey. If they do this, the God of peace will be with them.[8]

The book of Philippians also provides an insight into the motivations of Paul: "For to me, to live is Christ, and to die is gain" (1:21). Paul wanted Christ to be magnified in his body, whether through living or dying for Him. He later elaborated upon these goals (3:10–14).

CHAPTER 2

Opening Remarks
Philippians 1:1-2

Preview:

Both Paul and Timothy send greetings, as the servants of Christ to the church at Philippi, specifically addressing the leadership of the overseers and deacons. As Paul usually does, he calls the believers there "the saints in Christ." The rest of his greeting is typical of the great apostle; he wants the people to experience both grace and peace from God the Father and the Master, the Lord Jesus Christ.

The church at Philippi was anxious over Paul's welfare. They were afraid that his ministry might be over and that he might even be martyred by the Roman government officials. Their apprehension was heightened by an awareness of the severe illness of their messenger, Epaphroditus. These conditions caused within their own assembly a fear of persecution (1:28), a spirit of disunity (2:2-3; 4:2), a sense of dissatisfaction (2:14-15), an openness to false teaching (3:2, 17-19), and anxiety (4:6-7). Paul had to assure them that God was in control. They needed a change of perspective. Adverse circumstances had to be viewed as opportunities to proclaim the gospel (1:12). Selfishness had to be replaced by selflessness (2:4). A right relationship to God had to be established for both salvation and service (3:7-8, 13). And thanksgiving and contentment had to replace worry (4:6, 11-12).

The physical recovery of Epaphroditus and his return to Philippi thus provided Paul with an opportunity to inform the church about his response to the Roman imprisonment. Both the epistle and the homecoming of their friend were designed to produce a new joy within their hearts.

11

The Salutation (1:1)

The opening remarks contain what is normally found within a Pauline greeting: identification of self, associate, and readers; a blessing; and a prayer of thanksgiving (Rom. 1:1–8; Col. 1:1–3; 1 Thess. 1:1–2; 2 Thess. 1:1–3).

Paul's Name

In his pre-Christian life, Paul was known as Saul of Tarsus, the persecutor of the church (Acts 7:58; 8:1, 3; 9:1). When Christ revealed Himself to the young Pharisee, He addressed him as Saul (Acts 9:4). For the next nine years of his Christian life, he maintained the usage of his given name.

At the beginning of his first missionary journey, however, Saul changed his name to Paul (Acts 13:9, 13). On that occasion on Cyprus, Paul demonstrated his apostolic authority for the first time by blinding the sorcerer Elymas, who had resisted the gospel message. Through this miracle, Paul won his first convert, the Roman proconsul Sergius Paulus (Acts 13:7–12). Saul may have assumed the name of Paul as a constant reminder of the grace and power of God who can save sinners.[1]

The Latin *paulus* means "little" or "small." Before God, Paul saw himself as "the very least of all saints" (Eph. 3:8). Late in life, he still viewed himself as the "foremost" of sinners (1 Tim. 1:15). Thus, the name change may have manifested the change from the pride of Phariseeism to the humility of Christianity.

Born into the Jewish tribe of Benjamin, Saul was probably named by his parents after the first king of Israel (3:5; cf. 1 Sam. 9:1–2). King Saul, who was physically tall, was humbled by God because of his pride and arrogant self-will. Saul, the proud Pharisee, was also humbled by God to become a dedicated servant of Jesus Christ.

J. B. Lightfoot notes:

The official title of Apostle is omitted here, as in the Epistles to the Thessalonians. In writing to the Macedonian churches, with which his relations were so close and affectionate, St. Paul would feel an appeal to his authority to be unnecessary. The same omission is found in the letter to Philemon, and must be similarly explained. He does not enforce a command as a superior, but asks a favour as a friend. In direct contrast to this tone is the strong assertion of his Apostleship in writing to the Galatian churches, where his authority and his doctrine alike were endangered.[2]

Paul's Associate

Paul's associate was Timothy (Greek, *Timotheos*). His name is based on a combination of two Greek words meaning "honor" *(timē)* and "God" *(theos)*. He was one who honored God and who in turn was honored by God.

A native of Lystra, Timothy was the son of a Greek father and a Jewish mother (Acts 16:1). In his early youth he was influenced by the godly lives of his mother, Eunice, and his grandmother, Lois (2 Tim. 1:5; 3:15). He apparently was converted to Christ through the ministry of Paul during the latter's first missionary journey (1 Tim. 1:2, 18; cf. Acts 14:6-23). Paul's constant mention of Timothy as his son doubtless refers to the latter's conversion as well as to the close relationship that developed between them. Because of his spiritual gifts and maturity, he was selected by Paul to become a missionary team member during the apostle's second journey (Acts 16:1-3). At that time he was circumcised and ordained (Acts 16:3; 1 Tim. 4:14; 2 Tim. 4:5). He was circumcised not to gain justification but to increase his effectiveness as a witness to Jewish audiences who knew his racial background. Timothy shared in the establishment of the churches in Philippi, Thessalonica, and Berea (Acts 16:1—17:14).

During Paul's third missionary journey, he sent Timothy from Ephesus back into the provinces of Macedonia (where Philippi was located) and Achaia to minister to the churches in those areas and to prepare the way for a proposed visit by Paul (Acts 19:22; 1 Cor. 4:17; 16:10). Before Paul left Ephesus, Timothy rejoined him in that city (2 Cor. 1:1, 19; Rom. 16:21). He then traveled with Paul from Ephesus to Macedonia to Achaia back to Macedonia and on to the province of Asia (Acts 20:1-5).

The biblical record is silent about the presence of Timothy with Paul on the latter's trip to Jerusalem, his arrest in that city, his two-year imprisonment at Caesarea, and his voyage to Rome (Acts 21:1—28:16). Timothy must have rejoined the apostle at Rome in the early months of Paul's imprisonment there. Paul then dispatched Timothy to Philippi (2:19-24).

During Paul's second imprisonment in Rome, he requested that Timothy join him there (2 Tim. 4:9). It is difficult to say whether Timothy did go to Rome or whether he arrived before the apostle's martyrdom. Tradition says that Timothy was martyred during the reign of either Domitian or Nerva.

Timothy, therefore, was well known by the Philippians. He had been in that city on at least three occasions and was prepared to go again (2:19-23). Not only was he Paul's associate, but he also may have been the amanuensis who actually wrote the letter under the apostle's dictation and supervision.[3]

Paul and Timothy's Position

Both Paul and Timothy were "bond-servants of Christ Jesus." They were literally Christ's slaves (Greek, *douloi*), bought and owned by Him. This is the only epistle in which Paul uses such a descriptive word in apposition and applies it to both himself and his associate.

Paul later wrote that Timothy served (Greek, *edouleusen*) with him in the gospel ministry (2:22). The verb is related to the Greek word for slave. In ancient cultures, the sons born to slaves became slaves themselves. In like fashion, Timothy was Paul's spiritual son and thus inherited his slavehood status and motivation from the apostle.

To Paul and to the spiritually minded, the term *bond-servant* was a title of both dignity and humility. There was no greater position than to be the servant of Jehovah God. Moses was a servant (Ex. 14:31). So were the prophets of Israel (Amos 3:7). Christ called the aged apostle John His servant (Rev. 1:1). There is no conflict between being the servant of God and being the servant of Jesus Christ, because Jesus Christ is God the Son. Worship and service must always be joined and directed toward God only (Matt. 4:10).

This positional title is appropriate to the tenor of the epistle. Service is one of the dominant themes because it is the outward manifestation of inner humility and devotion. At His incarnation, Christ took "the form of a bond-servant" even though He was the sovereign Son of God (2:7). Paul, Timothy, and Epaphroditus all revealed the attitude of servanthood in their ministries (2:22, 25). The Philippians likewise needed to develop this Christlike attitude (2:3–5).

Paul's Readers

The saints. The title *saints* (Greek, *tois hagiois*) is descriptive of all genuine believers. It is not restricted to an elite group of spiritual persons, nor does it refer to a few who are declared to be saints years after their deaths. These saints were living lay members of the church at Philippi.

The term *saints* literally means "set apart ones." It is based on a Greek verb (*hagiazō*) that means "to set apart" or "to sanctify." The word *sanctify* applies to four different stages of the believer's salvation. It refers to the ministry of the Holy Spirit in the person's life before conversion (Gal. 1:15; 2 Thess. 2:13); the time of regeneration (1 Cor. 1:2; 6:11; Heb. 10:14); the present cleansing ministry by the Spirit through the Word of God (John 17:17); and the total separation from the effects of sin when the believer receives the incorruptible, immortal body at the rapture of the Church (Eph. 5:26–27).

A distinction must be made between being a saint and being saintly. The former refers to the believer's position in Christ, whereas the latter points to the believer's daily moral behavior. All believers are saints, but not all of them are saintly. However, all believers should try to put their sanctified position into practice. Sainthood is possible only because of one's position "in Christ Jesus." This is a distinctive sphere for every believer in this church age. A person gets *into* Christ and thus is *in* Christ by the baptism in the Holy Spirit, a ministry that first occurred on the Day of Pentecost (Acts 1:5; 1 Cor. 12:13).

These opening remarks are contrary to human expectations. Contemporary humans would see the apostles as saints and the church members as servants. But here the apostle is a servant writing to the saints. This approach further marks the joy of humility that is emphasized throughout the epistle.

The overseers. The "overseers" are the chief presiding officers of the local church. The term is based on a compound Greek word (*episkopos*) that literally means "oversight" (Greek, *epi*: "over" and *skopos*: "sight").[4] It is derived from a verb (*episkeptomai*) that translates "to look upon" or "to look after," thus to inspect as an overseer, comparable to the modern foreman.

In a nontechnical sense, the title is applied to Jesus Christ, who is "the Shepherd and Guardian" of our souls (1 Pet. 2:25). Christ has the oversight over the universal church as its living head (Eph. 1:22–23). The term was also used of the apostolic oversight that Judas forfeited by his unbelief and apostasy (Acts 1:20). The technical sense, however, is found in this passage. It is one of three Greek terms used to describe the position of the main church officers. The other two are *elder* (*presbuteros*)[5] and *pastor* or *shepherd* (*poimēn*). These three English terms are used interchangeably to describe the functions of this position (Acts 20:17, 28; 1 Pet. 5:1–2).

Although the three terms describe the same person, it is possible to isolate their distinctive emphases. First, the concept behind "pastor" is to shepherd and feed. The main responsibility here is the supply of spiritual nourishment through biblical teaching. A pastor must be a teacher, first and foremost (Eph. 4:11; 1 Tim. 3:2). Pastoral care has three goals delineated by Jesus Christ Himself: to teach the immature, new believers (John 21:15); to teach adult believers (John 21:17); and to guide all the flock (John 21:16).[6] Second, the essence of the "overseer" is to render oversight, to see that the work of the local church is done correctly by the members who have been trained by him. Third, the term *elder* refers to his position and respect due to him.

In the first century, the apostles and their authenticated representatives appointed elders to oversee those churches that were established by them (Acts 14:23; Titus 1:5). Christ assigned this prerogative to the apostles when He appointed them as the ones who would lay the foundation of the church age (Eph. 2:20). With the passing of the apostolic period, the responsibility for selecting elders rested with the churches themselves. They had the benefit of apostolic precedent plus the guidance of the inspired Scriptures that set forth the requirements of the office (1 Tim. 3:1–7; Titus 1:5–9).

The usage of the plural shows that one church could have more than one overseer-elder-pastor. Since one city might contain several house churches, it could indicate that each assembly had one overseer. All believers within one community constituted one church regardless of their respective meeting places. They were organically and organizationally joined together.

Only men were appointed to the position of overseer. The designated qualifications could apply only to men. No woman was to have administrative headship over the man in either the home or the church (1 Cor. 11:2–16; 1 Tim. 2:11–15).

The deacons. The "deacons" (Greek, *diakonois*) are those officers selected by the church to assist the elders. They should relieve the elders of lesser responsibilities so that the elders might be able to devote more time and energy to prayer and preaching (Acts 6:4). The concept of deacon probably originated out of a need created by the rapid numerical growth of the church at Jerusalem (Acts 6:1–7).

The qualifications of deacons are extremely high (1 Tim. 3:8–13). When the apostolic era ended, the local churches had to use these guidelines to choose their deacons. Just as the first deacons relieved the apostles of mundane cares, so the church office of deacon emerged to relieve the pastor of those responsibilities that could be assumed by lay members.

The term *deacon* (Greek, *diakonos*) is a compound word based on *dia* ("through") and *konis* ("dust"). The imagery suggests a man who quickly moves to perform his tasks and kicks up a trail of dust by his haste. Deacons, therefore, must be dependable servants of the church and faithful assistants to the pastor.

The Blessing (1:2)

The content of the blessing is twofold: "grace" and "peace." The first word reflects a Greek concept ("grace": *charis*), whereas the second manifests a Hebrew approach ("peace": *šālôm*). Grace always precedes peace and forms the foundation for the latter.

Grace. All believers are justified by grace through Jesus Christ (Rom. 3:24). Their acceptable standing before God is maintained by divine grace (Eph. 2:8–9). The doctrine of grace reveals that God bestows blessings on believing sinners apart from any merit within them.

In addition, God supplies daily grace to meet the needs of Christians, giving undeserved provision (John 1:16) and forgiveness (Rom. 5:20). This apostolic blessing stresses daily grace. Although Paul constantly glorified the grace of God in his life and ministry, the word occurs only three times in this epistle (1:2, 7; 4:23).

Peace. When sinners become believing Christians, they gain an unalterable standing of peace with God (Rom. 5:1). In the world, however, they need the peace of God for daily protection from hostile attacks upon their mind and heart. Paul began and ended the epistle with a request for this sustaining peace (1:2; 4:7, 9). If believers could only see that each day their lives begins and ends with God's grace and peace, they would have joy and stability. The word *peace* appears three times in this epistle (1:2; 4:7, 9).

The source of this blessing is from two persons within the divine being: God the Father and the Lord Jesus Christ. One preposition, "from" (Greek, *apo*) links the Father and the Son together as the common source.[7] Doubtless these gifts are mediated to the believer through the indwelling ministry of the Holy Spirit (Gal. 5:22).

Study Questions

1. Do any men approximate the life and ministry of Paul today? Is it possible to do today what he did in the first century? Why or why not?

2. How can modern Timothys be produced today? What should be the role of local churches in such development? Of seminaries? Of internships?

3. Do modern preachers see themselves as servants? Why or why not?

4. What kind of service should churches expect of their pastors? Should printed job descriptions be given to pulpit candidates?

5. What types of church government are permitted within the teaching of Scripture? What types are prohibited?

6. To what extent should pastors get involved in the lives of church members? How often should they visit in the homes? Are most churches too large today for proper pastoral care?

7. What areas of responsibility belong to the deacons? Should deacons be elected to short terms or to lifelong duties?

CHAPTER 3

The Prayer
Philippians 1:3-11

Preview:

The apostle Paul is extremely complimentary toward this church that seemed to care so much for him. He tells the Philippians that God will not cease doing His spiritual work in them. He mentions his imprisonment because of the gospel but still expresses a longing to be with them. This church must have been benefiting Paul in that he considers them partakers in his ministry.

The apprehension of the Philippians over Paul's welfare was natural, but they had forgotten what kind of man the apostle really was. He never permitted adverse circumstances to control his destiny or to rob him of his joy in the Lord. Whatever happened to him occurred for the furtherance of the gospel, not for its hindrance. His Roman imprisonment gave him time to write four inspired epistles: Ephesians, Philippians, Colossians, and Philemon.

In addition, Paul had a ministry of prayer. The Philippians should have known that the apostle would be engaged in this spiritual activity. Their own church started as a result of similar circumstances. Paul and Silas had been beaten and imprisoned for exorcising a demon out of a possessed girl in Philippi (Acts 16:22-23). They were fastened in the stocks within the inner prison, but they responded with prayer and the singing of praises to God (Acts 16:25). Prayers and praises! Instead of sobbing, they prayed. They knew that they were in God's will within that prison and that God was working out all things for His glory and their good. The prisoners and the jailer heard those joyful anthems, and presumably, many of them believed in Christ as the result.

At Rome the situation was no different. The apostle wanted his readers to know that he could pray in Rome and that his requests could be answered by God in Philippi and throughout the cities of the Roman Empire.

Paul's Heart Toward the Philippians (1:3–8)

Paul was not full of self-pity over his predicament; rather, he was concerned over the Philippians. Each verse in this section contains the mention of "you." In his most dire need, he was benevolent, altruistic, and other-centered. He was thankful for their concern, but more than anything he desired to pray for them. Paul was a giver by nature, not a taker.

Paul Thanked God for the Philippians (1:3)

Paul's gratitude was personal. Although Paul did not use the emphatic Greek first person personal pronoun *ego* ("I"), he did employ a first person singular verb. Timothy was included in the initial greeting, but the thanksgiving was exclusively Pauline. He wrote, "I thank," not "We thank."

Paul's gratitude was expressed "to my God." God was not distant or impersonal to the apostle; rather, He was a living Person who was directly and intimately involved in Paul's affairs (Acts 27:23). Paul's usage of this phrase should not be confused with the distinctive interpretation Jesus Christ attached to those words. Christ identified God the Father as "my Father" and "my God." God is the God and Father of the Lord Jesus Christ in a sense altogether different from the way in which He is the God and Father of believing sinners. The relationship between the Father and the Son is an infinite and eternal one within the divine being, whereas He is the God over His created world and the Father of His redeemed children. Paul willingly confessed the sovereign government of God over his entire life.

Paul's gratitude was constant. The verb "thank" (Greek, *eucharisteō*) denotes continuous action in present time.[1] Paul gave thanks for the Philippians repeatedly, not just once. The verb is a compound word based on two ideas: *good* (Greek, *eu*) and *grace* (Greek, *charis*). Whenever believers perceive the goodness of divine grace, they should instinctively respond with grateful thanksgiving.

Paul's gratitude was addressed to God. In ancient letters unearthed by archaeologists, the Romans and the Greeks began by giving thanks to their pagan gods. Here Paul directed his praise to the one and only God of the universe (cf. 1 Cor. 8:5–6).

Paul's gratitude was based on remembrance. Paul's thanksgiving rested on and was supported by memories. The phrase "in all my remembrance of you" has two interpretations. It could mean that he thanked God because the Philippians remembered him in his affliction by their prayers and gifts, or it could be interpreted that he gave thanks every time he remembered them.[2] Both concepts are true. When Paul thought of them, he considered what God had done in their midst and what they had done for him (4:15). Both concepts would provide sufficient grounds for thanksgiving.

Paul Made Request for the Philippians (1:4–5)

It is possible to be thankful for someone without ever praying for that person. This perspective marks the unsaved person, but Paul's outlook was altogether different. When he remembered a fellow believer, he thanked God for that person.

Circumstances of the request. "Prayer" and "request" are two translations of the same Greek word (*deēsis*). It refers to an entreaty or a supplication. Later the apostle used the general word for prayer (*proseuchomai;* 1:9). These prayers of need can go from person to person as well as from a person to God. In this passage the prayer is directed toward God only.

Five features about the prayer are given. (1) It occurred during the apostle's devotional period ("in my every prayer"). Whenever he prayed, he made supplication for the spiritual and financial needs of the church (4:19). The adjective "every" shows that the prayer was made often. (2) The adverb "always" indicates that Paul prayed whenever he remembered the Philippian church. They were not always on his mind, but when they were, he always made an entreaty for them. (3) Paul prayed for all of them. This included the saints, the bishops, and the deacons (1:1). He was no respecter of persons. He did not divide that local manifestation of the body of Christ. (4) He made request continually. The verb "making" (Greek, *poioumenos*) points out constant activity and duration.[3] Needs never go away and neither should the supplications for those needs. (5) The prayers were made "with joy." Here is the first mention of this key word that marks the main theme of the epistle. When needs arise, children of God should not manifest depression but should show complete exhilaration. This is possible because they can make supplication to a God who knows, cares, and provides.

Basis of the request. The foundation of the request was "fellowship," or "participation." The word "for" is not a connective, but a preposition (Greek, *epi*) normally translated "upon"; thus, the fellowship supported the request. There can be no joyful supplication resting on a faulty relationship.

Three integral features are set forth. First, the noun "participation" (Greek, *koinōnia*) denotes sharing, holding something in common. Biblical participation involves believers with one another and with God (1 John 1:3). Since light cannot have fellowship with darkness (2 Cor. 6:14), believers cannot have genuine fellowship with unbelievers.

Paul and the Philippians experienced a fellowship in the gospel (1:5), in grace (1:7), in the Holy Spirit (2:1), in the suffering of Christ (3:10), and in giving (4:14–15). True fellowship or participation must advance the cause of Christ and the spiritual growth of believers. In fact, two Christians do not have to be together geographically to have fellowship. Paul and the Philippians were miles apart, yet they experienced it.

Second, their participation centered "in the gospel." The preposition "in" is really "into" (Greek, *eis*). Both were *into* the gospel. Their fellowship advanced the message of redemption centered in Christ's death, burial, and resurrection (1 Cor. 15:1–4). The Philippians prayed for Paul and his missionary ministry, gave to him, and witnessed within their own city.

Throughout the Scriptures, the gospel is described in several complementary ways. Its source is God (Rom. 1:1), its Savior is Christ (Rom. 1:16), its standard is grace (Acts 20:24), its substance is salvation (Eph. 1:13), and its standing is peace (Eph. 6:15).

Third, the Philippians' participation was constant ("from the first day until now"). It began at the time of their conversion under his ministry, and it persisted until the sending of Epaphroditus and a financial gift (4:18). Actually, the financial support seems to have been at the forefront of this fellowship (2 Cor. 8:4; 9:13). They shared their substance with Paul when he labored in Thessalonica (4:14–16), and they did the same during his imprisonment at Rome.

Paul Had Confidence About the Philippians (1:6)

Man can disappoint, but God never fails. Paul did not place his confidence in the church per se; rather, he placed confidence in God who had saved them and who was working out His sovereign purpose through them. He knew that God always finishes what He starts. The verb ("am confident") actually refers to a settled persuasion of mind that was the continuing result of a crisis decision in the past.[4] Paul knew what God had done and was doing in his life, and he also knew that God would do the same in their lives.

God began a work in them. The nature of the confidence is indicated by the explanatory connective "that" (Greek, *hoti*). It is further described in answers supplied to three implied rhetorical questions: Who did it? What was done? Where was it done?

First, God did the work. The verbal construction ("He who began")[5] points to God's personal involvement in the Philippians' lives. Actually it started in His eternal choice of them to salvation (Eph. 1:4), but in this passage, the emphasis is on the time of their conversion when God began to work in them.

Second, the "good work" refers to the applied benefits of salvation secured by the gracious provision of Christ's substitutionary atonement. It includes a righteous standing before God (justification), a progressive deliverance from the power of the sin nature (sanctification), and the prospect of an immortal, incorruptible body (glorification). It is "good" (Greek, *agathon*) in that it corresponds to the very nature of God, who alone is good in and of Himself (Mark 10:18; Rom. 3:12). We become Christians because God has begun to do a good work in us, not because we are doing good works for God (Eph. 2:8–10).

Third, the work was begun in them ("in you"). The prepositional phrase shows the personal, subjective acceptance of Christ's redemptive death and resurrection and of the convicting, regenerating work of the Holy Spirit. Genuine salvation involves a human response to the divine inworking.

God will finish the work in them. Paul expressed two more features of his confidence. First, God will thoroughly bring to a purposeful end any work He has chosen to do. He is faithful to His promise and purpose (1 Thess. 5:24). None can stay His hand. The certainty of completion is seen in the verb ("will perfect"). It points to the achievement of a stated goal.[6] Second, the time of completion is "the day of Christ Jesus." This phrase points to the imminent rapture of the church before the seven-year period of tribulation, the seventieth week of Daniel's prophecy (Dan. 9:24–27; Rev. 6–19). It looks at the coming of Christ to take believers unto Himself (John 14:1–6). At that day it will involve the resurrection of the Christian dead and the translation of the living saved (1 Cor. 15:51–53; 1 Thess. 4:13–18). According to God's sovereign purpose, believers are already glorified in His sight (Rom. 8:30). People observe what is presently happening, but God looks at His people as what they will be when He has finished His work in them. It is a biblical axiom that God "calls into being that which does not exist" (Rom. 4:17).

Paul Had the Philippians in His Heart (1:7)

Since Paul often was separated geographically from his beloved spiritual children, he frequently expressed his affection through public correspondence (1 Cor. 5:3; 2 Cor. 7:3; Col. 2:5; 1 Thess. 2:17). He was always present in spirit, rejoicing and agonizing over what was taking place in their lives.

They were in his thoughts. The mind can never be divorced from the heart. True loving concern must stem from both as an expression of the total person. In this epistle, emphasis is placed upon a holy mind and right thinking (1:7; 2:2, 5; 3:15–16, 19; 4:2, 7, 8). The verb ("to think" or "to feel") means more than a mental exercise; it conveys a sympathetic interest and concern. The adjective ("right"; Greek, *dikaion*) shows that justified believers should manifest practical righteousness in their thoughts and attitudes.

They were in his actions. Genuine love is reciprocal. Paul had them in his heart, and they had him in their hearts. This heart possession was continuous, not sporadic.[7] Paul's concern occurred in two places—first, in his "chains," or "his imprisonment" (Greek, *desmois*). In his house, under arrest and chained to soldiers, Paul still thought about the Philippians. Second, Paul showed concern "in the defense and confirmation of the gospel." In the Roman court, he acted as a representative for all the churches. He thought of them through what he said ("defense") and what he did ("confirmation"). The word "defense" (Greek, *apologia*) refers to a logical, legal presentation of the truth (Acts 22:1; 1 Pet. 3:15). In Paul's evangelistic outreach, the gospel was confirmed by God through the performance of miracles and sign gifts (Mark 16:20; 1 Cor. 1:6-7; 2 Cor. 12:12; Heb. 2:3-4). Yet there is no biblical evidence that Paul performed such supernatural works before Caesar. Rather, he fostered a gracious deportment before the authorities.

> "Inasmuch as both in my bonds and in the defence and confirmation of the gospel" is a statement variously interpreted. Perhaps it is better to link the first words, "inasmuch as," with the expression, "ye all are partakers of my grace." Most scholars favour this and not the idea, "I have you in my heart both in my bonds and in the defence and confirmation of the gospel." Paul was a prisoner when he wrote this letter. Note the references to his bonds also in Ephesians 6:20; Col 4:18; Philem 1. The word "defence" *(apologia)* usually has the thought of an answer made in self-defence (Acts 22:1; 25:16).

> "Partakers" means "partners with" and is the word in v.5 connected with the preposition *sun*. It is again embracing them all. The grace is not so much the grace that saves us (Eph 2:5, 8), as the grace that enabled Paul to bear his chain and to defend and confirm the gospel. The saints at Philippi shared in it (1:29).[8]

They were in God's grace. Both Paul and the Philippians were "partakers" (Greek, *sugkoinonous*) of grace. The Greek word literally means "common with" or "sharers with." Both had been saved by grace, and both were experiencing sustaining grace in the midst of their respective trials.

Paul Longed for the Philippians (1:8)

It was witnessed by God. Paul used a solemn oath to support his loving concern for the church ("For God is my witness"). In his epistles, he often did this

(Rom. 1:9; 2 Cor. 1:23; 1 Thess. 2:5, 10). Paul knew his heart, and he also knew that God was aware of his inner feelings.

It was an intense desire. The two words ("I long") are the translation of just one Greek word *(epipothō)*. The preposition prefix *(epi)* intensifies this strong term of desire. It was used of the athlete who strained at the finish line to finish first. The object of this emotion was the church, not their money ("you all"). He could honestly say to them: "I do not seek what is yours, but you" (2 Cor. 12:14). Later he identified the Philippians as "my beloved brethren whom I long *to see,* my joy and crown" (4:1, emphasis mine).

Paul's Imprisonment for the Gospel

Paul and Silas singing and praying in prison (Acts 16:25)

The Holy Spirit testifies in every city, saying bonds await me (Acts 20:23)

A prisoner for Jesus Christ (Eph. 3:1; Philem. 1:9)

The prisoner of the Lord (Eph. 4:1)

My imprisonment for the defense of the gospel (Phil. 1:7)

Imprisonment for the cause of Christ (Phil. 1:13)

Imprisonment giving more courage to speak the word of God (Phil. 1:14)

Remember my imprisonment (Col. 4:18)

The prisoner of the Lord (2 Tim. 1:8)

Imprisoned as a criminal (2 Tim. 2:9)

The word of God is not imprisoned (2 Tim. 2:9)

A prisoner of Christ (Philem. 1:1)

I bore Onesimus while in prison (Philem. 1:10)

Onesimus ministered to me while imprisoned for the gospel (Philem. 1:13)

It reflected Christ. The sphere of desire was in "the affection of Christ Jesus." The term "affection" (Greek, *splagchnois*) refers to the viscera, the internal organs of the body, including the heart, liver, and intestines. Symbolically and spiritually, it came to mean the seat of emotions, with stress on the feelings of love, compassion, and tenderness. As Christ was compassionate, so was Paul. Christ was actually desiring the Philippians through him.

Abounding Love (1:9)

Paul's prayer for the Philippians was mentioned earlier (1:3–4). Now its content is set forth ("And this I pray"). Paul, like all believers, had to have an intense, loving concern for others before he could pray effectively. He expressed five goals for the Philippians within his prayer.

When sinners believe on Christ for salvation, the love of God is shed in their hearts by the initial infilling and permanent indwelling of the Holy Spirit (Rom. 5:5). They not only love God, but they also love the children of God in whom the same Savior abides (1 John 4:19). They are taught by God to love their spiritual brothers (1 Thess. 4:9), and this fact gives assurance of personal salvation (1 John 3:14). This implanted seed of love, however, must grow. It must be cultivated and manifested daily. It must not be limited or restrained.

Love's abundance. The imagery behind this verse is that of a river overflowing its banks during a flood. Love is the river, and the two banks that form its channel and direction are "knowledge" and "discernment." Christian love must not be a stagnant pool or a slow-moving trickle; it must be a raging torrent. According to the verb, love must constantly keep on overflowing ("may abound").[9] This concept is further reinforced by the descriptive adverbial phrase ("still more and more"). A flooding river grows wider as more water flows into its system.

Love's control. Love, however, must never be misdirected. Even a raging river is moving toward a destination within certain bounds. Two guidelines of genuine biblical love are now enumerated. First, love must be expressed in "knowledge" (Greek, *epignōsei*). This refers to a thorough mental grasp of spiritual truth. Elsewhere Paul prayed that believers might "be filled with the knowledge of His will in all spiritual wisdom and understanding" (Col. 1:9). True love does not act in ignorance. Believers must know *what* and *whom* to love. Second, love must be in "discernment." True love must discriminate between good and evil (Heb. 5:14) and between important and unimportant issues (1 Cor. 3:13–23). Believers must know *how* to love. Such love must reveal spiritual perception of divine beauty and worth.

Discerning Approval (1:10a)

Believers must "approve the things that are excellent." This action is the purpose or result of discerning love.[10] The verb "approve" (Greek, *dokimazein*) was used for assaying metals. It means to test with the sense of approval. All believers must internalize their convictions of what is right. In moral absolutes they must be committed to God's holy standards, but in ever changing cultural situations they must critically examine their soul liberty. The present tense of the verb indicates that believers must constantly reassess their opinions and lifestyle.

The "things that are excellent" are actually "the things that differ" (Greek, *ta diapheronta*). The difference is not between good and evil, because God has decreed that distinction. Rather, it is between the primary and the secondary, between eternal and temporal values. As situations of life change, so do the things that differ. Therefore, analysis must be done daily.

Blameless Deportment (1:10b)

Its description. Two qualities are given. First, the Philippians should be "sincere." The word literally means to be "judged by the sun" (Greek, *eilikrineis*). Ancient jars and vases were examined for disguised cracks by holding them up against the rays of the sun. Hypocrites can fool others, but God knows their thoughts and intents (Heb. 4:12). Second, they should be "blameless" (Greek, *aproskopoi*). They should not be like an uneven sidewalk against which a man could stub his toe and fall. Believers must not offend the saved or the unsaved (1 Cor. 10:32). Persons offend when they live selfishly.

Its duration. The active pursuit of this goal must last an entire lifetime. It is "until the day of Christ." Again, this event refers to the imminent coming of Christ at the rapture of the church and the subsequent Judgment Seat of Christ (1:6; 2 Cor. 5:10). If a believer lives in the light of the imminent appearing of Christ, he will live a godly life (1 John 3:1–3).

Righteous Character (1:11a)

Its nature. Righteous fruit can issue only from a righteous tree. Believing sinners have a justified position before a holy God, but they have the personal responsibility to put that new standing into practice (1 John 2:29; 3:7). Paul prayed that the Philippians might be permanently "filled with the fruit of righteousness."[11] This fruit includes the fruit of the Spirit (Gal. 5:22–23), the fruit of evangelism (Rom. 1:13), the "fruit unto holiness" (Rom. 6:22, KJV), the fruit of good works (Col. 1:10), and the fruit of thanksgiving (Heb. 13:15).

Its source. This fruit comes "through Jesus Christ." The Savior equated Himself with the vine and the believers with the branches (John 15:5). He said that they could do nothing apart from Him. A branch in and of itself cannot produce fruit; rather, it must allow the life of the vine to flow through it. In like manner, the believer must allow Christ to live His life through him or her (1:21; Gal. 2:20).

Glory of God (1:11b)

If the four goals of Paul's prayer would be achieved, then the ultimate result would be "the glory and praise of God." The glory of God magnifies who He is, and the praise of God rejoices over what He has done. You cannot have one without the other. His attributes and His actions can never be separated.

Study Questions

1. Why do Christians forget what other believers have done for them? For others? How can their memories be renewed?

2. Why are Christians not as thankful as they should be? Is there any solution?

3. What are the strengths of modern prayer meetings? What are their weaknesses?

4. In what areas of life should believers manifest confidence? Do Christians ever think that God has failed them? Why?

5. How can love be balanced by knowledge and judgment? Give some contemporary illustrations.

6. What steps should be followed in testing the things that differ? Are there objective criteria? Subjective?

7. Do Christians govern their behavior by a belief in Christ's return?

CHAPTER 4

The Opportunities of Obstacles
Philippians 1:12-19

Preview:
Paul's imprisonment caused him to be known among the elite praetorian guard, and it also emboldened many Christians to speak out for the word of God. Unfortunately, some believers shared the gospel out of envy and strife, thinking to cause Paul stress while in prison. Despite such selfish motives, Paul was still glad to see the proclamation of the gospel of the Lord Jesus Christ.

Jesus Christ taught that the godly life would involve tribulations (John 16:33), and Paul predicted that believers would face persecution (2 Tim. 3:12). Both evil men and demonic spirits oppose God and His children.

How should such opposition be viewed? How should it be received? Believers must always return good for evil (Luke 6:27–29; Rom. 12:17–21) and turn adversity into opportunities to glorify God. They should approach all obstacles with realism and optimism, not with pessimism.

The Principle Stated (1:12)

The church at Philippi became upset when it heard about Paul's imprisonment at Rome. The believers felt sorry for him and worried that his ministry had been seriously impaired and that he might die as a martyr. They thought that Paul's age and weak physical condition would slow down his effectiveness. To show their concern, the church sent Epaphroditus to make personal inquiry and to give Paul some financial assistance.

Things Will Happen to a Believer (1:12a)

Paul used the most common address to believers in Christ ("Brethren") to arrest the Philippians' attention (1:12; cf. 3:1, 13, 17; 4:1, 8). He wanted them to understand a fundamental principle in the will of God and to remember it always ("Now I want you to know").

The meaning of things. The general phrase "my circumstances" literally means "the according to me things" (Greek, *ta kat' eme*). Although many of Paul's friends accompanied him on his hazardous missionary journeys and were exposed to similar adverse circumstances, Paul did not include them directly in the expression of this principle.

The list of things. What had happened to Paul since he had last seen the Philippians? Although Paul did not itemize the obstacles in this letter, he did discuss them elsewhere (2 Cor. 11:23–27). Luke recorded the historical background of that period of the apostle's life (Acts 20:6—28:31).

At the end of his third missionary journey, Paul determined to go to Jerusalem with a special welfare collection given by the Gentile churches to the Jewish believers (Rom. 15:25–26). He fully expected to visit Rome and Spain after the project was completed (Rom. 15:23–24). At the same time, Paul knew that trouble awaited him in Jerusalem (Acts 20:22–23). Other Christians warned him not to go (Acts 21:4). Even the prophet Agabus predicted that Paul would be arrested and bound over to the Roman government authorities (Acts 21:10–11). Paul's travel companions also tried to prevent him from going but were unsuccessful (Acts 21:12–14).

At Jerusalem Paul consented to the request of the church elders to purify himself at the temple as a testimony to the Jewish believers who were still jealous for the law. When unbelieving Jews sighted the apostle in the court of the Israelites, they began to beat him (Acts 21:22–31). The Roman soldiers rescued him and bound him with chains (Acts 21:33). When a conspiracy to murder Paul was discovered by the authorities, he was secretly taken to the Roman garrison at Caesarea (Acts 23:23–33) where he remained a prisoner for two years (Acts 24:27).

Paul then appealed to have his case tried by Caesar in Rome; thus, he undertook a voyage surrounded by soldiers (Acts 25:10–12). He then encountered a storm, a shipwreck, and a desperate swim to safety (Acts 27:14–44). After a short stay at Malta, Paul finally arrived in Rome, where he spent the next two years under house arrest (Acts 28:16, 30–31). By this time, other churches were also concerned, so Paul sent Tychicus to both Ephesus and Colossae so that they might know what happened to him (Eph. 6:21; Col. 4:7).

Things Can Advance the Gospel (1:12b)

The adverb ("greater;" Greek, *mallon*) shows the contrast between the cause and the effect. To Paul, opportunity was on the other side of the obstacle. When believers view adverse circumstances from the divine perspective, they will use them for spiritual advantage.

The positive result of adversity is stressed here ("for the greater progress of the gospel"). The preposition ("for"; Greek, *eis;* cf. Rom. 1:20) indicates purpose, goal, or result. A believer must look at the result of the adversity, not the adversity itself. For example, the Israelites at the Red Sea saw in the onrushing Egyptian chariots a sign of destruction, but Moses recognized that predicament as an opportunity for divine salvation (Ex. 14:13).

The term *progress* (Greek, *prokopēn)* literally means "to cut toward." It is a military term used of engineers who would prepare a road for the advancing army by removing obstructions such as rocks and trees. Paul did not view difficulty with self-pity. Rather, he used problems to proclaim the gospel in distinctive ways. The verb ("have turned out") emphasizes the lasting effects of past difficulties.[1] It literally means "have come."

Personal Witness (1:13)

At this point, Paul wanted to show how God had used his arrest and subsequent two imprisonments to advance the gospel message. These results are indicated by the connecting words "so that" (Greek, *hōste*).

The nature of Paul's witness. Paul was no ordinary prisoner, a fact that soon became evident to those authorities who were involved in his case. The opening words are literally translated: "So that my bonds manifest in Christ might become. . . ." The prepositional phrase ("in . . . Christ") actually follows the adjective ("well known") rather than the noun ("imprisonment"). It was soon known that the apostle was before the Roman court because he was a Christian, not because he had committed a civil crime.

Paul was really "the prisoner of the Lord" (Eph. 4:1). He was an "ambassador in chains" (Eph. 6:20). Thus, Paul was in Rome as a witness, not as a defendant. He asked his friends to pray for this unique outreach opportunity (Eph. 6:19–20; Col. 4:3–4).

Its location. Two spheres of witness are mentioned. First, he spoke to "the whole praetorian guard." The Greek word *praitōrion* is normally transliterated as "praetorium" and can refer either to a place or to persons.

The term was used of the judgment hall where Pilate tried Christ in Jerusalem (John 18:28), of the judgment hall of Herod in Caesarea where Paul defended himself (Acts 23:35), and of the court of Caesar on Palatine Hill in Rome. Thus, the Praetorium was a place, the legal residence of Roman government officials. It may also refer to the barracks of the elite imperial guard.

More likely, however, this technical term referred to the Praetorium soldiers themselves.[2] Nine or ten thousand of these hand-picked soldiers served Caesar personally. They received double pay and special privileges. They soon became so powerful that the aspirants to the throne tried to solicit their support. Since Paul was chained constantly to a soldier during his two years of house arrest, he was able to witness to the guard. The guard also observed how Paul spoke to his friends, how he wrote, and how he prayed. The guards were changed every six hours; thus, in two years, the apostle may have been able to witness to nearly three thousand soldiers.[3]

Second, Paul spoke "to everyone else." Literally this means "to all the remaining ones." No doubt, he had the opportunity to give witness to other types of soldiers, to household servants, and to the government officials, including Nero. Paul's witness was successful, for he claimed that some of Caesar's household were believers (4:22). These people must have been saved though his testimony.

Encouragement of Preachers (1:14–18)

Many received boldness to speak (1:14). Paul's presence in Rome as a political prisoner caused a stir within the local church. A few became timid in their witness, but the majority were stimulated to intensify their evangelistic efforts. Four descriptions of them are given. First, they constituted the majority. Here "most" is literally "the more parts" (Greek, *tous pleionas*). The usage of the definite article (*tous*) shows that Paul was talking about a specific group. Second, they were definitely believers. Paul identified them as "brethren," and their standing before God is seen in the phrase "in the Lord." Third, they received inner confidence through Paul's example. The phrase "trusting in the Lord because of my imprisonment" shows that they were persuaded to make a decision to stand for the truth regardless of the consequences. Fourth, they had "far more courage to speak the word of God without fear." Fearing what people will think or do when we proclaim the Word is very natural, but this reluctance can be overcome. Christ encouraged His disciples not to fear (Matt. 10:28), and Paul did likewise to Timothy (2 Tim. 1:7–8).

Some preached out of bad motivation (1:15–16). The majority group was divided into two groups, indicated by the double usage of "some" (Greek, *tines*). Both preached the same redemptive message ("preaching Christ"), but each party had different reasons for doing so.

The faulty motivation of the first group is characterized in six ways. First, they preached "from envy." The word "from" (Greek, *dia*) is normally translated "because of"; thus, the cause of their proclamation was at fault, not its content. Envy (Greek, *phthonon*) is a work of the flesh, a sin caused by a lack of yieldedness to the Holy Spirit and a lack of love for the brethren (Gal. 5:16, 21, 26). It is an expression of the unsaved life, although Christians can also commit it (Rom. 1:29; Titus 3:3). Envy involves jealousy. These men were jealous of Paul's success and popularity and perhaps that of his friends.

Second, the result of envy is "strife" (Greek, *erin*). Envy is the inward emotion, whereas strife is its outward expression. It is also a work of the flesh (Gal. 5:20), a manifestation of the unsaved life (Rom. 1:29), and a result of false teaching (1 Tim. 6:4). Strife results when believers choose to follow certain leaders to the neglect of others (1 Cor. 3:3).

Third, they preached "from selfish ambition" (Greek, *eritheias*). Such lack of humility is the cause of personal rivalry (2:3). It is also a work of the flesh (Gal. 5:20).

Fourth, they did not preach "from pure motives" (Greek, *hagnōs*). This adverb is related to the adjective that means "pure, chaste, undefiled, and guiltless" (Greek, *hagnōs*). It was used of that which was holy and sacred, free from ceremonial defilement. These teachers preached because they loved their own reputations.

Fifth, they intended to aggravate Paul ("thinking to cause me distress in my imprisonment"). They hoped that Paul would become jealous when he saw them increasing their following. It was a subtle attack on the apostle's psychological stability. The word *distress* (Greek, *thlipsin*) literally means "friction." It carries a vivid image of the painful rubbing of iron chains against a prisoner's arms and legs.

Sixth, they spoke "in pretense" (Greek, *prophasei*; 1:18, pious hypocrisy, fake religiosity). The Pharisees used it as a cover for their sin and selfishness (Matt. 23:14; John 15:22). This is the term used of the fearful sailors who lowered the life boat for their own safety while pretending to be casting out the anchors (Acts 27:30).

Some preached out of good motivation (1:15b, 17). We have no indication as to which group constituted the majority. It would seem that the Roman church, to whom Paul wrote and which included a large group of his friends (Rom. 16), would have been very sympathetic toward the apostle.

Four features of the group are enumerated. First, they spoke from "good will" (Greek, *eudokian*). The word means "that which seems to be good." It involves free choice, a determination that brings a holy pleasure to oneself and a benefit to the object of that choice. This group loved to preach Christ, and they wanted to encourage Paul. This term refers to God's pleasure in choosing to reveal truth to spiritual babes (Matt. 11:25–26), to predestinate men to sonship (Eph. 1:5), to disclose His redemptive purpose to believers (Eph. 1:9), and to work within the lives of Christians (2:13). Paul used the term of his heart's desire for the salvation of Israel (Rom. 10:1).

Second, these people preached out of "love" (Greek, *agapēs*). In this context, their love was directed basically toward Paul. They loved him for who he was, for what he did for others, and for what he did for them. Love for the brethren always reflects love for Christ. They were also constrained to witness by the love of Christ (2 Cor. 5:14).

Third, these believers knew why Paul was in prison ("knowing that I am appointed for the defense of the gospel"). The apostle's trial was really a defense of the gospel message of redemption through Christ and thus a trial of Jesus Christ Himself. The defense (Greek, *apologian*) was a logical presentation of facts and arguments designed to show that Christianity was not a civil threat to the Roman government. The verb ("I am appointed"; Greek, *keimai*) is a military term used of a soldier who was on duty as a guard. The apostle, therefore, was a soldier of the cross who protected the integrity of the gospel message.

Fourth, they spoke "in truth." Truth is that which corresponds to the written Word of God (John 17:17). It also manifests God's essence and will. No error could be found in what they said, how they spoke it, and why they proclaimed it.

All preached Christ (1:18). In Paul's analysis of the preachers, he came to two conclusions. First, regardless of their motivation, the content of their message was orthodox. They did preach Christ (1:14, 15, 16, 18). They were theologically correct in the doctrines of Christology and soteriology. The content of Christ's person and redemptive work must be derived solely from a logical exposition of the inspired, written Word of God.

Second, Paul could rejoice over the proclamation of their message ("and in this I rejoice"). He could not rejoice over faulty motivation, but he could rejoice that their message was sound, that Christ was magnified, that sinners were regenerated, and that they were his brethren.

Paul's enemies were

> driven by the poisonous fantasies of jealousy and selfish ambition: in contrast to verse 16, their actions arise not from what they "know" but what they (wrongly) imagine. They also proclaim Christ, but theirs is a petty, territorial vision; their aim is naked self-advancement. The robe of "Christian ministry" cloaks many a shameless idolatry. Selfish ambition is

apparently a problem in Philippi, too (2.3; cf. 4.27); here as elsewhere, too many "look out for their own interests," 2.21.

Since Paul's concern is the defence not of himself but of the gospel, the adversaries' desire to cause him distress (or "affliction") can leave him relatively calm and unflustered.[4]

Increase of Support (1:19)

It was conceivable that the apostle could be found guilty and that he be martyred as a Roman criminal (1:20–21). However, he fully expected to be set free (1:24–25). He later expressed his hope to see the Philippians again (2:24–25). He even asked Philemon to prepare a guest room for him (Philem. 1:22). His conviction about his forthcoming release is here stated in the verb "I know" (Greek, *oida*), an inner persuasion conveyed by the indwelling Holy Spirit. The fact of Paul's release is seen in the phrase "my deliverance." The Greek term *sōtērian* is normally translated "salvation." Here, however, it does not refer to spiritual salvation, but to his deliverance from a four-year period of custody by the Romans. Such things as a release from prison do not happen on their own. Paul knew that and predicated his freedom on two means of support.

By man. One means of support was the intercession of believers ("through your prayers"). Some believers have questioned whether they should pray since God has already determined what He will do. These people fail to recognize that God has also chosen to work through human instrumentality. The word *prayers* (Greek, *deēseōs*) refers to intense intercession, the same ministry Paul was conducting in their behalf (1:4). When believers lovingly pray for one another, God will accomplish His work. He works in and through people, not apart from them. Paul even asked Philemon to pray for his release from prison (Philem. 1:22).

By God. In the program of redemption, God and humans are colaborers (1 Cor. 3:9). The prayers of saints and the provision of God are two complementary sides of the same divine-human activity. Divine help is here called "the provision of the Spirit of Jesus Christ." The word *provision* (Greek, *epichorēgias*) is a double compound word (Greek, *epi, choros,* and *hēgeomai*) that means "to furnish supplies for a musical chorus." In ancient times, a benefactor would pay for the singers and dancers at a festival. The word later came to mean "to provide generously." In medical terminology, it was used of the joints and ligaments that joined two bones (Eph. 4:16). The imagery is very clear. Paul and the Philippians, two members of the body of Christ, were joined together by prayer and the omnipresent, indwelling ministry of the Holy Spirit in spite of geographical distance.

The Holy Spirit is called "the Spirit of Jesus Christ" because He was sent by the Son as well as by the Father and because He has glorified Jesus Christ at all times (John 15:26; 16:14).

Study Questions

1. What specific adversities can happen to believers? Can believers ever be prepared to meet such adversity?

2. How can the gospel be furthered by adversity? By death? By illness? By accident?

3. Why do Christians suffer depression? What can be done to gain victory over self-pity and frustration?

4. How can Christians encourage other believers? In what ways do they sometimes discourage them?

5. In what ways can a person with a faulty motivation proclaim truth? Should we cooperate with such individuals?

6. Should Baptists rejoice over the successes of Presbyterians? Methodists over that of Pentecostals? In what areas do denominational distinctions disrupt mutual rejoicing?

7. Why should believers pray for one another? How can such intercession be encouraged? Why don't more believers attend prayer services?

CHAPTER 5

The Blessings of Life and Death
Philippians 1:20-26

Preview:

Paul did not want to be shamed for the sake of the gospel, but he was ready to die if necessary. Death to him was gain! He realized that to remain on earth and serve the Lord was important for the cause of the gospel but also for serving and encouraging the believers. In all of this Paul admitted being "hard-pressed."

To Paul, death was the bridge between two distinct expressions of life. It was the end of the old life, but it was also the beginning of a new life. Thus, he could rejoice in either circumstance and could use both for the glorification of God.

The Philippians wanted the apostle to live, but they were afraid that he would soon be martyred. For them, only Paul's living would bring advantages. They needed to look at his life and death options through his eyes and from the divine perspective.

For Paul (1:20-24)

In Philippians 1:20-24 the church is not mentioned. Rather, the apostle is giving his analysis of his imprisonment, the possibility of his death, and the expectation of his release.

Paul's Testimony (1:20)

Paul had hope. The opening preposition "according to" (Greek, *kata*) shows the standard behind Paul's confession. The outward manifestation of hope is "expectation," whereas the inward conviction of heart is "hope." The former is the effect, and the latter is its cause.

The noun "expectation" (Greek, *apokaradokian*) is unique. It is a double compound word made up of *apo* ("from"), *kara* ("head"), and *dokeō* ("to suppose or think"). In ancient times it was used of the spectator who sat on the edge of his seat and stretched his neck to see the outcome of an athletic event. Thus, it meant to watch eagerly with strained expectancy and longing. Elsewhere it is used of all of creation, which anticipates a deliverance from the curse when the children of God receive their new bodies (Rom. 8:19).

The word *hope* (Greek, *elpida*) denotes one of the three main Christian virtues (1 Cor. 13:13). It refers to a settled assurance of heart caused by a firm conviction that what is believed will come to pass (Rom. 8:24–25). All committed believers are looking for the "blessed hope," the coming of Jesus Christ (Titus 2:13). Thus, hope is not a crossing of the fingers, a naïve wishful thinking against great odds; rather, it is a divinely implanted response to the sure promises of God.

Consequently, Paul had an expectant hope that he would be released, that he would see the Philippians again, that he would live to have further ministry, and that he would see Christ, either at his death or at Christ's coming.

Paul was not ashamed. Shame should not become a blot upon the family of God. God is not ashamed to be called their God (Heb. 11:16). Christ is not ashamed to call believers His brothers (Heb. 2:11). Thus, believers should not be ashamed of God. They should not be ashamed to confess the name of Christ in salvation (Rom. 10:10), to share the gospel (Rom. 1:16), nor to identify themselves with other Christians (2 Tim. 1:8).

The inclusive phrase "in anything" refers to both good and bad times, to situations of life or death. In Paul's case, it denoted both freedom and imprisonment.

Paul magnified Christ, who sits in the third heaven at the right hand of the Father in His resurrected, glorified human body. At the same time, Christ is spiritually present in the world through His divine attribute of omnipresence. He also dwells within the life of each Christian (Gal. 2:20). Thus, the only way for an unsaved person to "see" Christ today is in and through the life of a believer. In that connection, Paul expressed five features about his magnification of Christ.

First, its manner was "with all boldness." The idea behind "boldness" (Greek, *parrēsia*) is a total freedom of speech before God, friends, and foes (Heb. 10:19). Paul prayed that he might have boldness to testify (Eph. 6:19–20).

Second, Paul magnified Christ consistently ("even now, as always"). He had magnified Christ through the success of his three missionary journeys, and he was not about to change now that he was a prisoner in Rome. In the past, he had forthrightly stood for Christ before sorcerers (Acts 13:8–11), enraged synagogue Jews (Acts 13:44–45), polytheistic heathen (Acts 14:11–18), Judaizers (Acts 15:1–2), city officials (Acts 16:20–22), philosophers (Acts 17:18–34), and materialistic silversmiths (Acts 19:23–41). After Paul's arrest in Jerusalem, he gave a bold witness five times: before the Jewish multitude at the temple (Acts 22:1–24), before the religious council (Acts 23:1–10), at Caesarea before the Roman governors Felix and Festus (Acts 24:1—25:12), and later before Herod Agrippa II (Acts 26:1–32). During his voyage, shipwreck, and subsequent arrival at Rome, the apostle remained constant and steadfast in his testimony (Acts 27—28).

Third, Christ was magnified in Paul by the agency of the Holy Spirit. The passive voice of the verb ("shall . . . be exalted") suggests an outside influence. Since the Holy Spirit was sent into the world to glorify Christ (John 16:13–14), He was the One who controlled the apostle.

Fourth, Paul exalted Christ in his "body." The body, of course, is the arena in which natural life occurs and which death so forcefully attacks. It is the most observable feature of human existence. It is impossible to talk about the magnification of Christ in one's thoughts and feelings without seeing a visible demonstration. There can be no glorification of God in the spirit without the body being involved (1 Cor. 6:19–20).

Fifth, the magnification of Christ had a double means of accomplishment ("whether by life or by death"). To Paul, death was just as much a means to glorify Christ as was life. Most people view death with a pessimistic, defeatist outlook, but Paul saw it as a victory to be won. He wanted people to say, "Look at how he lived! Look at how he died!"

Paul's Creed (1:21)

The connective *for* (Greek, *gar*) introduces the explanation for Paul's strong testimony. He had an intense, personal philosophy of life and death. The prepositional phrase "to me" is actually just one Greek word (*emoi*).[1] In the sentence, it is very emphatic because it stands first and also because it is the emphatic form of the personal pronoun. Paul thus stressed his own outlook.

For life. Paul's creed was simple yet profound: "to live is Christ." Literally, the Greek reads, "The act of living: Christ." Paul's thoughts, feelings, and actions were fixed on Christ and controlled by Him. The Savior was both the center and the circumference of Paul's daily existence.

For death. The emphasis of the phrase "to die" (Greek, *to apothanein*) is on that split second of time when death actually occurs, when the self is separated from the body. That event is instantaneous, whereas life is constant.[2]

The process of death, which is often long and painful, is not contemplated in this concept.

When believers die, they are immediately free of suffering and are directly present with Christ in the third heaven. From that point on, they will be with the Savior forever. This is why Paul could call the instantaneous act of death "gain" (Greek, *kerdos*). God views the death of His children as precious (Ps. 116:15). Thus, when believers pass away, earth's loss is always heaven's gain.

Paul's Choices (1:22–23)

No person can will his or her own death (Eccl. 8:8). Only one person, Jesus Christ, had the delegated authority to release His spirit at death and to resurrect Himself (John 10:18). Nevertheless, the apostle could express his preferences, leaving the actual choice with a sovereign God. He stated the ramifications of two distinct possibilities for his immediate future.

To be on earth (1:22). Three aspects of this possibility are given. First, Paul knew that he would continue to live. The usage of the conditional particle "if" (Greek, *ei*) does not mean that his future was uncertain; rather, it introduces a condition of reality on which he could base a conclusion.[3] The phrase "in the flesh" denotes life on earth in the natural body; it has no connotation of sinful flesh here.

Second, Paul knew that his ministry would be successful. The demonstrative pronoun "this" (Greek, *touto*) refers to the continuation of his natural life. To Paul, living meant more working, and more working meant more fruit bearing. "Fruitful labor for me" specifically refers to the results of Paul's missionary activity (Rom. 1:13). It included the salvation of sinners, the edification of saints, the establishment of churches, the training of new leaders, and the writing of inspired Scripture.

Third, Paul did not disclose his personal preference ("and I do not know which to choose"). Death would be a personal gain to him, but an extended ministry would have value both for him and for others. He knew what course he would choose for his life if he would have had that prerogative, but he determined not to reveal his inner feelings to others.

To be in heaven (1:23). Most people want life without death rather than life with death. The natural desire of humans is to live, not to die. Paul's case, however, was much different. He had to determine where he wanted to live—on earth or in heaven. Either location had advantages.

Paul gives three reasons why he preferred heaven. First, it was an inner compulsion ("But I am hard-pressed from both directions"). The Greek verb *sunechomai* literally means "to have with." It refers to pressure being imposed upon someone from two different directions. Paul elsewhere used the word to describe the constraint of the love of Christ on his life (2 Cor. 5:14). Christ used the same term to describe the pressure on Him as He faced the cross (Luke 12:50). The two constraints that pushed at Paul were the necessity to abide on earth and the desire to depart. Both compulsions were valid and equally strong.

Second, he had a "desire" (Greek, *epithumian*), an intense passion or drive for heaven. This desire was no mere whim. The verb "having" shows that it was a constant part of Paul's feelings at this time in his life.[4] Age, physical exhaustion, persecution, and imprisonment had quickened his interest in heaven. Paul's desire for heaven had a single purpose with two aspects within it.[5] He first wanted "to depart." This unusual Greek verb *(analusai)* is used of the releasing of prisoners, the removal of the yoke from an ox, the breaking up of a tent, and the loosing of a ship from its moorings. Later, when the apostle did expect to be martyred during his second Roman imprisonment, he confessed that the time of his "departure" (Greek, *analuseōs*) was at hand (2 Tim. 4:6). Second, Paul wanted "to be with Christ." Thus, death was not an escape for Paul; rather, it meant that he would be with the most important person in his life. The verb "to be" (Greek, *einai*) indicates eternal fellowship.[6] The Bible says nothing about a soul sleep after death or a temporary residency in purgatory. At death a believer goes into the presence of Jesus Christ and continues to live (2 Cor. 5:6–8).

Third, Paul preferred heaven because it was "very much better." Actually, there are three comparative adjectives in this phrase (Greek, *pollō mallon kreisson*). Literally, it reads "much more better." In quantity, quality, or any other comparative values, heaven and the presence of Christ are far superior to earth.

Paul's Concern (1:24)

Paul's inner struggle was whether to depart or to abide. His preference for heaven and Christ, though sincere and holy, manifested a slight selfishness. After all, Paul was foremost a servant, and a servant must live to meet the needs of others. He knew what he wanted to do, but he also recognized what he had to do.

Three aspects of Paul's concern are enumerated. First, he accepted the fact that he would "remain on in the flesh." The verb means "to remain upon" (Greek, *epimenein*). Thus, he planned to remain on the earth in his natural body. Second, his continued living was "more necessary" (Greek, *anagkaioteron*). People who make decisions out of love and humility will always do what is best for others, not what is best for themselves. In this fashion, Paul could again prove himself to be an example to them. Third, Paul wanted to abide for them ("for your sake"). Since he had them in his heart (1:7), he had to think of them when he contemplated his own personal future.

Paul's Teaching on the "Flesh"
Christ's physical lineage was traced to David (Rom. 1:3).
Human physical works cannot appease God (Rom. 3:20).
The sinful weakness of the flesh enslaves people to impurity (Rom. 6:19).
With the flesh people follow sinful impulses (Rom. 7:25).
The Law was weak because of human "fleshly" effort (Rom. 8:3).
Human wisdom is but "fleshly" wisdom (1 Cor. 1:26).
No flesh can glory before God (1 Cor. 1:29).
Flesh and blood cannot inherit the kingdom of God (1 Cor. 15:50).
A thorn in the flesh was a physical illness (2 Cor. 12:7).
Flesh cannot bring about justification before God (Gal. 2:16).
The believer needs liberty from "fleshly" sin (Gal. 5:13).
Sinful "fleshliness" is at war with the Holy Spirit (Gal. 5:17).
Christians can lust by the flesh (Eph. 2:3).
Paul desired both to remain in his human body and to be with Christ (Phil. 1:22–24).
Christians can have a "fleshly" mind (Col. 2:18).
Christ took upon Himself a body of flesh (1 John 4:2–3).

Paul could see value in both his life and death, but the Philippians would only receive benefit if the apostle lived. That factor alone gave the apostle an inner conviction that he would be spared from a Roman death (note his words "being confident of this"). Paul knew that his return to active missionary service would produce two major blessings for the church—an increase in their faith and the joy of reunion.

The Increase of Faith (1:25)

Paul's knowledge. Paul knew intuitively by the indelible conviction of the Holy Spirit that he would be set free. The verb "I know" (Greek, *oida*) stresses an innate knowledge in contrast to an experiential, learned wisdom. No objective criteria produced by the trials themselves would have caused the apostle to have a glimmer of hope. He viewed his imprisonment and legal appeals from the standpoint of the divine will and human necessity.

Paul's knowledge manifested itself in two predictions. He knew he would remain alive ("I shall remain;" Greek, *menō*), and he knew he would return to Philippi ("continue with you all"). The Greek verb here literally means "to remain with them beside them" (Greek, *sumparamenō*, TR). It was one thing to get out of prison; it was another to be able to travel to their city once again.

The Philippians' faith. The word "for" (Greek, *eis*) introduces the reason behind Paul's release. Two results could be achieved.[7] First, their faith would advance ("your progress . . . in the faith"). Just as adverse circumstances furthered the outreach of the gospel (1:12), so the good news of Paul's release would increase their faith in God, who can deliver believers from all difficulties. In addition, their faith would be full of "joy." Faith not only must be intellectual and volitional; it also must be emotional. Belief must cause tears of happiness. An anticipating faith should shout and sing at the fulfillment of redemption. When faith becomes married to sight, joy will officiate.

The Joy of Reunion (1:26)

Paul saw four possible features in the Philippians' proud confidence in him. (1) It would "abound." It would be full and running over constantly. (2) Their confidence would rest "in Jesus Christ." He would get the glory and praise for what would be accomplished. (3) Their confidence would also reside in Paul ("in me"). A believer can rejoice at the presence of another believer and of the omnipresent Savior at the same time. Such rejoicing is complementary, not contradictory. (4) Their confidence would be caused by Paul's personal return ("through my coming to you again"). Neither Epaphroditus's return nor Timothy's visit would generate the joy that the apostle's physical presence in their midst would produce.

Study Questions

1. In what ways are some Christians ashamed today? What can help them to correct this weakness?

2. Can speaking boldly be done improperly? How? How do courtesy and tact fit into one's witness?

3. Are believers consistent? Why do they have highs and lows in their experience? Is constancy a mark of leadership?

4. How can Christ be magnified in the home? At school? At work?

5. What is the first thing that comes into a person's mind when he

or she hears your name? For what do you want to be known?

6. Do all Christians have a healthy outlook toward death? How can a believer fail Christ in his death? In his funeral? In his will?

7. What are the values of separation? Of reunion? Can such lessons be learned apart from hard human experience?

CHAPTER 6

The Challenge to the Church Philippians 1:27–2:4

Preview:

Paul urges the Philippians to remain firm in one spirit and to strive for the faith of the gospel. He reminds them that they were called to believe and suffer for Christ and to experience the conflict that comes in regard to the truth. He calls on the Philippians to remain united, avoid selfishness and empty conceit, and maintain humility of mind.

In the opening section of this epistle, Paul dealt mainly with events that affected his own behavior. He now turns his attention to the spiritual condition of the church. From Epaphroditus and subsequent church messengers,[1] the apostle realized that the church needed encouragement and exhortation. In this passage, he develops his instruction around two basic appeals (1:27; 2:2).[2]

Be Good Citizens of Heaven (1:27–30)

Definition of Citizenship (1:27a)

The believer is a citizen of heaven. The exhortation "conduct yourselves" is better translated: "Behave constantly as citizens." The Greek verb *politeuesthe* ultimately comes from the word for "city" (*polis*) found within the names of several American cities[3] and also transliterated into the English word "politics." The Philippians understood this term well because they were free Roman citizens possessing all of the rights and privileges thereof (Acts 22:28). In his defense before the Jerusalem council, Paul used this term of himself (Acts 23:1). All believers have heavenly citizenship (3:20). The Philippian believers never become citizens of the covenant nation Israel when they became saved (Eph. 2:12); however, they did became fellow citizens of heaven with all other believers in this age (Eph. 2:19).

The believer must be a worthy citizen. Paul elsewhere encouraged believers to walk worthy of the divine calling (Eph. 4:1), and of God (1 Thess. 2:12), and to please God in all respects (Col. 1:10). A worthy walk recognizes the double citizenship of every believer. Paul admitted his Roman citizenship and used those rights at times (Acts 22:28; 25:10); but such citizenship is temporary, limited to this life. He also knew that he was primarily a citizen of heaven, a position that would never end. Worthy citizenship therefore obligates all believers to both governments and God (Matt. 22:21).

The believer must represent the gospel. The behavior of a heavenly citizen must be worthy of "the gospel of Christ." All Christians are Christ's ambassadors to bring the good news of divine reconciliation to a lost and hostile world (2 Cor. 5:20). They therefore should do nothing to antagonize the very people God is trying to save. They must not give offense (1 Cor. 10:32–33).

The believer must be a devoted citizen. A good citizen will behave properly with or without supervision. Therefore, Paul's presence ("whether I come and see you") or absence ("or remain absent") should have nothing to do with the way the Philippians live. After all, they were ultimately responsible to God, who was always watching them (Col. 3:22).

Goals of Citizenship (1:27b–30)

The aim of heavenly citizenship is steadfast living on earth. The verb "standing firm" indicates that the Philippians were the true church (1 Cor. 12:13) and were to maintain their stand throughout their earthly residency.[4] Some believers, unfortunately, stand but do not work, whereas others work but do not stand. Paul provides five characteristics of the God-pleasing stand.

1. *Stand in unity.* The Philippians were to stand "in one spirit" (Greek, *en heni pneumati*). The "spirit" may refer to the Holy Spirit or to the oneness of purpose created within the human spirit by the Holy Spirit. There can be no unity within the brethren apart from the sovereign control of the Spirit. All believers have been baptized in that one Spirit into the body of Christ, the true church, and they have drunk by faith of the Spirit (1 Cor. 12:13). They are indwelt by the Holy Spirit (1 Cor. 6:19–20), and they have access by Him unto the Father (Eph. 2:18). They must endeavor "to preserve the unity of the Spirit in the bond of peace" (Eph. 4:3). That unity is marked by one body, one

Spirit, one hope, one Lord, one faith, one baptism, and one God and Father of all (Eph. 4:3–6).

2. *Stand in evangelism.* Paul gives three marks of this stance. First, they needed to be of "one mind." The Greek literally reads "one soul" *(mia psuchei).* Their souls were to be joined together even as those of David and Jonathan who loved each other (1 Sam. 18:1). Second, they needed to strive together, to cooperate as teammates. The word "athlete" comes from the Greek verb translated "striving together" *(sunathlountes).* Each believer must execute his or her own assignment at the right time and in the right way (cf. 2 Tim. 2:5). Third, their goal was to be "the faith of the gospel." Continuing with sports metaphors, like a good defensive unit in football, the believers must not let Satan and false teachers penetrate their assembly. Like a good offensive unit, they must drive forward to victory. They must defend the truth and win converts at the same time.

The phrase "the faith" points to the specific body of spiritual truth the local church must preserve and propagate (cf. 1 Tim. 3:15).[5] Paul predicted that some would depart from the faith (1 Tim. 4:1), and Jude encouraged believers to "contend earnestly for the faith which was once for all delivered to the saints" (Jude 1:3). The entire phrase "the faith of the gospel" points to all of the truth necessary to be understood and believed for salvation. It includes a clear biblical exposition of the redemptive work of Jesus Christ.

3. *Stand without fear.* The manner of the Philippians' stand was to be without fear ("in no way alarmed by *your* opponents"). The verb "alarmed" (Greek, *pturomenoi*) is used of horses spooked into an uncontrollable stampede. Inner fear is usually caused by an outside stimulus.

Double citizenship has advantages, but it also brings misunderstanding and conflict. A believer is in the kingdom of God but also lives among the kingdoms of the world that are ruled by Satan (Luke 4:5–6). The "opponents" included the Judaizers, the self-righteous legalists who had invaded the church (3:2). Other adversaries were pagan idolaters, the evil world system, Satan, and demonic spirits. The Roman government and citizenry also attacked believers. But Jesus Christ cautioned believers not to fear men (Luke 12:4). He predicted that believers would have tribulation within the church age, but He also assured them that He had overcome the world (John 16:33).

Such opposition must be seen for what it really is. It has two sides. First, it is to the unsaved "a sign of destruction." The word *sign* (Greek, *endeixis*) is an ancient legal term for a demonstrable proof. The hostility of the opponents revealed that they were unregenerate and would receive the judgment of God because of their unbelief and their unrighteous persecution of believers. Their sinful practice manifested their sinful position before God. The concept behind "destruction" (Greek, *apōleias*) is that of lostness, the very antithesis of salvation. Second, deliberate adversity from the unsaved is to believers a proof of salvation. The world loves its own, but it hates and persecutes those who have turned to Christ (John 15:18–19). In one sense, Christians should rejoice when opposition comes, because they can conclude that the world sees Christ in them, thus assuring that they are genuinely saved. The qualifying phrase "and that *too*, from God" shows that God is the source of salvation and that He has permitted the persecution to occur within the limits prescribed by Him.

4. *Stand in suffering.* Persecution by the world affords believers the blessing of being able to suffer for the sake of Christ and for divine righteousness (Matt. 5:10–12). Such opposition should not be viewed as a punishment but as a gift ("For to you it has been granted for Christ's sake"). The verb "granted" (Greek, *echaristhē*) is based on the word for "grace" (Greek, *charis*). Since grace is unmerited divine favor, people do not deserve to suffer for Christ any more than they deserve to be saved through Him.

The two divine gifts imparted to all believers are listed in chronological order. First, it was given to them "to believe in Him." Salvation is of the Lord from the beginning to the end (Jonah 2:9). As objects of divine choice, believers know they will be in the eternal presence of God because of what Christ has done for them, not because of what they have done for Christ. All are saved by grace alone through faith alone in Christ alone (Eph. 2:8–9). The entire program of salvation is a gift from our loving God. Second, it was given to them "also to suffer for His sake." Most believers want glory apart from suffering, faith without conflict. However, suffering for Christ produces assurance (1 Pet. 4:14), rewards (1 Pet. 4:13), evangelistic fruit (1:12–14), and glory to God (Acts 9:16).

A distinction must be made between suffering per se and Christian suffering. A believer must suffer "for His sake." The text literally reads, "in behalf of Him" (Greek, *huper autou*). Just as Christ once suffered for believers on the cross, so should children of God suffer for Him. Believers must follow the example of Christ (1 Pet. 2:21). Suffering for wrongdoing or stupid mistakes is deserved and will bring no reward (1 Pet. 2:19–20).

5. *Stand with Paul.* The church was experiencing "the same conflict" they saw in Paul. The term "conflict" (Greek, *agōna*) transliterates as "agony." It was used of the strenuous struggles of athletes and gladiators. Paul challenged Timothy to fight the good "fight" (Greek, *agōna*) of faith (1 Tim. 6:12) and confessed that he himself had fought a good fight (2 Tim. 4:7). All believers are engaged in spiritual conflict with the demonic forces of Satan (Eph. 6:11–12). To stand, they must put on the defensive armor of God (Eph. 6:10–18).

This conflict resembles that of Paul in two ways. First, it was like that which Paul endured at Philippi during his initial ministry ("which you saw in me," cf. Acts 16:19–40). They saw what happened to him, namely, his beatings and imprisonment. They also observed his spiritual response to the shameful abuse (1 Thess. 2:2). Furthermore, it was like that which Paul was presently experiencing in Rome ("and now hear *to be* in me"). The church had only secondhand reports of the apostle's predicament. They therefore dispatched Epaphroditus to gain firsthand information.

Bring Joy to Paul (2:1–4)

The Philippians lost some of their joy when they heard about the arrest and subsequent imprisonments of Paul. Their joy was further decreased when they heard about the sickness of Epaphroditus (2:26–28). They were totally unaware that Paul was rejoicing in the midst of his adversity. They wanted the apostle to have joy; but instead, they were in need of it. The apostle, of course, could not have total joy as long as the church was marked by sadness. In addition, whenever believers are not rejoicing in the Lord, they are disposed toward divisiveness, pride, and selfishness. To correct the situation, Paul issued a direct command (2:2) that can be translated, "Fill full my joy" (Greek, *plērōsate*).[6] They needed to replenish what had evaporated from the apostle's cup of joy.

Conditions for Joy (2:1)

Joy is based on attitudes and relationships. Paul could not have joy if the Philippians' attitude was right toward him but wrong toward others. He set forth four grounds for joy.[7]

Encouragement in Christ. The word *encouragement* (Greek, *paraklēsis*) can refer either to an exhortation or to the comfort produced by that appeal. As comfort, it is both an attribute of God and a gift from Him (John 14:16; 2 Cor. 1:3–4). As exhortation, it becomes the basis of appeal for Paul. There can be no real joy when disputing believers fail to obey Christ's command to be one (John 17:21).

Comfort of love. The "consolation of love" will produce joy and unity when believers love Christ as they should and when they love one another as Christ has loved them (John 13:34–35). The term *consolation* (Greek, *paramuthion*) conveys the idea of persuasive address, incentive, or stimulus. Acting out of love, believers should encourage others with their words of comfort, their friendship, and their deeds of mercy.

Fellowship of the Spirit. All believers share in this communion (Greek, *koinōnia pneumatos*). The Holy Spirit dwells in each of them, and He joins them all within the one body of Christ. Genuine submission to Him will produce the ninefold fruit of the Spirit (Gal. 5:22–23).

Compassion. The two sides of brotherly compassion are seen in the phrase "affection and compassion." The term *affection* (Greek, *splagchna*) is based on the Greek word that refers to the inner organs of the body, thus indicating the seat of human emotions. The concept of "compassion" (Greek, *oiktirmoi*) points to outward deeds of mercy caused by inner concern. Compassion is the opposite of indifference. Where there is no compassion, there can be neither love nor joy (1 John 3:16–18).

Nature of Joy (2:2–4)

Paul admonished the church to increase his joy. Joy is not mere laughter or a happy smile. Happiness can be manufactured, but joy must be grown. It involves time and obedience. Three of its essential qualities are expressed in this passage.

Unity (2:2). Four descriptions of unity are given. First, believers are to be "of the same mind." The phrase literally reads, "that you keep on thinking the same thing" (Greek, *hina to auto phronēte*). Paul later gave Euodia and Syntyche the same charge (4:2). God was glorified through the Philippians' joint evangelistic efforts and holy thought patterns (1:27; 4:8). Second, the believers needed to have "the same love." They must love whom and what God loves. They must love each other with the same love. They must love God with their total beings, their neighbors as themselves, and their spiritual brothers and sisters as Christ sacrificially loved them (Matt. 22:37–39; John 13:34). Third, believers are to be "united in spirit." This phrase literally means "joint souls" (Greek, *sumpsuchoi*). As a chain, one believer must be linked together with another child of God. Fourth, believers must be "intent on one purpose." Literally, this translates, "thinking constantly the one thing" (Greek, *to hen phronountes*). The one thing is later explained as the selfless mind of Christ (2:5).

Humility (2:3). Humility has both a negative and a positive quality. Negatively, believers should not possess a selfish, competitive spirit. The opening words read, "Do nothing from selfishness or empty conceit" (Greek, *mēden kat' eritheian mēde kata kenodoxian*). Someone has said that conceit is the disease whereas selfish ambition is the symptom. The former is inward and the latter is outward.

The sin of selfish ambition is a work of the flesh (Gal. 5:20, NIV). It characterizes those who preach out of a faulty motivation (1:15). It also marked the disciples as they argued over which of them was the greatest (Luke 22:24). The concept behind conceit is that of empty glory (Greek, *kenodoxian*). In appearance it may seem to be impressive, but inside there is no substance. It is like a balloon; the larger it stretches on the outside, the larger the emptiness on the inside. Such vain glory marked the Pharisees and Diotrephes (Matt. 6:1–18; 3 John 1:9).

Positively, believers should have a high opinion of others. This does not mean that Christians should have a poor self-image; rather, they should try to lift others up without exalting themselves. They must have a servant mind, humbling themselves in order to serve others. They must not think of themselves more highly than they ought to think (Rom. 12:3). They should recognize that they are what they are by the grace of God (1 Cor. 15:10). True humility is the mark of spiritual greatness (Matt. 20:26–27). It will rejoice in what God has made of them and what He has done through them (1 Cor. 1:26–31; 4:6–7).

Concern for others (2:4). The verb *look* (Greek, *skopountes*) is the basis of the English word *scope*. It means to keep one's eye constantly focused on an object. Believers should not merely look out for their "own personal interests."[8] They should not have a selfish outlook, asking, "What's in it for me? What will I get out of it?" Instead, believers should look out for "the interests of others." The adversative "but" (Greek, *alla*) is very emphatic, showing the contrast between selfishness and selflessness. Believers should thus ask, "What are the needs of my brother? What can I do to help him?" We should please others for their edification (Rom. 15:1–2).

Study Questions

1. In what ways do believers manifest that they are good citizens of heaven?

2. Are Christians consistent? Should they be faithful in church attendance when they are away on vacation? Should Christian college students observe the school regulations when they are home for the summer?

3. Should Christians cooperate in evangelistic efforts with all others regardless of moral and doctrinal differences?

4. In what ways do believers fear spiritual opposition? Physical? Social? How can they be encouraged?

5. In what practical ways can believers manifest unity? What is the difference between conformity and unity? Unity and union?

6. What are the marks of pride? Of humility? Of concern for others? Do modern church programs foster vainglory?

CHAPTER 7

The Humiliation and Exaltation of Christ
Philippians 2:5-11

Preview:

In this section, Paul sets forth some of the strongest arguments for the deity of the Lord Jesus Christ. He argues that Christ shares the same characteristics of God and that He is equal with the Father. Because of Jesus Christ's relationship with the Father, the Father highly exalted Him and gave Him the highest name, which "is above every name." As all confess the Lordship of Jesus, God the Father receives the glory!

The perfect example of servanthood is Jesus Christ. In Him can be seen the manifestation of unity, humility, and concern for others. Paul has here contributed one of the greatest Christological passages in the entire Bible (cf. John 1:1–18; Col. 1:15–19; Heb. 1:1–3).

The Illustration of Christ (2:5)

The command. The command literally reads, "Think this in you." The present imperative (Greek, *phroneite*) shows that a humble, altruistic concern must be a daily practice and that it must originate within a submissive mind and will that are determined to obey God. It is not something God develops within the lives of Christians without their knowledge or permission. It also is not achieved through a nonrepeatable crisis decision. The concept behind the verb is that of a mind fixed on a specific purpose.

The demonstrative pronoun "this" (Greek, *touto*) points to the attitude that Christ possessed when He became incarnate in order to die on the cross.

The example. Jesus Christ is often seen in the Scriptures as the supreme example of suffering in the will of God (1 Pet. 2:21), of living in holiness (1 John 2:6), of leadership (1 Cor. 11:1), and of humble servanthood (John 13:15). Theory must be put into practice, and Christ provides the best pattern in that pursuit.[1]

The Humiliation of Christ (2:6–8)

The world views humiliation as forced embarrassment, a reduction of self-respect. Christ, however, elevated the concept to a positive holy virtue that should be cultivated in the lives of all believers. He completely manifested it through His incarnation, earthly ministry, and subsequent death on the cross.

Christ's Deity (2:6)

A sovereign God cannot be humbled, because there is no one or nothing outside Himself that could force Him into that situation. He could, however, humble Himself as a free choice of His will, and He did just that. In the divine program of redemption, God the Son humbled Himself before humankind.

Christ was in the form of God. The phrase "in the form of God" (Greek, *en morphē theou*) refers to the basic essence of the divine being. It denotes the inner nature, not the external appearance. All that God is, Jesus Christ was, is, and ever shall be. What can be said about the Father and the Holy Spirit can also be said of the Son. The Father is God, the Son is God, and the Spirit is God, yet there is only one God (Deut. 6:4). God is a trinitarian oneness. Christians do not worship three Gods, nor are the three persons simply three parts of the one God. There are three distinct persons within the divine being yet an intrapersonal oneness.

The participle *existed* (Greek, *huparchōn*) literally means "to be under beginning" (Greek, *hupo* and *archō*) and denotes prior existence. Christ not only existed in the beginning; He existed before there was a beginning (John 1:1). He did not begin to be in the form of God, because as God He was eternally in the form of God. To say that Jesus was God and that He was in the form of God is to say the same truth.

Christ was equal to God. Christ was not the most God-conscious man who ever lived; nor was He simply like God. Rather, He was "equal with God." His equality to God extended to all of the essential attributes. The Son is just as holy, omnipotent, omniscient, and sovereign as the Father. Christ asserted that God was His Father in a sense in which He is not the Father of anyone else. The

Son and the Father share the same divine nature within an eternal relationship (John 10:30). The Jewish critics understood Christ's claims of equality with the Father, but they rejected them, accusing Jesus of blasphemy (John 5:18; 10:33). The articular infinitive "to be" (Greek, *to einai*) shows that Christ always has been equal to God. If Paul wanted to say that Christ desired to become equal to God, he would have used a different verb form (Greek, *genesthai*).

Christ did not selfishly grasp His deity. The enigmatic phrase "a thing to be grasped" can more easily be translated, "Who . . . did not consider the fact of being equal to God a prize to be selfishly grasped." The verb *consider* (Greek, *hēgēsato*) looks at a logical time in the past when God the Son resolved to surrender the divine prerogative to be served in order to serve the human race as its Savior.

The noun *grasped* (Greek, *harpagmon*) has both an active and a passive meaning. As active, it would refer to the act of seizing or grasping, whereas the passive would emphasize the result of grasping. The active would imply that He wanted to become equal with God, but the passive would see the equality as a reality already held.[2] In this context, the passive is the theological preference.

When Christ did not esteem His equality with God as a prized possession, he literally did not look "on his own personal interests" (cf. 2:4). Instead, He viewed "the interests of others," namely, the sinful plight of the human race. He did not contemplate what He would gain for Himself, but rather what He could do for others.

Christ's Incarnation (2:7)

The strong adversative *but* (Greek, *alla*) contrasts Christ's refusal to be proud as God with His willingness to be humble as man. The prior verse (2:6) gave His attitude, whereas this verse describes His action.

Christ emptied Himself. The translation of the two Greek words *heauton ekenʔse* literally means "Himself He emptied." This points to the historical event of the conception when God the Son entered the body of the virgin Mary, who was overshadowed by the ministry of the Holy Spirit (Luke 1:26–38).

Of what did Christ empty Himself? Several views have been put forth. Some claim that He gave up His deity when He became man; however, God cannot diminish His being. He cannot become less than what He is. He is immutable (Mal. 3:6). Others assert that Jesus emptied Himself of His relative attributes, defined as omnipresence, omnipotence, and omniscience. It is true that Christ went through normal human experiences such as learning (Luke 2:52), exhaustion (John 4:6), and geographical, bodily limitation. This does not mean, however, that He did not possess these essential characteristics of deity. Today Christ's resurrected, glorified human body is in the third heaven, yet He is able to indwell every believer by His Spirit (Col. 1:27) and to be with all believers everywhere at the same time (Matt. 28:20). Some wrongly say that Christ did not use His divine attributes when He lived on earth. He created food, walked on water, and forgave sins.

The proper explanation is that God the Son surrendered the independent exercise of His divine attributes. In the incarnation, He yielded His will to that of the Father. He was God manifest in the flesh. He possessed the attributes, but He used them only under the control of the Holy Spirit and within the will of the Father.

Concerning Christ, Albert Barnes writes that Paul's purpose is not to show

> that he aspired to be equal with God, or that he did not regard it as an improper invasion of the prerogatives of God to be equal with him, but that he did not regard it, in the circumstance of the case, as an object to be greatly desired, or eagerly sought to retain his equality with God. Instead of retaining this by an earnest effort, or by a grasp which he was unwilling to relinquish, he chose to forego the dignity, and to assume the humble condition of a man.[3]

Christ took a servant attitude. His self-emptying is further explained by the fact that He took "the form of a bond-servant" (Greek, *morphēn doulou labōn*). The noun "bond-servant" (Greek, *doulou*) refers to a slave rather than to a hired domestic (Greek, *diakonos*). The Greek participle *labōn*, translated "taking," looks at the time when He emptied Himself, namely, His incarnation at the conception.

A contrast must be seen between Christ's eternal existence in the form of God and His decision to take the form of a servant. As God, He was sovereign, deserving to be served, but He became a slave in order to serve. The active voice of the verb (Greek, *labōn*) reveals that He willingly took the role of slave; it was not forced on Him. Jehovah called Him "My Servant" (Isa. 42:1). Christ Himself claimed that He came to do God's will (Heb. 10:7).

Although there is an ontological equality of persons within the divine essence, there is a voluntary subordination to carry out the redemptive purpose. Within the oneness of a married couple, there is an ontological, personal equality of husband and wife, yet there is a functional headship of the husband over the wife to carry out the purposes of marriage (1 Cor. 11:3). That relationship reflects the functional headship of the Father over the Son.

A servant has no outward display of glory. As the preincarnate God, the glory of the Son radiated from His divine personhood (Isa. 6:1–5; John 12:41). That glory, when veiled within human flesh, manifested itself through servile acts of grace and truth (John 1:14). On one occasion, though, Christ "was transfigured" (Matt. 17:2). Literally, he was "metamorphosed" (Greek, *metemorphōthē*)—that is, He experienced a change of form. The glory of His divine person shone through the flesh of His humanity in which He came to serve.

Christ became human. The Son of God inwardly took the form of servanthood, but outwardly He was made "in the likeness of men." The verb "being made" (Greek, *genomenos*) again looks at the incarnation, namely, the conception in the womb of Mary. The conception was supernatural, but Christ's fetal development, birth, and physical-psychical growth were all normal human experiences (Luke 2:52). The verb means to become what one presently is not. God the Son was an eternal spirit, but He became a flesh and blood person (John 1:14; Gal. 4:4).

The phrase "likeness of men" does not imply that Christ was less than a real man. The word *likeness* (Greek, *homoiōmati*) means that He appeared as real men appear. He walked and talked as ordinary men do. He did not have a halo around His head, nor did a glow emanate from His body. In their dealings with Christ, people treated Him as another man.

Jesus came "in the likeness of sinful flesh" (Rom. 8:3). He was a real man, yet He inherited no sin nature from His mother. A sin nature, however, is not an innate part of the human nature. Adam was a perfect man when God created him, and he did not have a sinful tendency. He later acquired it when he deliberately disobeyed God. Christ neither inherited nor obtained a sin nature; nevertheless, His humanity was just as complete as that of any person. He was very man of very man yet apart from sin (John 8:46; 2 Cor 5:21; Heb. 4:15; 1 Pet. 2:22; 1 John 3:5).

Barnes writes:

> The natural and obvious meaning of the language is, that there was an equality of nature and of rank with God, from which he humbled himself when he *became* a man. The meaning of the whole verse, according to the interpretation suggested . . . is, that Christ, before he became a man, was invested with honour, majesty, and glory, such as was appropriate to God himself; that there was some manifestation or splendour in his existence and mode of being then, which showed that he was equal with God. . . . The fair interpretation of this passage, therefore, is, that Christ before his incarnation was equal with God.[4]

His Crucifixion (2:8)

Christ was treated as a man. He was "found in appearance as a man." The word *appearance* (Greek, *schēmati*) deals with external appearance. People had a sense perception of Jesus, but they did not see Him as He really was. They saw a mere man, not the God-man.

Christ's enemies saw Him as a blaspheming man. If they had known who He really was, they would not have crucified Him (1 Cor. 2:8). His half-brothers hurled sarcasms at Him (John 7:3-5). His hometown neighbors gave Him no honor (Mark 6:1-6). Even the leading apostle, Peter, wrongly rebuked Him (Matt. 16:22).

Humans receive both their personhood and human nature from their parents. God the Son was a divine person with a divine nature who acquired a human nature. He did not receive a personality from Mary. As a result of the incarnation, He was one person with two natures—one divine, the other human.[5]

Christ humbled Himself. Christ was not humbled by others; rather, He "humbled Himself" (Greek, *etapeinōsen heauton*), voluntarily submitting of His will to the directive will of the Father. Jesus' humble submission can be seen in His prayer in the Garden of Gethsemane (Matt. 26:39) and in His arrest, trials, and mockeries. Even Pilate marveled at Christ's quiet acceptance of His predicament (Matt. 27:14). He was the sacrificial Lamb of God, the fulfillment of messianic prophecy (Isa. 53:7). Christ thus possessed a lowliness of mind, a quality Paul wanted all believers to have (2:3).

Christ became obedient to death. The fact of His death is seen in the phrase "becoming obedient to the point of death." Christ knew that His incarnation in a human body presupposed death in that same body (Heb. 10:5-10). His blood had to be shed to produce remission of sins (Heb. 9:22). The type of death was "death on a cross." To the Jew, this was an accursed way to die (Deut. 21:23; Gal. 3:13). To the Roman, it was the execution of a criminal. No Roman citizen had to die this shameful death. It was both painful and embarrassing. The extent of the humiliation of Christ can be seen in His descent from being in the form of God to the lowest form of human death.

William Hendriksen comments:

> From the very beginning of his incarnation he bowed himself under the yoke. Implied in this act of humbling himself is: **and became obedient,** namely, to God the Father, as verse 9 clearly indicates (note, "Therefore *God,*" etc.). Moreover, his obedience knew no bounds: **even to the extent of death.** In that death he, functioning both as Priest and Guilt-offering, gave himself as an expiatory sacrifice for sin (Isa. 53:10). Hence, this death was not just an ordinary death. Says Paul, **yes death by a cross.** Such a death was very *painful.* It has been said that the person who was crucified "died a thousand deaths."[6]

The Exaltation of Christ (2:9–11)

Christ's exaltation came as a result of His total submission to the Father's will. The verb *exalted*, used only here in the New Testament and only of Christ, means to lift above or to lift beyond (Greek, *huperupsōsen*). The adverb *highly* (Greek, *huper*) is actually the preposition prefixed to the verb. This act of God fulfilled the prophecy that spoke of the exaltation of the suffering servant (Isa. 52:13), which involved both the resurrection of Christ from the realm of death and His ascension into the very presence of the Father within the third heaven. Today He is seated at the Father's right hand (Heb. 1:3).

Christ's exaltation involves supremacy over the natural creation because He is its divine creator (John 1:3). It also involves headship over the church because He is the divine-human redeemer (Col. 1:15–19). His exaltation made possible the sending forth of the Holy Spirit (Acts 2:33), intercession for believers (Rom. 8:34), the conferral of spiritual gifts (Eph. 1:20–23; 4:7–11), and representation before God (Heb. 4:14–16).

Paul and the Deity of Christ
Christ is the image of the invisible God (Col. 1:15).
Christ created all things (Col. 1:16).
Christ is before all things (Col. 1:17a).
In Christ all things hold together (Col. 1:17b).
He poured out upon us richly through Jesus Christ our Savior (Titus 3:6).
The LORD your God is the God of gods, and the Lord of lords (Deut. 10:17).
Christ is King of kings and Lord of lords (1 Tim. 6:15).
Our great God and Savior, Christ Jesus (Titus 2:13).
Every knee shall bow to God (Rom. 14:11).
Every knee shall bow to Christ (Phil. 2:10).
In Christ all the fullness of Deity dwells (Col. 2:9).

As part of Christ's exaltation, the Father gave Him "the name which is above every name." The concept of name points to the total person. It refers to the office, rank, and dignity attached to the person because of his or her position. The names of God, for example, reveal His essence and attributes (Gen.

17:1; Ex. 3:14). Since Christ's given name is above every name, it denotes exalted supremacy over all of creation.

Every knee will bow. The bowing of the knee implies a sincere act of reverence, respect, and submission. The reverence has a threefold scope. *First,* the adoration in heaven comes from holy angels and redeemed people who have died (Eph. 1:21; Heb.12:2–24; Rev. 4:9–11; 5:11–12). *Second,* the submission on earth comes from all living people. *Third,* the genuflection under the earth comes from fallen angels and unregenerate people existing in Hades (Luke 16:19–31), Hell (2 Pet. 2:4; Greek, *tartaroō*), or the lake of fire (Matt. 25:41; Rev. 20:11–15).

Every tongue will confess. Both the content and the goal of the confession are set forth. First, the content is the name. It can be translated as "Jesus Christ is Lord" or "Lord Jesus Christ." In either case, every tongue will confess the deity, the humanity, and the redemptive office of the Savior. For some (holy angels and saved men), this confession represents their worship and praise, whereas for others (fallen angels and unsaved men), it designates their total submission to His absolute sovereignty.

Second, the goal of the confession is the glory of God the Father. The time of the confession is not stated. It could occur at the beginning of the millennial reign of Christ or at the time of the Great White Throne Judgment when the old system passes away to make room for the new (Rev. 20:10—21:2).

Study Questions

1. How can the mind of Christ be developed daily? What factors attempt to prevent this expression?

2. How can the deity of Christ be proved to a Jehovah's Witness? To a Jew?

3. How can believers empty themselves today? What are the marks of genuine humility?

4. What are the characteristics of true servanthood? How can churches foster the spirit of service?

5. Are enough sermons preached on the hypostatic union, the truth that Christ is one person with two natures? Can Christians theologically express themselves in the right way?

6. Should modern worship include the bowing of the knee and the confession of the mouth?

CHAPTER 8

The Marks of Humble Service
Philippians 2:12-16

Preview:

Paul is concerned with the spiritual walk of the Philippians. He praises them for their obedience but wants them to continue their growth by working out their salvation. God is sovereignly controlling their lives, so they are to do all things without grumbling or dispute. They are to show constantly that they are innocent in a crooked world and to stay close to the Word of Life, which is the revealed Word of God.

Christians play both an active and a passive part in their relationship with God. They must believe, yet they must be quickened. To grow spiritually, it is imperative for them to walk in holiness yet to be led by the Spirit as well. Human accountability and divine sovereignty thus form two sides for the channel of redemptive purpose.

In this section, Paul further develops his admonitions to the church (cf. 1:27—2:4). The illustration of Christ's humility only heightened their obligation to become true servants of the gospel. This portion is structured around two main commands: "Work out" (2:12) and "Do" (2:14).

Human Responsibility (2:12)

Genuine effort involves God and humans as colaborers. Believers cannot become spiritual by themselves, nor can Christ live His life through unyielded vessels.

The vocative "my beloved" reveals Paul's personal concern for the church. Earlier he identified them as "brethren" (1:12); later, he used this same description (3:1, 13, 17; 4:8). He joined the two titles in a subsequent outburst (4:1). Thus, he regarded them as genuine believers and with great affection.

Obedience. The Philippians' obedience was known to all. They always obeyed. The adverb *always* shows the stability of their Christian walk. The verb *obeyed* (Greek, *hupēkousate*) is a compound form of two words: "under" (Greek, *hupo*) and "hear" (Greek, *akouō*). Thus, people obey when they put themselves under the authority of one who is speaking. The Philippians obeyed God, His word, Paul, and their church officers (1:1). Their obedience manifested Christ's obedience (2:8).

Work. The imperative "work out" literally means "keep working down" (Greek, *katergazesthe*). It involves a constant process of self-initiated activity.[1] When a believer is thoroughly working at his spiritual development, he is working out what God is working in. He is putting his position into practice (Eph. 2:10). The prefix *kata* intensifies the verb and means that the work should be brought to a proper finish. Believers should complete what God has started.

Three features of this work are set forth. First, the time of the work is seen in the phrase: ". . . not as in my presence only, but now much more in my absence." The "presence" could refer either to the past during the apostle's first visit to their city or to his anticipated return (1:27; 2:24). Paul had observed the Philippians' rapid spiritual growth, and he also was convinced that they would prosper under his future ministry. He knew, however, that their advancement could not be dependent on his personal supervision of their lives. The strong contrast manifests his concern that they must learn to mature without his personal help. They needed God to grow in grace and knowledge, but they did not need Paul (2:13).

Second, the object of the work was the Philippians' own salvation. People cannot work for their salvation, but they can work out their spiritual position (Rom. 4:5; Eph. 2:8–10). Biblical salvation involves deliverance from the penalty of sin (2 Thess. 1:9), from its power (Heb. 7:25), and from its presence (Rom. 13:11). The Philippians were saved people (1:6; 3:1); thus, "salvation" (Greek, *sōtērian*) here refers to the daily struggle for victory over the sin nature. Each believer is responsible for his or her own success or failure. He cannot achieve growth for others, nor can he blame others for his carnality.

Third, the attitude of work must be "with fear and trembling." When believers perceive God as He is and what He wants to do through them, these good emotional responses will be produced. They do not mean a psychological frailty nor a fear of hostile people and adverse circumstances. Paul preached with fear and trembling (1 Cor. 2:3). The Corinthian revival was marked by those emotions (2 Cor. 7:15), and so were the lives of obedient Christian slaves (Eph. 6:5). Obedience and holy emotions are companions.

Divine Responsibility (2:13)

People must work because God is working. Four aspects of this divine work are set forth in this verse.

Subject of the work. All persons of the triune Being are actively involved in the life of each believer. The Father is the husbandman who prunes and cleanses each saint (John 15:1–2). The Holy Spirit produces His fruit within the child of God (Gal 5:22–23). Christ lives by faith through each Christian (Gal. 2:20). It appears, though, that the name God (Greek, *ho theos*) here refers to the Father (2:9). The divine activity is literally an "in-working" (Greek, *ho energōn*). The transliteration is "the one who energizes." God's inner work deals with enablement and character, whereas a person's outer work manifests his or her conduct.

Location of the work. God works within the human life ("in you"). This involves the total personality—the intellect, emotions, and will. God does not want to be excluded from any area of human experience. He is not content just to indwell the body of each believer; He wants to energize the new life He has quickened.

Purpose of the work. The two infinitives ("to will and to work") show the two goals of the divine inworking. First, God desires "to will" (Greek, *to thelein*). The will of God manifests His purpose. It includes that which He has unconditionally determined to do within the lives of all believers regardless of their faithfulness (Rom. 8:28–30). It also includes that which He wants to do within each Christian; however, it is conditioned upon the believer's obedience and submission to His will (Rom. 12:1–2; 1 Thess. 4:3). God does not force spirituality on anyone who refuses to have it, but He still continues to work out His purpose. Instead of blessing, He may chastise a disobedient child (Heb. 12:5–11). The commands to repent and to be reconciled are constantly set forth before His erring children. Second, God desires "to work" (Greek, *to energein*). The energy of God manifests His power to accomplish His purpose. God never commands a believer to do something without supplying the ability to do it (4:13). Divine grace and sufficiency are always available for people to do the tasks appointed them (2 Cor. 3:5).

Goal of the work. God works for His own glory ("for *His* good pleasure"). All aspects of salvation are executed for the praise of the glory of divine grace

(Eph. 1:6, 12, 14). They are decreed according to the good pleasure of the divine will (Eph. 1:5, 9). Believers must find pleasure in what brings God pleasure. When they do, they will have joy and satisfaction.

The Explanation of the Command (2:14)

The first command (2:12–13) dealt with the believers' vertical relationship to God, whereas the second imperative concerns their horizontal relationships to people and situations. The first was to be obeyed with a positive attitude; the second is to be discharged without a negative outlook.

The action. Paul simply declared: "Do all things." The present imperative (Greek, *poieite*) stresses the necessity to keep on doing at all times and in all situations. The believer must always be a doer of the Word (James 1:22).

The direct object ("all things") includes all that God has commanded. Love for God manifests itself in the keeping of His directions (1 John 5:2). God's commands are not burdensome (1 John 5:2). Life outside God's will is oppressive, but voluntary conformity to the divine will brings rest to the soul (Matt. 11:28–30).

The attitude. Christians are to avoid "grumbling and disputing." When adversity comes, people have a tendency to blame others or God for their difficulties rather than faulting themselves or rejoicing in tribulation. When the first sin occurred, Adam blamed God and Eve faulted the serpent (Gen. 3:11–13).

The noun *grumbling* (Greek, *goggusmōn*) comes from a verb that means to mutter or grumble. It is an "outward expression of an inner lawlessness and rebellion that shakes the fist in the face of God and repudiates His right to rule, that questions His love and wisdom."[2] The children of Israel constantly complained when they wandered in the wilderness (Ex. 14:10–12; 15:24; 16:3; 17:3; Num. 14:2). Their complaining actually was directed at God through Moses (Ex. 16:9).

The noun *disputing* (*dialogismōn*) conveys the ideas of dialogue and argument. It emphasizes mental murmuring, whereas complaining reflects an emotional response.

Both attitudes, of course, reveal a spirit of carnality. They constitute rebellion against what God wants people to do, when He wants them to do it, where it should be done, and why it should occur. In essence, they are like the clay that questions the potter as he fashions it (Rom. 9:19–21). Such constant bickering will lead to divine chastisement.

The Purposes of the Command (2:15–16)

A holy reason can always be found behind a divine command. The verb ("that you may prove yourselves") shows that there is a difference between being a Christian and living out the Christian life. The former refers to position, the latter to practice. Four purposes are expressed.

Blameless behavior. The concept "blameless" (Greek, *amemptoi*) means a freedom from censure. To be blameless means to be judged by others to be innocent and pure (1 Thess. 2:10; 5:23). To be "innocent" (Greek, *akeraioi*) is to be unmixed or unadulterated.[3] The term was used of solid gold jewelry that was without any alloy. In medicine it referred to a prescription that was useful but harmless. Such spiritual purity, unmixed with sin or hypocrisy, can be attained only by the heat of testing through adversity.

Spotless children. Paul called the Philippians to be "children of God." Sinners become children of God by regeneration through the Holy Spirit (John 1:12) and they inherit the divine nature of their heavenly Father. Paul also wanted them to become "above reproach." This negative adjective literally means "without spot or blemish" (Greek, *amōma*). Believers have been washed of the guilt and filth of their sin so that they are clean in God's sight (John 13:10; 1 Cor. 6:11). Nevertheless, they still must be cleansed from the daily defilement of the world (John 13:10; 1 John 1:9). The Philippians' environment was not conducive to holiness, because they lived "in the midst of a crooked and perverse generation." The word *crooked* (Greek, *skolias*) implies that which is curved in contrast to that which is straight. The adjective *perverse* (Greek, *diestrammenēs*) denotes that which is permanently distorted or twisted.[4] The world is full of ungodly people who will never be reformed or regenerated; rather, immorality will increase (2 Tim. 3:1–7). Believers should not expect to convert the entire world, nor should they permit the world to change them.

Lights in the world. Christians should be separated from the world but not isolated from it. They must "shine as lights in the world." Christ, as the Light of the World, shone in the world of spiritual darkness (John 1:4). Believers, as light, should also let their lights shine (Matt. 5:14, 16). Light must function where it is needed—in the darkness.

Word bearers. Believers must "hold fast the word of life." The Greek verb *epechontes* means not just to hold fast to oneself, but also to hold forth to others. A person can only witness to that which he or she already possesses.

Jesus Christ is the Word of Life (1 John 1:1); however, each portion of Scripture is a word of life about Him. The written Word reveals the living Word to those who are dead in spiritual darkness.

The Results of the Command (2:16)

Boastful rejoicing. Paul knew that he would appear "in the day of Christ." This event includes both the return of the Savior and His subsequent judgment of believers. It involves the reunion of the saints with each other and with the Lord (2 Thess. 2:1). In that day, Paul wanted to rejoice over what his ministry had accomplished in the lives of the Philippians. "To glory" (Greek, *kauchēma*) includes a pride of achievement and should not be limited to mere joy. There is joy when a sinner receives salvation, but there is greater joy when spiritual children walk in truth (3 John 1:4). Unfortunately, the joy of parenthood is readily lessened by the disobedience of children (Heb. 13:17).

Productive labor. Paul was not content with merely a good start. He wanted his spiritual children to go on to maturity and holiness, to be right both in position and in practice. He determined the success of his ministry by two concepts. First, he did not want to find out at the Judgment Seat of Christ that he had "run in vain." This would occur if he preached a faulty or partial message (Gal. 2:2) or if he harbored carnal motivations or immoral behavior (1 Cor. 9:26–27). Furthermore, he did not want the future to reveal that he had toiled "in vain." Both legalism and Satan could cause this result (Gal. 4:11; 1 Thess. 3:5).

Paul's race and toil were correct. He knew that God would reward his integrity and faithfulness, for no genuine labor is in vain in the Lord (1 Cor. 15:58). All Christian workers have wondered about the value of their work in the lives of others, especially when those people persistently refuse to follow their leadership. They must, however, finish their course with joy and expectation (Acts 20:24; 2 Tim. 4:7).

Study Questions

1. Do Christian leaders love their people as they should? Do they express it in their words and actions?

2. Do Christians fear God today? If not, what can be done to produce genuine reverence?

3. When do the human and the divine conflict? When do they harmonize?

4. Why do believers often complain? Cite some examples of times when Christians may murmur when the unsaved do not.

5. What are the characteristics of a crooked people? In what ways does our country manifest these?

6. How can believers be more effective in their witness?

7. Why do Christian workers often get discouraged? How can they be helped?

CHAPTER 9

The Three Examples of Humility
Philippians 2:17-30

Preview:

Not knowing his fate, whether release or death at the hands of his captors, Paul still rejoices in his service to the Lord and asks his readers to do the same. He prepares to send two men back to the Philippians with his letter. The first is Timothy, who, according to Paul, has a tender heart for the Philippians and who has been a faithful servant to both Paul and the gospel. The second is Epaphroditus, who brought the original message to Paul from Philippi. Epaphroditus suffered much, almost to the point of death, for the gospel and still had a great concern for his fellow Christians in Philippi.

Theory must be put into practice and ideas must be dressed in flesh. Learners want to be shown as well as to be told. The apostle thus cited three men—himself, Timothy, and Epaphroditus—who manifested the mind of Christ and who were working out what God was working in. All three exhibited the joy of unity, humility, and concern for others.

Paul (2:17-18)

Paul was not afraid to point people to himself nor to list himself as the first example (cf. 4:9). Leaders must be, know, and do all that God expects before they can require commitments from others. Good teachers, leaders, or parents should be able to ask others to observe them as well as to listen to them (Ezra 7:10).

His Offering (2:17)

In the past. The phrase "upon the sacrifice and service of your faith" points to that time when Paul completely surrendered his life to God. All believers should present themselves to God as a living sacrifice (Rom. 12:1–2). This priestly function can occur at conversion, but it is usually made in a postregeneration experience. It can be reaffirmed subsequently many times. Unfortunately, many believers never make this decision to lose their lives for Christ's sake (Matt. 16:24–25).

The "sacrifice" (Greek, *thusia*) refers to the Jewish rite of the burnt offering in which an animal was totally consumed on the altar to show the complete and voluntary dedication of a person to God. Offerers made this sacrifice because they were thankful for all that God had done for them. Thus, Paul gave his life entirely over to God to live for His glory (1:20).

A commitment to God also brings a commitment to others. Paul knew that his service to God would involve service to others ("and service of your faith"). The term *service* (Greek, *leitourgia*) transliterates as "liturgy"; thus, helping others is actually a religious ministry. The apostle served them by declaring how they could have saving faith and by encouraging them to grow in faith.

In the future. The conditional clause "if I am being poured out" reveals the strong possibility of imminent martyrdom for the apostle.[1] The Greek verb (*spendomai*) was used of the drink offering that was poured out on the burnt offering (Ex. 29:38–41; Lev. 23:12–13; Num. 15:1–10). Paul had given his life to live for God and others; now he was willing to give his life to die for them. In this way he emulated the self-emptying of Christ and His obedience unto death (2:7–8). Paul elsewhere confessed his willingness to die for Christ as a drink offering (Acts 21:13; 2 Tim. 4:6).

Even those who had been saved from a pagan background would have understood this figure of speech. They were acquainted with the libation of wine or perfume poured out in the concluding rites of a sacrifice to a polytheistic deity.

His Rejoicing (2:17–18)

Rejoicing has two directions. First, Paul said: "I rejoice and share my joy with you all." He rejoiced in the prospect of a death that would glorify God and advance the believers' faith. Second, he called upon them to rejoice with him (*"I urge you,* rejoice in the same way and share your joy with me"). They were saddened by his imprisonment, but he wanted their despair to be turned into joy by the truth of his letter and by the personal witness of Timothy and Epaphroditus.

Timothy (2:19-24)

Timothy assisted Paul in the original evangelization of the city. He was also a cosender of the epistle (1:1). Now he is mentioned as a second example.

Paul's Purpose for Timothy (2:19, 23-24)

Paul always made his travel plans in total submission to God's will (Acts 18:21; Rom. 15:32). His human desire is seen in the verb "I hope" (Greek, *elpizō*). His acknowledgment of the divine will is evident in the phrase "in the Lord Jesus."

At the beginning and the end of this section, Paul presented three purposes concerning Timothy. In between, he discussed the character qualifications of his young associate.

To send him to the church (2:19, 23). Paul hoped to send Timothy to the church "shortly." The Greek adverb *(tacheōs)* conveys the idea of imminent quickness.[2] The fact of sending was sure; only the time of sending was indefinite. The latter is clarified in the conditional statement: "as soon as I see how things go with me" (2:23). Paul was awaiting the disposition of his appeal before Caesar and the Roman authorities. He fully expected that it would be favorable and that it would be given at any moment. Although the apostle needed Timothy in Rome, he was more concerned about the spiritual needs of the church. Thus, he planned to give up one who belonged to him. This attitude reflected the mind of Christ who gave up what was His to reach others.

To be encouraged (2:19). The conjunction *that* (Greek, *hina*) shows the second purpose: "that I also may be encouraged when I learn of your condition." Timothy would be the first to be cheered by the response of the church to Paul's letter; then he would report back to Paul either by personal visit or by a representative.

The verb literally reads: "I may have a good soul" (Greek, *eupsuchō*). To have an effort of joint souls (1:27; 2:2), those souls must be spiritually healthy and pure. This condition, however, must be based on knowledge. It would happen when Paul received the report about the condition of the church.

To prepare for the visit of the apostle (2:24). Paul then expressed confidence that he would be able to visit Philippi. The verb ("I trust;" Greek, *pepoitha*) is different than the one used for the sending of Timothy (2:19). It denotes a settled assurance and conviction of heart produced by the indwelling God. Both the intensive pronoun *myself* and the adverb *shortly* reinforced that inner persuasion. Such news, of course, would bring joy to the hearts of the Philippians and would stimulate them to obey the directives of Paul's letter.

Paul's Preference for Timothy (2:20–22)

Why did Paul decide to send Timothy? Why not one of his other coworkers? The apostle saw in Timothy some qualities that the Philippians needed to develop.

He was "of kindred spirit" (2:20). The term literally means "equal soul." Just as Jesus Christ was equal to the Father in deity (2:6), so Timothy was equal to Paul in the characteristics of unity, humility, and concern for others. This is a stronger and slightly different term than that used in his appeal to the church members (2:2; Greek, *sumpsuchoi*). Both Paul and Timothy shared the mind of Christ, thought the same things, and had the same spiritual goals.

He had concern (2:20). Three concepts are described here. First, Timothy was a caring person. The verb *care* can be used of a self-destructive worry that profits no one (4:6; Matt. 6:25). Timothy, however, manifested the same care for the churches that Paul showed (2 Cor. 11:28). He prayed, taught, and counseled others. Second, his concern was genuine, the adverb normally translated as "genuinely" or "truly" (Greek, *gnēsiōs*). Later, Paul called him "my genuine child in the faith" (1 Tim. 1:2; Greek, *gnēsiō*). He was legitimate in his spiritual birth and development, and he manifested the same nature as Paul, his spiritual father. Third, Timothy had concern for the church. The phrase "your welfare" can be translated "the things concerning you" (Greek, *ta peri humōn*). Timothy shared the apostle's concern over the weaknesses of the believers. He wanted to be the human instrument by which God would remedy the situation.

He was not selfish (2:21). Paul then pronounced a general indictment on the motivation of some gospel preachers (1:15–16). The words "for they all seek after their own interests" have a ring of sadness in them. Selfishness, a trait of sinful humanity, unfortunately permeates the Christian world as well. Timothy, however, was not in the ministry for what he could get out of it. He was a giver, not a taker.

He manifested Christ (2:21). Selfish persons do not seek the things "of Christ Jesus." These things include the mind of Christ as seen in humility, obedience, and concern for others. Christ emptied Himself, Paul was willing to pour out himself, and Timothy was determined to seek the glorification of the Savior in his ministry to the church.

He was a servant (2:22). Timothy was first of all a proven servant. The Philippians were aware of his character ("you know"), for they had had contact with him on at least four occasions. He was in their midst when the church was started (Acts 16:12–40), when Paul sent him from Athens to Thessalonica (Acts 18:5; 1 Thess. 3:1–2), and twice during the third missionary journey (Acts 19:22; 20:3–6). They had proof (Greek, *dokimēn*) that

Timothy was a faithful worker. The word *proof* was used of the testing of precious metals by the heat of fire. All church leaders should be proved so that people will have confidence in their leadership (1 Tim. 3:10).

Timothy was also a cooperative servant. Paul said of Timothy, "he served with me." Some servants can work effectively when they labor alone but cannot get along with others to serve in a team effort. Timothy, however, served "like a child serving his father." Timothy was Paul's son in the faith and thus inherited the apostle's servant nature. There was no competition between the two, nor did Timothy seek to displace Paul.

Third, Timothy was a servant of the gospel. He determined to further the outreach of the redemptive message in the lives of both sinners and believers. This dedication reflected Christ's willingness to lay the foundation of the gospel through His death and resurrection (2:5–8).

Epaphroditus (2:25–30)

The name Epaphroditus means "lovely" or "charming." It is probably based on Aphrodite, the pagan goddess of love and beauty. His name occurs only twice in the Scriptures, both times in this book (2:25; 4:18). The church had sent Epaphroditus to Rome to give Paul some money (4:18). Now the apostle planned to send him back home with his letter.

His Character (2:25)

The verbs indicate that Paul sent Epaphroditus at the same time he dispatched the letter.[3] He deemed it necessary because the epistle was finished (2:25). Epaphroditus was now well enough to travel. Paul listed five positive characteristics of this outstanding believer.

Brother. Relationship is more crucial than responsibility; thus, Paul first described Epaphroditus as his brother. They were both in the family of God through regeneration, and they were joined together with the brothers and sisters at Philippi (1:12; 3:1).

Worker. Epaphroditus was also a fellow worker (Greek, *sunergon*). Both he and Paul were working out what God was working in. Paul never permitted his apostolic status to foster a superior spirit within himself. Rather, he saw himself as a coworker with God and with other believers in a common effort to reach people with the gospel.

Soldier. Epaphroditus was a "fellow soldier" as well. He had put on the armor of God to war against sin and the devil (Eph. 6:10–17). He endured hardship as a good soldier of Jesus Christ (2 Tim. 2:3–4). He took his stand with Paul in aggressive defense of the gospel (1:7).

Messenger. Furthermore, Epaphroditus was the "messenger" (Greek, *apostolon*) of the church. This term is normally translated "apostle," but he was not an apostle in the technical sense. Only those who saw the resurrected Christ and who were commissioned directly by Him to preach the gospel were regarded as the authoritative apostles (1 Cor. 9:1–5; 15:7–9). In a general sense, however, he was sent by the church to Rome with a commission to execute. He was an apostle of the church but not technically of Christ.

Minister. Finally, Epaphroditus was also a minister to the needs of the apostle. The phrase "the one who ministered" is actually a noun (Greek, *leitourgon*). It is used of official and sacred service. In this context it is also used of the service of both Paul and the church (2:17, 30). The gift of money sent by the church was a sacrifice to God offered as a priestly function of believers (4:18). Just as Paul was willing to live or die in his service to the church, so Epaphroditus came close to death in his service to Paul.

His Concern (2:26–28)

Epaphroditus truly looked on the interests of others (2:4), as is clearly demonstrated in the details surrounding his sickness.

His compassion (2:26). Two inner emotions are described here. First, he longed after his home church. It was a prolonged duration of intense desire. This desire was of the same type that Paul expressed to the church (1:8). Second, he "was distressed." This is the same term used of Christ's agony in Gethsemane (Matt. 26:37; Mark 14:33). It stresses mental, emotional, and spiritual anguish.

The reason for these two emotional concerns is seen in the causal clause "because you had heard that he was sick". In his labor at Rome, Epaphroditus became deathly ill. Word of this sickness somehow got back to the church at Philippi. Subsequently, he became informed that the church knew about his physical weakness. He then became concerned over their concern for him.

His healing (2:27). The church knew that their member had become ill, but they apparently did not know the severity of the weakness. Paul now informed them that Epaphroditus was sick "to the point of death." No indication is given of the nature of the sickness. But God in His mercy graciously healed him. God extended physical mercy to Epaphroditus and psychological mercy to Paul ("and not on him only but also on me"). The negative purpose clause shows the real explanation behind the healing ("lest I should have sorrow upon sorrow"). The first sorrow came when the coworker became sick, and the second would have come if he had died.

His reunion (2:28). As soon as Epaphroditus was healed, Paul sent him in haste to the church. The adverb "more eagerly" (Greek, *spoudaioteros*) connotes speed and diligence. The appearance of Epaphroditus at Philippi doubtless caused both surprise and joy, because the church thought that he was still ill in Rome. They had not heard about his miraculous recovery. His return would accomplish two good results: The church would rejoice at his coming and Paul would be less sorrowful in that the anxious concern of all parties would be turned into joy.

His Commendation (2:29)

Receive him. The conjunction "therefore" (Greek, *oun*) shows what response the church should have toward Epaphroditus in the light of his dedicated service and return. The two imperatives call for two positive reactions. They should first receive him in the Lord with all gladness (cf. Matt. 10:40–41).

Honor him. They should also "hold men like him in high regard." The plural ("men") points them to esteem highly all men who were like Epaphroditus. The phrase "in high regard" (Greek, *entimous*) literally means "in honor." The word is used of a precious, prized possession and of money (1 Tim. 5:17). The adjective is used of Christ as the precious cornerstone of salvation (1 Pet. 2:4, 6). Humble servants of the Lord must be appreciated, and such honor should be given publicly.

His Commitment (2:30)

He worked for Christ. Epaphroditus's motivation was the gospel ministry. He declared the redemptive work of Christ, namely, His death and resurrection (cf. 1 Cor. 16:10). In addition, his labor took him to the door of death. Just as Christ obeyed unto the death of the cross, so Epaphroditus followed his Savior to the threshold of physical death.

He did not regard his life. The participle "risking" (Greek, *parabouleusamenos*) was used of people who exposed themselves to danger. The thought is that Epaphroditus risked his life. In his concern for Paul's needs, he did not look on his own needs, namely, the progressive weakness of his body.

He offered substitute service. Epaphroditus was aware that the gift of the church was not enough to meet the apostle's needs, so he worked to earn money. The more he worked, the weaker he grew. He tried to make up that difference between the actual amount of the gift and the needed total. We know the lack was not created by a deliberate attempt to withhold funds, for the church was later applauded for its generosity (4:10–19).

Study Questions

1. What does it mean to offer oneself as a living sacrifice to God? How many Christians have done this? Have you?

2. What motivates a person to die for a cause? What prevents that person from doing so?

3. In what ways do Christians make plans without consulting God? How can human and divine plans be harmonized?

4. In what ways do Christians manifest personal ambition and greed in the work of the Lord? How are they encouraged in this unwholesome pursuit?

5. Is it wise for members of the same family to work together in the same Christian effort? Are there advantages? Disadvantages?

6. Does God perform works of healing today? Are there genuine faith healers today?

CHAPTER 10

The Danger of Legalism
Philippians 3:1-6

Preview:

Although Paul starts with a command to rejoice, he immediately follows with a warning about false teachers, both Jew and Gentile, who would pervert the gospel message, putting faith in their flesh and working for their salvation. To magnify the futile nature of fleshly position or accomplishments, Paul shows how he had been the perfect fleshly example of righteousness.

In the third chapter of Paul's letter to the Philippians, he discusses the threefold aspect of salvation against the background of doctrinal error. The exposition of this basic truth centers around three verbal concepts. First, Paul wanted to be "found in Him"; that is justification (3:9). Second, his ambition was to "know Him;" that is sanctification (3:10). Third, he desired to "wait for a Savior"; that is glorification (3:20). These three theological verities deal with the past, present, and future experiences of all believers.

In this treatment of the doctrine of justification, Paul distinguishes between salvation by works through human effort and salvation by grace alone through faith alone. In this section, two major contrasts between Paul and the false teachers are set forth.

In Circumcision (3:1-3)

The adverb *finally* (Greek, *to loipon*) does not signal the end of the letter; rather, it designates an abrupt change in subject matter. The transitional thought translates: "As far as the rest is concerned."

Necessity of Warning (3:1)

The opening command to "rejoice in the Lord" sets the tone for the entire chapter. They were not to rejoice in who they were or what they had done. They were to rejoice in all that Jesus Christ is and in all that He had graciously provided through His redemptive death and resurrection. Such holy joy, however, can be threatened by the onslaught of doctrinal and moral error.

For Paul. Faithful preachers must not only declare truth, but also expose error. Like Nehemiah, they must build and protect at the same time (Neh. 4:18). Paul knew that he had "to write the same things" he had taught them during his past visits to their city (3:18). Repetition and reinforcement are basic laws of pedagogy.

Such warnings were not "trouble" (Greek, *oknēron*), that is, not an irksome task, to Paul. This adjective comes from a verb that means to delay or to hesitate; thus, the apostle did not shrink from his responsibility to point out error. Paul determined to declare the whole counsel of God at all costs (Acts 20:26–31).

For the church. Paul's writing the same warnings over again was a "safeguard" for the Philippians. This adjective comes from a verb (Greek, *asphallō*) that means not to totter or to reel. Paul wanted them to be forewarned, to be alert to danger, and to be watchful for their souls.

Nature of Warning (3:2)

The imperative "beware" is repeated three times. This verb (Greek, *blepete*) simply means to keep looking out, to continue watching, or to persist in seeing.[1]

Some have concluded that Paul was talking about three different groups: Gentiles, greedy teachers, and Jews. It seems better, however, to see the descriptions as three characteristics of the same group. They doubtless were the Judaizers who taught that a Gentile had to be circumcised to be saved (Acts 15:1). They should not be equated with the preachers who spoke the truth with faulty motivations (1:14–18).

Beware of dogs. This warning depicts their character. The title "dogs" (Greek, *kunas*) is applied to the unsaved who are filthy and vulgar (Prov. 26:11; 2 Pet. 2:22), who mock at God (Ps. 59:6), who are contemptible (2 Sam. 9:8), and who will be outside the holy city (Rev. 22:15). Jews used the term as a synonym for Gentiles (Matt. 15:26). The metaphor in this verse, however, refers to Jewish teachers who tried to impose legalism on Gentile believers. They are like the false prophets within ancient Israel (Isa. 56:10–11).

Beware of evil workers. This warning describes the conduct of the false teachers. They were workers in that they aggressively promoted their beliefs.

They were working to gain their own salvation, and they attempted to influence others to accept legalism as an additional requirement to faith as the grounds for divine acceptance. The Judaizers were "evil" (Greek, *kakous*), deceitful workers and false apostles (2 Cor. 11:13), whose work was marked by a heretical message and selfish motivations. They were ministers of righteousness based on human pride and effort, not proclaimers of the divine righteousness that is imputed by grace through faith alone (2 Cor. 11:15).

Beware of the false circumcision. This warning denotes their creed. The term "false circumcision" (Greek, *katatomēn*) refers to severe mutilation, a thorough cutting. This descriptive title must be seen in contrast to genuine circumcision (Greek, *peritomē*), which is based on the same verb stem. The Judaizers were cutting down (Greek, *kata*), whereas circumcision involved a cutting around (Greek, *peri*). Physical mutilations, practiced in pagan idolatry, were prohibited by God through Moses (Lev. 21:5; 1 Kin. 18:28).

In their zeal to physically circumcise their converts, the Judaizers were spiritually castrating them. They harmed people by their false teaching. They proclaimed salvation by faith and works, a concept that really is a "works only" human religion. They were unsaved and under the curse of God (Gal. 1:6–9). They perverted the gospel by removing its gracious character.

Reason for Warning (3:3)

The connective "for" (Greek, *gar*) gives the reason for the three warnings. In this verse there is a contrast between the true circumcision and the false circumcision.

Definition of true circumcision. The personal pronoun *we* (Greek, *hēmeis*) has special stress. We believers in Christ, including circumcised Jews, circumcised Gentile proselytes, and uncircumcised Gentile converts, are the true spiritual children of Abraham (Gal. 3:26–29). The pronoun, of course, includes both Paul and the church.

The verb *are* (Greek, *esmen*) manifests a dogmatic conviction that Paul was absolutely sure of the spiritual standing of his converts and himself. It was a present possession enjoyed by all of them.

The phrase "the *true* circumcision" (Greek, *hē peritomē*), is a synonym for the body of Christ, the true church, the family of God in this present age. It manifests the work of the Spirit of God within the heart of each believer at the time of regeneration (Col. 2:11). In the flesh, the presence or absence of physical circumcision distinguished between the Jew and the Gentile (Eph. 2:11), but spiritual circumcision involves the heart and the spirit (Rom. 2:28–29). True circumcision removes the sin of the heart, not the skin of the flesh (Jer. 4:4).

Explanation of true circumcision. Three aspects are given. First, genuine believers "worship in the Spirit of God." Constant worship is part of their daily behavior.[2] Jesus Christ declared that God is spirit and that people must worship Him in spirit and truth (John 4:24). The noun *spirit* can refer to either the Holy Spirit or to the human spirit. Regardless, both concepts are true. Believers worship God the Father in their human spirits by the Holy Spirit who indwells them.

Second, genuine believers "glory in Christ Jesus." All saved people glory continually in the finished redemptive work that the God-man accomplished through His death and resurrection (Gal. 6:14). To glory in Christ also means to admit that He is Jehovah God (Jer. 9:23–24; 1 Cor. 1:29–31).

Third, genuine believers "put no confidence in the flesh." When people have such confidence, they think they are good enough in themselves and that they have sufficient ability to do whatever it takes to gain entrance into heaven. Self-abasement is absolutely necessary to gain divine exaltation, a truth seen in the parable of the publican and the Pharisee (Luke 18:9–14).

In Confidence (3:4–6)

The mention of "confidence" (3:3; cf. 3:4) serves as a transition from the first contrast to the second. On what basis can confidence be established? In this section, Paul sets forth criteria for spiritual excellence, which he once trusted in his unsaved life.

Comparison of Confidence (3:4)

Paul never altered his message, but he did change his methods in order to minister to different groups (1 Cor. 9:19–23). He reluctantly involved himself in boasting to disprove false allegations against him (2 Cor. 11:1—12:11). To portray graphically the folly of self-confidence, he now used himself as an example. He set forth two claims. He asserted that he could have confidence. The pronoun *I* (Greek, *egō*) puts great emphasis on the self. The adverb *far more* (Greek, *mallon*) links him with the Judaizers who built their ministries on self-confidence. The prepositional phrase "in the flesh" makes it clear that this was a confidence based on human standards, not on divine and biblical evaluations. Paul then charged that he could have more confidence than anyone else in the world. He did not just match the Judaizers or any other self-righteous group; he surpassed them. This boast did not originate from any pride on his part. He actually used this evaluation of his past as an argument to show the fallacy of such egomania.

Demonstration of Confidence (3:5–6)

Before Paul became a Christian, his life was a spiritual paradox. He was at the same time both one of the best men and one of the worst men who had ever lived. He hated Christ and His followers; thus, he became a blasphemer and a persecutor (1 Tim. 1:13). In this passage, however, he sets forth seven points of his human merit. The first four were a result of his genetic inheritance, whereas the last three were a reflection of his personal choices. All of them, nevertheless, manifested his pride. Here can be found pride of race, family, patriotism, orthodoxy, zeal, and self-righteousness.

Circumcision. Circumcision was a sign of faith in the fulfillment of the Abrahamic covenant (Gen. 17:1–14). When the rite was first instituted, Abraham was ninety-nine years old and Ishmael was thirteen (Gen. 17:24–25). From that point on, a Jewish male child had to be circumcised on the eighth day after his birth (Gen. 17:12; Lev. 12:3). In conformity to the law, Jesus was circumcised on the eighth day (Luke 2:21), and so was Paul. Gentiles became proselytes when they submitted to this religious surgery in their adult years.

Stock of Israel. Paul could trace his genealogical ancestry to the patriarchs, including Jacob, whose name was changed to Israel by God (Gen. 35:10). The term *nation* (Greek, *genous*) denotes kind, race, or generation. The term *Israel* came to be seen as the covenant name of the elect nation (Rom. 11:1).

Tribe of Benjamin. Benjamin was the last of the twelve sons to be born to Jacob. In fact, Jacob's beloved wife Rachel died as she gave birth to this son (Gen. 35:16–18). This tribe gave Israel its first king, Saul. It is very plausible that Paul's parents named him after this royal member of the tribe.

Hebrew of the Hebrews. Paul was a Hebrew son born to Hebrew parents. Neither Paul nor his parents ever submitted to the influences of Hellenistic culture. He learned the Hebrew language and orthodox customs at an early age in his hometown of Tarsus and later received his rabbinical education in Hebrew at Jerusalem under the respected Gamaliel (Acts 22:2–3). Although he grew up in a Gentile city and learned both Greek and Aramaic, he did not become Hellenized as so many Jews had done (Acts 6:1).

Pharisee. After Paul's three journeys as a Christian missionary, he still confessed that he was a Pharisee (Acts 23:6). He thus contrasted himself with the other dominant Jewish sect, the Sadducees, who denied the existence of angels, the reality of the spirit, and the physical resurrection of the dead (Acts 23:8). Phariseeism was the strictest sect within Judaism (Acts 26:5). Paul was not only a member of this legalistic, orthodox group, but he was also its most zealous member (Gal. 1:14).

Zealous. In his zeal for legalistic Phariseeism, Paul had persecuted the church. He honestly thought that the killing of Christians was a noble and meritorious service for God (cf. John 16:2). He was responsible for the martyrdom of Stephen (Acts 8:1), for forcing the apostles out of Jerusalem (Acts 8:1), and for imprisoning believers both in Jerusalem and in Damascus (Acts 8:3; 9:21). Believers were terrified by him (Acts 9:26). Although Paul's zeal and sincerity could never be questioned, he was sincerely wrong. He was reckoned within the spiritual blindness of national Israel (Rom. 10:2–3).

Blameless. Legal righteousness can only be achieved by meticulous conformity to all of the positive and negative commandments. It can only be granted to those who deserve it.

Paul asserted that he had become "blameless" (Greek, *amemptos*). He loved God and tried to serve Him to the best of his ability. No one could accuse him of being slothful in his attempts to keep the law. He was not perfect. In fact, he sinned, but he doubtless offered a proper sacrifice for his atonement.

Study Questions

1. Are Christians given enough warnings about false teachers and erroneous doctrine? What are the best ways to alert them?

2. What is involved in declaring the whole counsel of God? How does this relate to the correct procedure of discipleship?

3. What contemporary groups correspond to the ancient Judaizers? What are the modern equivalents to the issue of circumcision?

4. How can God be worshiped in the spirit? What is the difference between proper order and legalistic formality?

5. In what ways do people put confidence in the flesh? How can their pride be exposed?

6. How do people recite their religious pedigrees today? Is this possible through pride of denomination?

7. How can people be sincerely wrong in their religious practice? How can such people be won to Christ?

CHAPTER 11

The Joy of Salvation
Philippians 3:7–14

Preview:

After pointing out his earthly credentials as a righteous man, Paul explains that all of his accomplishments are worthless compared to the righteousness "which comes from God on the basis of faith." Paul speaks of his great desire to one day be resurrected in Christ but also points out that, until that day, we all must work toward that goal. We are not to dwell on our past, whether glorious or infamous, but constantly press onward in service to our Lord.

In the first part of Philippians 3, Paul contrasts himself with the legalistic Judaizers, but in this middle section he reveals his new relationship to Jesus Christ. Two aspects of his salvation are given here: justification (3:7–9) and sanctification (3:10–14).

Justification (3:7–9)

Justification is the act of God whereby He declares to be righteous that sinner who has received the imputed righteousness of God by faith in Jesus Christ. Its essence is grace (Rom. 3:24), its source is God (Rom. 3:26), its means is faith (Rom. 3:28), its foundation is the blood of Christ (Rom 5:9), its sphere is Jesus Christ (1 Cor. 6:11), its agent is the Holy Spirit (1 Cor. 6:11), and its evidence is works (James 2:24).

At the time of justification and conversion, a sinner must reject the proud efforts of self and accept the gracious provision of Christ. Paul did exactly that. The strong adversative ("but") shows the contrast between Paul's past and his present spiritual life.

Paul Rejected Self

The phrase "whatever things" (Greek, *hatina*) refers to the seven points of Paul's past religious experience (3:5–6). They had produced a legalistic sense of confidence within his life. The noun *gain* (Greek, *kerdē*) is in the plural and should be read as "gains." The apostle had looked upon each individual achievement as a separate gain.

Paul esteemed his gains as loss (3:7). His assets became liabilities. His credits suddenly were transferred into debits. The verb phrase "I have counted" indicates that he made a conscious decision to repudiate his religious successes and racial inheritance and that he continued to view his part in an unfavorable light.[1] This new outlook occurred at the time of his repentance.

The word *loss* (Greek, *zēmian*) is in the singular, signifying that Paul grouped all of his gains together into one and treated them as a unified loss. There was nothing meritorious in any one of them. This word was also used of the loss suffered by the ship on which Paul was taken as a prisoner to Rome (Acts 27:10, 21). The cargo was thrown overboard and the ship broke up (Acts 27:38, 41). In like manner, sinners must discard their pride in order to rescue their souls. The prepositional phrase "for Christ" gives the reason for the radical rejection of self. People must do it to receive the righteousness of the Savior.

Paul suffered loss. At his conversion, Paul also "suffered the loss of all things." It cost the young Pharisee to become a Christian. He lost his status within Judaism, his reputation, and his opportunity for wealth and fame. He experienced ostracism, bodily harm, death threats, and property destruction (cf. Heb. 10:34). He may have forfeited his Jewish birthright and family inheritance. The inclusive phrase "all things" goes beyond the areas listed as gains (3:5–6) and embraces all spheres of human experience. Paul's conversion produced radical changes in all of his personal and social relationships.

Why did Paul give up so much? He did it because Christ had done something for him. To have everything without Christ is to have nothing, but to have Christ is to possess everything. The reason behind Paul's conversion was neither intellectual nor psychological; rather, it was Christological—for the sake of Christ.

Paul esteemed his gains as rubbish (3:8b). In these verses, Paul revealed his present attitude toward his past by using the same verb (Greek, *hēgeomai*) three times; however, he made a sharp contrast by twice changing the verb tense from past ("counted") to present ("count"). After twenty-five years of Christian experience, Paul still deprecated his self-righteous effort in the same way he did when he was born again. In genuine conversion, a believer repudiates legalism for both the imputation and the maintenance of his salvation.

The graphic term *rubbish* (Greek, *skubala*), sometimes translated "dung," has two possible derivations. It could come from the noun stem for body excrement (Greek, *skor*), or it may refer to the food leftovers that were thrown to the dogs (from Greek, *ek kunas ballō*). In either case, it points to that which must be discarded as useless waste.

Paul rejected his righteousness (3:9a). Paul had boasted about his achievements in his attempt to become righteous before God and humans. He once saw himself as blameless concerning legal righteousness (3:6). He knew that he had righteousness, but he now recognized that he had the wrong kind. He needed to rid himself of his self-righteousness. He finally perceived that no one is righteous in oneself before God; thus, no one can produce righteous acts that can bring salvation (Rom. 3:10).

Paul Accepted Christ

The exclamation "More than that" shows the intensity of Paul's new conviction. It sets up a striking contrast between the old and the new outlooks on righteousness. His acceptance of salvation through Christ is now seen in four aspects.

Paul now knew Christ (3:8a). He repudiated his past legalistic efforts "in view of the surpassing value of knowing Christ Jesus my Lord." Salvation is not based on ignorance; it involves knowledge. Sinners must know something to be saved, and they also must know someone. They must know intellectually that Jesus Christ is both divine and human, that He died for the guilt and penalty of their sin, that He rose physically from the dead, that He is the only Savior of humankind, and that humans cannot do anything to save themselves. They must then know Christ experientially by believing in Him, by entrusting themselves completely to the saving care of the Lord.

The essence of eternal life is relationship that exists from knowing God and His Son (John 17:3). It consists of a reciprocal knowledge. Believers know God, and God knows believers (Gal. 4:9; 2 Tim. 2:19). When salvation occurs, people know God as their Father and Christ as their Savior, and God knows believing sinners as His children. Such knowledge has more "surpassing value" than all of the self-righteous acts of all people put together.

Paul won Christ (3:8b). The apostle lost that he might gain. He lost self and gained Christ. He lost sin and gained righteousness. He lost that which was human and gained that which was divine. He lost temporal things and gained eternal things.

The conjunction *that* (Greek, *hina*) gives the purpose for Paul's rejection of his selfish gains. The verb phrase "I may gain" is actually based on the same stem as the noun *gain* (3:7; Greek, *kerdē*); thus, Paul wanted to gain (Greek, *kerdēsō*) Christ. He not only gained Christ in that one crucial event, but also

for an entire lifetime. The active voice of the verb shows the human responsibility in the appropriation of salvation. In salvation, people gain Christ, not
just things from Him. The eternal destiny of believers is to be with Christ, not
just to be in heaven (1 Thess. 4:17).

Paul was found in Christ (3:9a). The passive voice of this verb (Greek,
euretho) shows that a believing sinner has been put into Christ by God. The
human gaining and the divine placing occur at the same moment. The sphere
of acceptance comes from one's position in Christ. When a person is in Him,
he or she has been blessed with all spiritual blessings (Eph. 1:3). In Christ, a
believer has divine election, predestination, acceptance, redemption, forgiveness, inheritance, and sealing (Eph. 1:4–14). That person can now rejoice in
his or her new spiritual position (2 Cor. 5:17).

> Paul's desire to "be found in him" probably has an eschatological aspect.
> Paul wants the divine scrutiny he will undergo at Christ's return to reveal
> unquestionably that he had been in vital spiritual union with Jesus
> Christ. For this to be so, it could not be on the basis of a righteousness he
> could call "my own" . . . , that is, the kind of righteousness one might
> achieve through general conformity to the Mosaic law. Such might win
> the admiration of men, but it could never achieve the absolute perfection
> God requires (Gal. 3:10, 11; James 2:10). In strong contrast (*alla*, "but"),
> to be found in Christ requires the righteousness that has its source not in
> man but in God who has provided Jesus Christ, the "Righteous One"
> (Acts 3:14; 1 John 2:1).[2]

Paul possessed the righteousness of God (3:9b). Four aspects of this possession are set forth. (1) Its means is through faith in Christ. The person and
redemptive work of Jesus Christ are the means of saving faith (Rom. 3:22,
28–31). (2) Its source is God. In salvation, people become partakers of the
divine nature; thus, God imputes positional righteousness to them (2 Pet.
1:4). Believing sinners are just as righteous as Christ because they have been
made the righteousness of God in Him (2 Cor. 5:21). God now sees believers
in and through Christ and His righteousness. (3) Its basis is faith. The righteous position rests upon (Greek, *epi*) the foundation of faith or trust, not
upon pride or self-effort. (4) Its sphere is in Christ. Before God, persons are
found either in Adam or in Christ (Rom. 5:12–21). The former brings condemnation, whereas the latter guarantees justification.

James White further explains justification:

> This act of justification is undertaken by God (God is the One who justi-
> fies) and is not based in any way upon anything wrought in believers or
> done by them. Rather, the action is undertaken "for Christ's sake alone."

Justification, then, is a free act of God's grace and is in no way dependent upon human actions, works, merits, or dispositions. And the Bible puts it, God is the justifier. It is a divine act, not a human accomplishment.

If it is by the imputation of Christ's righteousness that the believer is justified, what is the instrument of this action? The instrument is said to be faith, but this is no bare intellectual assent to the facts of the gospel. This is a faith that results in the person "believing and resting on him and his righteousness." This faith is supernatural in origin, for it is "not of themselves, it is the gift of God." This is a living faith, one that looks to Christ alone for salvation. . . . No religious rite or activities can justify.[3]

Righteousness by Faith

Righteousness comes through faith (Rom. 3:22).

Righteousness is imputed to the sinner by the work of Christ (Rom. 4:3).

Righteousness is a gift—it cannot be earned (Rom. 5:17).

Righteousness comes from God (Rom. 10:3).

Righteousness comes by faith (Rom. 10:8–10).

The fruit of righteousness comes through Jesus Christ (Phil. 1:11).

The child of God is to pursue righteousness (1 Tim. 6:11).

The righteousness of the Law cannot save (Gal. 2:21).

Human beings do not have a righteousness acceptable to God (Phil. 3:9).

In Sanctification (3:10–14)

Christ came that we might have life and that we might have it abundantly (John 10:10). When believing sinners have justification, they have life (3:7–9), but when they work at sanctification, they gain the abundant life (3:10–14). Getting saved is like getting married; it is just the beginning of a growing, knowing, and sharing relationship.

The Goals of Sanctification (3:10)

The words of purpose ("that I may know")[4] cannot be fulfilled unless the truth of the prior verses is a living reality (3:7–9). A person must be in Christ in order to know Him. Justification must precede sanctification. The verb indicates personal, experiential knowledge. Three objects of that knowledge are now set forth.

To know Christ. There is a difference between objective and personal knowledge of a person. The former deals with facts about a man, whereas the latter stresses intimate acquaintance. For example, all Americans know who the president of the United States is, but very few know him personally. Paul knew that he had salvation; now he wanted to know the Savior. This goal is a lifelong pursuit, because the divine person of the Son of God is inexhaustible. People are not known as objects are known. People are known as they reveal themselves to others (John 14:21).

Believers can grow in grace and in the knowledge of Christ through a diligent study of the Scriptures that testify to Christ (John 5:39; 2 Pet. 3:18). As they see Him and begin to know Him through the written Word, that truth will transform their personalities into conformity to Christ (2 Cor. 3:18).

To know the power of Christ's resurrection. The same "power" (Greek, *dunamin*) that raised Jesus Christ out of physical death also raised believing sinners out of spiritual death. This power presently operates within believers to give them daily victory over sin (Eph. 1:18—2:7). Paul prayed that believers might perceive this truth (Eph. 1:15–20).

By spiritual identification with Christ through the baptism in the Holy Spirit, all believing sinners are crucified, buried, and raised together with Christ (Rom. 6:3–10). Just as sin and death no longer have dominion over the living, resurrected Savior, so believers should claim by faith that divine victory for themselves (Rom. 6:11).

To know the fellowship of Christ's sufferings. Jesus predicted that the apostles would suffer and die in the will of God (Matt. 20:23; 26:36–46). All of them did. Paul wanted to experience that fellowship of suffering. Believers cannot die for sins as Christ did, but they can suffer for the sake of righteousness as they permit Christ to live out His life through them. All believers who deny themselves, take up their crosses daily, and follow Christ will share in His sufferings (Matt. 16:24; 1 Pet. 2:21). This unique fellowship will involve suffering according to God's will (1 Pet. 4:19) for doing good (1 Pet. 3:14), for the name of Christ (1 Pet. 4:14), and for being a Christian (1 Pet. 4:16).

Such total resignation to God's will manifests total conformity to the death of Christ. It reveals the submission of the human will to the divine will. Just as Christ was in the form (2:7; Greek, *morphēn*) of God, so the believer should be conformed (Greek, *summorphizomenos*) to Christ's death. In effect, the believer must constantly affirm, "I die daily" (1 Cor. 15:31). The order of the verse reflects the experience of the believer. Christ suffered before He was raised, but believers will suffer if they manifest resurrection power in their daily living.

The Expectation in the Goals (3:11)

This verse has two possible interpretations. Both are consistent within the context of the teaching of this epistle.

To be sensitive in the present. The emphasis here is on a spiritual resurrection (Rom. 6:7–10; Eph. 5:14). Paul knew that he would have to keep fighting against his sin nature (1 Cor. 9:27). He wanted to be spiritually alert and alive.

To be accepted in the future. The emphasis here is on a physical resurrection (1 Cor. 15:50–58; 1 Thess. 4:13–18). The term literally translates "out resurrection" (Greek, *exanastasin*). When Christ returns, living believers will be translated and dead Christians will be raised. The unsaved will be resurrected later; thus, this would be a resurrection out from among the unsaved who would remain dead (Rev. 20:5).

Paul did not doubt the reality of Christ's return, the translation of living saints, or the resurrection of the dead. The conditional character of this verse ("in order that") points to the uncertainty as to whether he would be alive or dead in that day. Since the return of Christ was imminent, Paul wanted to be spiritually ready at all times. He wanted to be praised before the Savior, not ashamed (1 John 2:28).

Paul's Doctrine of Resurrection

Believers will experience resurrection like Christ (Rom. 6:5).

The body is sown perishable, it is raised imperishable (1 Cor. 15:42).

We shall bear the image of the heavenly (1 Cor. 15:49).

The dead will be raised imperishable (1 Cor. 15:52).

Mortal will put on immortality (1 Cor. 15:53).

The metaphor of a building from God is used to represent a believer's new body (2 Cor. 5:1).

Believers long for their bodies to be clothed with their dwelling from heaven (2 Cor. 5:2).

The dead in Christ shall rise first (1 Thess. 4:16).

Believers have a hope laid up for them in heaven (Col. 1:5).

The Attitudes Behind the Expectation (3:12)

Paul was neither complacent nor apathetic. In honest introspection, he revealed three basic attributes that controlled his holy ambition.

Paul had not received everything. He admitted that he had not yet obtained God's completed work in his life. Literally, the Greek reads "received" *(elabon)*. He had not yet received everything God had in store for him. In the thirty years since his conversion, Paul had enjoyed many times of blessing, but still more productive experiences lay ahead. God is a giving God, and He will continue to give abundantly to those who want more.

Paul had not become everything. He admitted that he was not yet "perfect." This is actually a verbal construction: "have been perfected" (Greek, *teteleiōmai*).[5] The verb conveys the idea of a decisive past event with the results of that experience continuing into the present. He knew that he was not in a perfected state with no room for personal, spiritual development. If Paul, the greatest of the apostles, had not yet achieved perfection after thirty years of Christian experience, then no believer can ever reach this plateau in this life. This verse repudiates the concept of sinless perfectionism.

Paul had not done everything. He had ambition to improve. The verb phrase "I press on" indicates hard pursuit, such as a hunter following his prey. Paul wanted to to lay hold of (Greek, *katelēphthēn*) and pull down that purpose for which he had been saved. He wanted to do everything God had planned for him to accomplish.

The Ambition in the Attitudes (3:13–14)

The abrupt insertion of the vocative ("Brethren") is used to draw attention to Paul's conclusion. The Judaizers did not have the joy of either justification or sanctification. Paul definitely had the former, and he was in the process of gaining the latter. The joy of sanctification is based on daily ambition and achievement. It is described here in four concepts.

To be honest about oneself. Paul knew that he had not yet achieved the totality of the divine purpose for his life ("I do not regard myself as having laid hold of *it* yet"). The Greek verb *logizomai* means to think something through to a conclusion. The pronouns "I" (Greek, *egō*) and "myself" (Greek, *emauton*) are very emphatic. They stress that Paul had evaluated his own spiritual condition, not that he had accepted the opinions of others.

To forget the past. Paul daily was "forgetting what *lies* behind." No person can erase from the memory what has transpired before, but he or she can keep the past from controlling the present and the future. When God forgives our sins, He still remembers what they were, but He does not hold them against us. Believers thus must not permit the past to cause them depression or overconfidence in the present.

"What *lies* behind" includes Paul's past Pharisaical life that he had just recounted. In progressive sanctification, believers must not look upon their unsaved past with so much shame or pride that they fail to see Christ. In the same sense, they must not view their Christian past with either disdain or satisfaction.

To reach for the future. Someone has said: "Today is the first day of the rest of your life." For believers, the best is yet to come. They should face the future with anticipation and joy.

Paul was "reaching forward to what *lies* ahead." The verb *reaching* (Greek, *epekteinomenos*) denotes an athlete who runs without swerving off course and who strains his entire body to cross the finish line (Acts 20:24; 1 Cor. 9:26). It was a spiritual exercise that occurred every day in the apostle's life.[6]

The things that lay ahead for Paul included a personal knowledge of Christ, victory over sin and self, and more personal achievement. Paul, had at least three more epistles to write (1 and 2 Timothy, Titus), a work on Crete to establish (Titus 1:5), and life to give in martyrdom.

To press toward the goal. With all of his holy ambition, the apostle wanted to do "one thing" (3:13). He earnestly desired to "press on toward the goal for the prize of the upward call of God in Christ Jesus." The verb *press* (Greek, *diōkō*) describes vigorous, concentrated pursuit. Paul was a man with a goal. He knew who he was and where he was going. He realized that both God and others were watching him; but at the same time, he fixed his eyes on Christ (Heb. 12:1–2), for his goal was to be like Him.

A "prize" (Greek, *brabeion*) will be given for success. At the Greek games, the winner of a race was summoned from the stadium floor to the judge's seat and a wreath of leaves was placed on his head. At Athens, the winner was also given five hundred coins, free meals, and a front-row seat at the theater. These prizes were temporary, but believers can obtain an eternal and incorruptible prize (1 Cor. 9:26).

This human endeavor has been made possible by the "upward call of God in Christ Jesus." God has chosen people in Christ Jesus to be saved and sanctified. The prize itself is a gracious gift, but attainment of the goal requires human effort. God's goals for believers are always forward and upward, designed to strengthen and improve them.

Study Questions

1. Do people suffer the loss of anything today when they profess salvation?

2. What is the difference between spiritual position and spiritual practice? Which is more important?

3. What is involved in genuine saving faith? Is repentance essential? How would you define imputation of righteousness?

4. How can believers know Christ personally? How much time is involved? How can church programs help or hinder?

5. Are all Christians victorious over sin today? Why not? What can be done to attain this goal?

6. Why are believers sometimes depressed? Apathetic? Why do they often lack ambition?

7. How can you press toward the mark for your life? Name some of your failures. How can these be overcome?

CHAPTER 12

The Joy of Maturity
Philippians 3:15-21

Preview:

Paul now addresses the walk of mature believers, the ones who stay in the Word of God constantly striving to do His will. Mature believers are to be consistent in their walk, holding to the standard set by the Word. To make this easier, Paul says to emulate those who are godly examples but to beware of those who are ungodly examples. He ends with a joyous statement on the eventual glorification of each believer.

Each Christian should make the appeal: "Please be patient with me; God is not finished with me yet." Spiritual birth presupposes growth into maturity. Such advancement implies deficiencies that need correction, weaknesses that need strengthening, and ignorance that needs education. The local church that prospers has members with mutual forbearance and understanding toward one another.

In this section, the apostle challenged the believers to experience the joy of maturity.

The Goals for the Church (3:15-16)

The conjunction *therefore* (Greek, *oun*) joins this section to the previous one. Paul wanted his personal aims to become goals for the Philippians. Two aims are given.

Same Mind (3:15)

The command. Three features of this command are set forth. First, it included both Paul and his readers. The exhortation ("Let us . . . have this attitude") shows that the apostle identified himself with the church and needed to be stimulated to further growth just as they did.[1] It literally reads, "Let us keep on thinking."

Second, Paul's directive could be obeyed only by those who were mature and were maturing. The qualitative adjective "as many as" (Greek, *hosoi*) shows that only a select group of believers would respond to the appeal. The term *perfect* (Greek, *teleioi*) does not contradict Paul's earlier denial of personal perfection (3:12). Mature believers know where they are in the divine order of spiritual progress and perceive that they can still develop further. For example, a perfect eight-year-old child is at the right stage of physical, emotional, and intellectual maturity for his age bracket, but he is still maturing toward a nine-year-old goal.

Third, the command to be like minded was directed toward one purpose. The demonstrative pronoun *this* (Greek, *touto*) points back to Paul's intent of pressing toward the goal and of believers doing all that God planned for them to do and becoming all that God has designed for His children.

The correction. Some Christians blindly think that they do not need to improve or that they can mature through legalism ("and if in anything you have a different attitude"). They take a position other than that lived or prescribed by Paul. Someone has said that a person convinced against his own will is of the same opinion still. After all that Paul had taught in this epistle and after describing his own spiritual condition that still needed improvement, what more could the apostle say to change his readers' wills? Did they actually think they were better than he was? In this situation, he simply turned them over to divine conviction ("God will reveal that also to you"). The means of illumination would be the teaching of the Holy Spirit, the observation of the growth of mature believers in grace, and the rod of chastisement.

Same Walk (3:16)

Paul said that both the church and he had made significant progress in their spiritual lives. They had moved into a doctrinal position and a behavioral pattern that were being threatened by the legalists. The verb phrase "we have attained" shows that they had arrived at this plateau after much effort and experience.[2] The Judaizers, however, charged that they had to advance beyond simple faith to a complex legalistic system (cf. Gal. 3:3).

God has only one way of salvation, and he likewise has only one means of sanctification. Both Jews and Gentiles alike are saved by faith alone in

Christ alone, and they become holy by total submission to the Holy Spirit who produces His fruit through them (Gal. 5:16, 22–23). The standard of the Christian walk is here described as "that same standard." The noun *standard* is *kanoni* in the Greek and is the source of our English word "canon." Just as the Bible alone is the basis of evangelical faith and practice, so these standards should provide the guidelines for daily living.

The two verbs argue for constant obedience to Paul's directions.[3] First, he wanted the Philippians to walk according to the same principles he had just discussed. A Spirit-controlled walk is void of dissension and jealousy; rather, it is marked by love and concern for others (Gal. 5:22—6:5). Second, Paul desired them to be of the same mind (cf. 2:2). There can be no joy if there is static immaturity and selfish competition within the bounds of legalism.

The Apostasy of the Judaizers (3:17–19)

Paul ended this chapter just as he began it—with a warning (3:1–2). The direct address ("Brethren") served to alert them and to form a transition to this new subject. Apostasy is a departure from a moral and doctrinal standard. Paul established himself as the spiritual yardstick by which the apostate legalists were to be measured.

The Standard of Orthodoxy (3:17)

Paul. With all humility, the apostle could confidently exhort, "Join in following my example." He wanted the Philippians to become what he was. He knew that God had done great things in his life, that his theology and practice were sound, and that the Philippians needed an objective, visible, human goal. Paul could make this pronouncement with all of his apostolic authority because he knew he was following Christ (1 Cor. 11:1).

Others. The charge "observe" (Greek, *skopeite*) calls for careful scrutiny. The English word *scope* comes from this Greek term. Its present tense suggests that the Philippians were to set their sights constantly on those who were in their midst, especially since Paul was absent from them. Paul wanted them to follow such men as Timothy and Epaphroditus, the godly bishops and deacons in their assembly (1:1), and dedicated men and women within the congregation. Paul offered his associates and himself as a pattern by which others should be tested.[4] The Greek word for *pattern (tupon)* is normally translated "type," the impression or stamp made by an industrial die. It was used of the nail prints in Christ's hands (John 20:25). Paul and his associates thus became a mold into which the lives of others could be poured and conformed.

The Violation of Orthodoxy (3:18–19)

The conjunction *for* (Greek, *gar*) states the reason for the two commands given (3:17). Imitation and vigilance were needed because many false teachers were present. Believers must perceive the difference between the spirit of truth and the spirit of error (1 John 4:1–6). They should not be gullible and accept all preachers as genuine. Whenever Paul was in their church, he told them about the imminent invasion of heretics ("of whom I often told you"). In this letter, he warned them once again ("and now tell you"). His love for Christ, the truth, and the Philippians can be seen in his compassionate concern. Tears streamed down from his eyes as he dictated his letter (cf. Acts 20:31).

Paul then describes this unscrupulous group of false teachers in five ways.

Enemies of the cross of Christ. They manifested their hostility to the redemptive message of Christ's death and resurrection by insisting that faith alone in Christ alone is not sufficient to save. They expressed faith in the person of Christ but not in his finished work. They contended that circumcision and obedience to the Mosaic law needed to be added to faith in order to receive justification (Acts 15:1). If righteousness, in total or in part, is dependent on legalism, then the value of Christ's death is negated (Gal. 2:21). The concept of salvation by works is contrary to the principle of divine grace (2 Cor. 11:13–15; Gal. 5:10).

Their end is destruction. These legalists are lost and destined for perdition. The "end" (Greek, *telos*) refers to the conclusion of the acceptance of the legalistic message. When persons who have embraced legalism die, they go to Hades to await the final resurrection, the Great White Throne Judgment, and consignment to the eternal lake of fire.

The term *destruction* (Greek, *apōleia*) is based on the same stem that is used to form such words as "perish" and "lost" (Luke 19:10; 1 Cor. 1:18). The unsaved treat the message of the cross with intellectual contempt because they already are perishing (1 Cor. 1:18). If they do not exercise repentant faith in Christ, their living convictions will be confirmed at their death. In Hades they will not experience extinction but the total loss of well-being. They are destructive men destined for destruction (2 Peter 2:1–3).

Their god is their belly. These false teachers were in the ministry for what they could get out of it. Both Paul and Peter warned against greedy elders (1 Tim. 6:3–10; 1 Peter 5:2). Their belly became their god in that they served their worldly appetites (Rom. 16:18).

One reason why Paul surrendered his right to be supported financially by his converts was to avoid the suspicion that he was only interested in their money (1 Cor. 9:1–18). To show that salvation was a free gift from God, he offered his apostolic services at no charge. Unfortunately, his critics turned this gracious gesture into an argument against his apostleship (2 Cor. 11:7–9; 12:13). They claimed that God financially prospered all successful preachers (1 Tim. 6:5). This assertion is ridiculous in that Christ Himself experienced no material gains from His earthly ministry.

They glory in their shame. The false teachers gloried in things of which they should have been ashamed. They boasted in the flesh, in the physical rite of circumcision, and in the legalistic efforts of self. They bragged about the number of people they were able to get to submit to circumcision (Gal. 6:13).

They mind earthly things. Believers frequently are castigated for being so heavenly minded that they are no earthly good. The converse, however, is more usually true. People are often so earthly minded that they never think about heavenly matters. The Judaizers attempted to spoil the church by human traditions and worldly religious concepts (Col. 2:8). They tried to force a legalistic calendar on believers (Gal. 4:3, 9–10) and to impose a restricted diet in which certain foods could not be touched, tasted, or handled (Col 2:21–22). This legalistic conformity replaced grace and faith as the basis for justification and sanctification. People who trust themselves must always look down at the earth rather than up into heaven.

The Glorification of Believers (3:20–21)

Legalism may tell people how to live, but it cannot prepare them for death. Since it is based on self-effort, it is powerless to raise people out of death. It is at this very point that the insufficiency of legalism is laid bare. In contrast, believing sinners have put their trust in Christ, who conquered death and hell through His resurrection. Christians can look forward to new bodies that will be both immortal and incorruptible.

Our Citizenship Is in Heaven (3:20)

Its meaning. The residents of Philippi were actually citizens of Rome. They constituted a Roman colony within the region of Macedonia. Away from Rome they were still Romans (Acts 16:12, 21); thus, they fully understood the significance of this spiritual metaphor.

Christians likewise constitute a colony of heaven on earth. They have double citizenship (Greek, *politeuma*). Paul was in the kingdom of God, yet he claimed the rights of his Roman citizenship (Acts 16:37; 22:25–29). The possessive pronoun *our* is very emphatic and stresses the joint possession of heavenly citizenship by Paul and the church in contrast to the earthly domain of the Judaizers.[5]

Its location. Our citizenship literally is "in the heavens" (Greek, *en ouranois*).[6] In a general sense, the Philippians were heavenly citizens, but specifically their residency was the Holy City (Rev. 21:2, 10). People of faith, like Abraham, have looked for this city built by God (Heb. 11:10). Jesus Christ has prepared rooms for believers within this city (John 14:2–3; Heb. 11:16).

The verb *is* (Greek, *huparchei*) indicates that this citizenship was a present possession. The same verb is used to describe Christ's "being" in the form of God (2:6; Greek, *huparchōn*). Just as the deity of Christ can never be diminished, so the heavenly citizenship of the believer can never be taken away. It exists now and forever.

Our Savior Can Come at Any Moment (3:20)

Christ's relationship to believers. Paul makes three points about Jesus Christ. First, He is the "Savior" (Greek, *sōtēra*). The angels declared Him to be such before the shepherds at His birth (Luke 2:11). He was the Savior of both Jews and Gentiles (John 4:42). This title is also a direct proof of the deity of Christ, because the titles "God" and "Savior" are used interchangeably (1 Tim. 4:10). The Old Testament openly declared that only Jehovah could be the Savior of His people (Ps. 106:21; Isa. 45:21; 49:26). Since Jesus Christ bears the name of Savior, He must also be Jehovah God (Titus 2:13).

Paul remarks that our citizenship, or "commonwealth," is in heaven. R. C. H. Lenski adds:

> The contrast with the Judaizers and their following does not present a list of opposite items which match those stated in v. 18, 19. Paul's contrast is summarized in the vital one of the vast difference obtaining between "those minding the earthly things" over against whom we stand whose "commonwealth exists in heaven." This enables him to bring in the resurrection, at which he in v. 11 says he wants to arrive and in v. 14 calls "the prize of the lofty calling of God in Christ Jesus." For the Judaizers "the end is perdition," for true believers the Savior who will transform our bodies. So plainly does Paul link together v. 11–14 with v. 20, 21 that we cannot think of two sets of errorists.[7]

Second, His full name is "Lord Jesus Christ." This is the name every tongue will confess and at which every knee will bow (2:10–11).

Third, He will come from the heavens, namely, the third heaven where He is seated at the right hand of the Father.

The relationship of believers to Christ. Believers should "wait" (Greek, *apekdechometha*) for Him because of who He is and what He has done. The verb stresses an earnest longing, an eager expectation, and an anxious waiting. It connotes an imminent coming, a possibility in one's own lifetime.

Our Change Will Come from Christ (3:21)

The present nature of the human body is suited to temporal life on this planet. It must therefore be changed before it can function properly in the eternal state (1 Cor. 15:50). This change can occur in one of two ways: The bodies of believers alive at the time of the rapture of the church will be glorified (1 Thess. 4:13–18). The bodies of believers who die before Christ's coming and the Rapture will be raised from the dead and be made immortal and incorruptible (1 Cor. 15:51–57).

The object of the change. The object of the change is the "body of our humble state." The literal translation is "the body of our humiliation." It refers to the mortal, corruptible body that was the result of the introduction of sin into the human race by Adam. It is thus subject to disease and death and is marked by dishonor and weakness (1 Cor. 15:43). Nothing is more humbling than a diseased body hooked up to a life-support system or a lifeless body in a coffin. In such a body, Christ humbled Himself to die on the cross (2:8), and in the same type of body believers will one day die.

On "our humble state," W. E. Vine comments: ". . . the body of our humiliation—that is to say, the body which is ours in our low estate, as being subject to sufferings and indignities and all the effects of sin. There is nothing here or elsewhere in Scripture to support the Manichaean theory of the vileness [KJV 'vile'] of our frame [or body], as that for which a contempt is to be entertained. See 1 Thessalonians 5:23."[8]

Jesus Christ will "transform" (Greek, *metaschēmatisei*) this body at His return. The verb emphasizes outward appearance. Through the incarnation, God the Son took on the appearance (Greek, *schēmati*) of man in order to change the appearance of man (2:8). Believers thus are promised new bodies not subject to disease or death. The limitations of this temporal, earthly body will also be eliminated in the new body that is suited for eternity.

The goal of the change. When the change occurs, believers will be "conformed" to the resurrected, glorified, immortal, incorruptible body of Jesus Christ (1 Cor. 15:49; 1 John 3:2). The Greek term *summorphon* refers to the inner essence of the new body. Believers will not become little gods, nor will they look exactly like the Savior. There will be no sin nature in this new body. It will be controlled by the spirit, not by the soul (1 Cor. 15:44).

The guarantee of the change. The divine power that enabled Christ to conquer death through His resurrection and that will enable Him to force all of His enemies into total submission is the same power that will change the bodies of believers. The resurrection change will happen because God has decreed that it will occur. God always does what He says He will do.

Study Questions

1. Are Christians sometimes stubborn? In what areas? How can they be changed?

2. Why do evangelicals differ over the standards of the Christian walk? Can unity ever be achieved in this area?

3. How can we tell whether we should follow a human leader? If such leadership is not followed, is that disobedience?

4. Who are the enemies of the cross today? What are the means by which this judgment can be made?

5. From what things has Christ saved us? Do people restrict the application of salvation to certain areas of their life?

6. What should be the Christian approach to funerals? To cremation?

CHAPTER 13

The Joy of Peace
Philippians 4:1–9

Preview:

Paul starts with a direct address to two of the members of the Philippian church, asking that they resolve their differences and walk in Christian unity. He follows once again with a command to rejoice and gives them a message on attaining a lasting personal peace through "prayer and supplication with thanksgiving." Paul finishes with instruction on how to order one's thought life to bring glory to the Lord.

Problems inevitably come to all people, including Christians (Job 5:7). Christ predicted future trials for His own, but He also promised the protection of His peace (John 14:27; 16:33). When believers are controlled by the Holy Spirit, they will manifest both joy and peace (Gal. 5:22).

In this passage, Paul gave his final commands to the church. He wanted them to experience love, joy, and peace in three distinct areas.

In Human Relationships (4:1–3)

In Philippians 4:1–3, Paul addresses the church collectively (4:1), two women (4:2), and his coworker (4:3). He reveals three aspects in which the joy of peace can be seen.

Through Love (4:1)

The conjunction *therefore* introduces Paul's longing to be with the Philippian church, with whom he had such kinship and joy.

Their description. Paul expressed his affection for the Philippian believers with five forms of address. (1) They were his "brethren." Both he and they had been born again into the family of God. He was their spiritual father, but they were still brothers. He had no doubts about their salvation. (2) They were "beloved" (Greek, *agapētoi*). This description occurs twice in the verse. He not only loved them because they were his brothers, but because he wanted to (1 Thess. 4:9–10). (3) They were longed for (Greek, *epipothētoi*). Paul earlier had expressed that he longed after them (1:8). He did not desire their money; rather, he wanted them. This adjectival title placed great emphasis on an inner emotional longing. (4) They were his "joy." Paul felt this way about all of his converts (1 Thess. 2:19–20). He rejoiced in them personally, not just in what they had done for the Lord. Real joy is rejoicing in people. (5) They were his "crown" (Greek, *stephanos*). A victorious runner in the Greek games received a festive garland on his head (1 Cor. 9:24–25). At the Judgment Seat of Christ, believers will receive different crowns for distinctive achievements (2 Cor. 5:10). To the apostle, the Philippian believers represented his joy of victory because he knew that his race and labor in Philippi had not been in vain (2:16).

Their defense. Paul preceded his warning about the legalists with a command to rejoice in the Lord (3:1). He then defined the acceptable position as being found in the Lord (3:9). He now issued an imperative to stand fast in the Lord. Paul's admonition (Greek, *stēketo*) means to take a stand and to remain firm in that position.[1] He did not want the Philippian believers to yield to the pressures of the Judaizers. His personal testimony and doctrinal explanation provided the church with adequate spiritual weapons to resist the attacks. Their stand was to be *in the Lord,* not in a minor theological point or a denominational distinction. They were to relate everything to His divine-human person and to His redemptive death and resurrection, within their justified position.

Through Unity (4:2)

Objects of the appeal. The two women mentioned here were the thorns in the apostle's crown. Since Paul constantly encouraged unity (1:27; 2:2; 3:16), these women must have possessed strong divisive influence on others. Their identity remains a mystery. They may have been among the women who were saved when Paul first preached at Philippi; if so, they would have been two of the charter members of the church (Acts 16:13). Quite possibly they may have been deaconesses or women of financial wealth. In any case, the friction between these two women had to be eliminated.

Purpose of the appeal. To show no partiality, Paul used the same verb of appeal twice ("I urge"). Both shared equal blame for their disruptive conduct.

The fact that the apostle criticized them in this public letter shows that the entire church must have known about their personal conflicts. Apparently even the church was unable to resolve the problem.

Although believers have distinctive personalities and will naturally have differences of opinions, they should strive for unity in spiritual issues. Thus, Paul charged them "live in harmony in the Lord." Literally, they were to think the same thing (cf. 2:2; 3:16). Refusal to do so indicates a spirit of carnal divisiveness and disobedience (3:15). No church or leader can have the joy of peace when members are bickering.

Through Help (4:3)

The giver of help. These women needed assistance to resolve their differences. Paul then made a personal request to a close friend to give such help. There is an obvious contrast between the firm appeal to the women (Greek, *parakaleō*) and this gracious request (Greek, *erōtaō*).

The identity of the "comrade" (Greek, *suzuge*) remains a mystery. Some assign the title to a woman, perhaps Lydia; however, the adjective *true* is masculine, not feminine. A plausible view is that the term should be seen as a proper name (Greek, *Suzugus*), since names of other individuals are given in the context. The addition of the adjective (Greek, *gnēsie*) indicates that the comrade was in character what his or her name meant. A *suzugus* was a crossbar with loops on the end through which the heads of two oxen were placed. Paul thus regarded Suzugus as a genuine coworker in the ministry.

The request was direct and simple: "Help these women" (Greek, *sullambanou autais*). The verb was used of seizing (Matt. 26:55), conceiving (Luke 1:24), and of taking hold together with someone (Luke 5:7). The verb prefix (Greek, *sun*) may indicate that others, perhaps Clement and the fellow workers, were already trying to help them.

The recipients of help. In spite of the friction between the two women, Paul still appreciated who they were and what they had done for the Lord in the past. First, they had labored with him in the gospel ministry. The Greek verb *sunēthlēsan* was used earlier of striving together for the advance of the gospel (1:27). Second, their names were in the Book of Life, meaning that they had received eternal life from God through faith in His gracious provision by Jesus Christ (Luke 10:20; Rev. 20:15).

In the Human Heart and Mind (4:4–7)

Complaint and anxiety are the opposites of joy and peace. God wants His children to have the latter, but they must also want them so badly that they will do what the Bible says they must do to get them. The joy of inner peace will come automatically if one's behavior follows this fivefold procedure.

1. *Rejoice in the Lord always* (4:4). The joy of the Lord gives strength to the people of God (Neh. 8:10; Prov. 15:13; 17:22). Constant rejoicing should be an integral part of the believer's inner response to both life's pleasant and difficult situations. The repetition of the imperative *rejoice* and the use of the adverb *always* prove that principle (1 Thess. 5:16).

Rejoicing must always be "in the Lord." Christians should experience sorrow when a loved one is sick or dies. It would be wrong and contrary to wholesome human instinct for a person to be happy at that time. Happiness can occur only when outward circumstances are pleasant, but inner joy can be present at all times. It is a positive action of the will in obedience to the divine command, not a reaction to outward pressures. The fruit of the Spirit-filled life is always joy (Gal. 5:22). Believers can rejoice in the Lord because they know they are saved, that God cares, and that God is working out His sovereign plan for His glory and for the spiritual good of His people (Rom. 8:28).

2. *Be gentle* (4:5). The term "forbearing spirit" (Greek, *epieikes*) encompasses reasonableness, magnanimity, forbearance, goodwill, and a friendly disposition. A forbearing person bears trouble calmly and rejects revengeful meanness. Jesus Christ was both meek and gentle (2 Cor. 10:1). His forbearance should not be equated with moral softness nor His meekness with authoritative weakness. The same Christ who beckoned the little children also drove the religious racketeers out of the temple with a scourge. Such forbearance has its source in divine wisdom and is a requirement for a pastor (1 Tim. 3:3; James 3:17).

The spirit of nonviolence must be manifested to all people, both friends and enemies (Titus 3:2). Christ manifested this virtue on the cross (1 Pet. 2:23). People who retain spite are simply winding up the watch spring of their emotions for a breakdown. If they have no peace with God or others, they can never have inner peace. A forbearing person, however, will be both a glad and godly person.

3. *Be alert to divine presence* (4:5). In the midst of four imperatives, Paul inserted a promised truth: "The Lord is near." The presence or absence of inner peace will be in direct proportion to one's awareness of the presence of Jesus Christ.

The expression "near" (Greek, *eggus*) refers to a nearness, either of time or space. First, it could refer to the immanency of Christ's return (James 5:7–8). Paul had just discussed the blessed hope of believers in which they will see Christ and receive new bodies (3:20–21). If Christians are looking up and ahead, they will not be depressed by looking down or back. Anxiety is often caused by an uncertain future, but believers know they could be with Christ at any moment.

> Quite evidently Paul expects a speedy return of Christ. It was natural in the beginning of the Church's history. . . . This solemn fact which governs the whole of Paul's thinking, and has especially moulded his ethical teaching, readily suggests "reasonableness." The Lord, the Judge, is at the door. Leave all wrongs for Him to adjust. Forbear all wrath and retaliation (cf. Rom. xii. 19 ff.).
>
> But further, in view of such a prospect, earthly bickerings and wranglings are utterly trivial. Cf. I John ii. 28, "Abide in Him, so that if He be manifested, we may have boldness and not be ashamed before Him at His coming."[2]

Second, "near" could refer to the omnipresence of Christ. He is not only in believers, but also with them at all times and in all circumstances (Matt. 28:20). God is the constant environment of all His children. Christians are never alone, but when they think God has deserted them they will become fearful. They must believe that God is where he is and that God can meet their every need.

4. *Do not worry about anything* (4:6). There is a difference between genuine care and false anxiety. The verb ("be anxious") and its noun ("care") are used in both a positive and a negative sense. Timothy had a constructive concern for the church (2:20). Paul knew that his associate would pray, witness, teach, and counsel effectively. The apostle himself asserted that the care of all the churches was upon him (2 Cor. 11:28). He prayed for them, wrote to them, visited them, and sent his associates to them. Asking God and doing what he could formed a positive, loving care for others.

A false care is self-destructive. Christ taught that a believer should not worry about the basic necessities of life that the heavenly Father promised to provide (Matt. 6:25), about things that cannot be changed (Matt. 6:27), and about the problems of tomorrow (Matt. 6:34). Such worry is caused by a lack of faith and by a wrong set of values and priorities (Matt. 6:30–33). Such cares, like weeds, choke the application of God's Word to one's life and make one insensitive to the imminent coming of Christ (Matt. 13:32; Luke 21:34). False cares should be cast on the Lord because He genuinely cares for His own (1 Pet. 5:7).

5. *Pray about everything* (4:6). The strong contrast between worry and faith is seen in the transitional adversative *but* (Greek, *alla*). A worrying Christian will waver, but a trusting believer will be stable and triumphant.

Paul's Cure for Anxiety

Prayer

Be devoted to prayer (Rom. 12:12).

Devote yourselves to prayer (1 Cor. 7:5).

Pray at all times (Eph. 6:18).

Pray and watch (Col. 4:2).

Labor earnestly in prayer (Col. 4:12).

Pray without ceasing (1 Thess. 5:17).

All people should pray (1 Tim. 2:8).

Supplication (Petition)

Petition God (Rom. 10:1).

Help others by petition (2 Cor. 1:11).

Petition God for others (2 Cor. 9:14).

Pray with all prayer and petitions at all times in the Spirit (Eph. 6:18).

Continue in entreaties and prayers night and day (1 Tim. 5:5).

Remember others in prayer night and day (2 Tim. 1:3).

Thanksgiving

Overflow with gratitude to God (2 Cor. 9:12).

Abound with thanksgiving (Col. 2:7).

Be alert with an attitude of thanksgiving (Col. 4:2).

Render thanksgiving to God for others (1 Thess. 3:9).

Make intercessions and thanksgivings for all (1 Tim. 2:1).

Four concepts of prayer are set forth as the divine remedy for a troubled soul. (1) The "requests" (Greek, *aitēmata*) are specific petitions addressed to God. If a person needs wisdom, he or she should ask for it (James 1:5). (2) "Prayer" (Greek, *proseuchē*) is the general invocation of God in which believers give their adoration, devotion, and worship. (3) "Supplication" (Greek, *deēsei*) refers to the desperate cry for help arising from need. (4) All prayer must be accompanied by "thanksgiving." Believers must thank God for the answers in advance, for His loving concern, and for access into the divine presence through Christ's meritorious work (1 Thess. 5:17–18).

When believers have joy within, gentleness around, and prayer above, they will experience peace.

Description of peace. True peace is "the peace of God." When believing sinners have been justified by God, they possess positional peace before God (Rom. 5:1). Jesus Christ thus becomes their peace (Eph. 2:14). In the world, however, they also need the daily, practical application of the peace of God. Divine peace, with God as its source, manifests that attribute of His eternal being (Isa. 26:3).

God's peace "surpasses all comprehension" and is totally foreign to the experience of the unsaved. Even when believers rest in its presence, they cannot verbalize what has happened. Christ said that His peace is different from that given by the world (John 14:27).

Paul's Doctrine of Peace

The peace of God comes to those who practice peace (Phil. 4:9).

Christ is our peace (Eph. 2:15).

The gospel is called peace (Eph. 6:15).

Peace comes with God through Christ (Rom. 5:1).

The Holy Spirit is life and peace (Rom. 8:6).

The fruit of the Spirit is peace (Gal. 5:22).

Peace comes through the blood of Christ (Col. 1:20).

The world thinks it has "peace and safety" (1 Thess. 5:3).

The Lord is called "the God of peace" (1 Thess. 5:23).

Christians should be like-minded and live in peace together (2 Cor. 13:11).

Christians should live at peace with all people (Rom. 12:18).

Defense of peace. Paul sets forth three facts about divine peace. First, it will "guard" (Greek, *phrourēsei*) the believer. The derivation of this verb (Greek, *pro* and *horaō*) means to see before or to look out. It is a military term used of a garrison of soldiers or sentries on duty (2 Cor. 11:32). Just as soldiers of the praetorian guard were assigned to keep Paul under protective custody, so the peace of God can stand in constant vigilance over the children of God. Second, the peace of God will guard the hearts and minds of believers. Christians can enjoy emotional and mental stability if they rest in this divine protection. Third, it will guard believers "in Christ Jesus." They must have both their position and practice in Christ. If they are disobedient or carnal, they cannot expect to have inner tranquility. They must abide in Christ and permit Him to manifest Himself through their inner life (Ps. 90:1).

In Human Endeavor (4:8–9)

Faith must lead to constructive action. Negative anxiety must be replaced by positive habits (Eph. 4:25–29). After praying, believers must get involved in right thinking and doing. The two imperatives ("meditate/think" and "do") give these two directives.

By right thinking (4:8). Paul lists six objects of right thought. Each is introduced by the qualitative adjective "whatever" (Greek, *hosa*). The plural indicates that many thoughts could be grouped under each category.

First, "true" things are the opposite of lies and false witness. A true issue is that which corresponds to the true nature of God (Rom. 3:4). Believers must surround their hearts and minds with the girdle of truth (Eph. 6:14), must produce the fruit of the Spirit in truth (Eph. 5:9), and must speak the truth in love (Eph. 4:15, 25). Second, the adjective *honorable* (Greek, *semna*) comes from a verb that means to worship or revere (Greek, *sebomai*). Thus, honorable thoughts are dignified and serious, prompted by holy morals and motives. Believers should be marked by such honorable thinking and conduct (1 Tim. 2:2; 3:4; Titus 2:2, 7). Third, those things that are correct in relation to God and man are "right" (Greek, *dikaia*). Fourth, "pure" (Greek, *hagna*) things are those that will not contaminate oneself or others. They are stainless and morally chaste. Fifth, a pleasing thought is "lovely" (Greek, *prosphilē*). It is ethically beautiful and attractive, and it produces concord, peace, and rest. Sixth, wholesome, constructive thoughts are "of good repute" (Greek, *euphēma*). They contain no immoral or sexually suggestive innuendo (Eph. 5:4).

All of these objects of right thought are characterized by virtue and praise. The imperative "let your mind dwell" or think (Greek, *logizesthe*) stresses the idea of a constant thought process. Believers must strengthen daily the moral integrity of their thought life (Prov. 23:7).

By right doing (4:9). The verb *practice* (Greek, *prassete*) emphasizes *constant* practice, the development of a habitual lifestyle.[3] Paul wanted the Philippian believers to emulate him. The church had a fourfold contact with the apostle, evidenced by the four verbal actions described. (1) They "learned" from his oral instruction in their midst. He discipled them. (2) They "received" truth as it was transmitted to them by way of this epistle and by his associates who had ministered to them. (3) They "heard" from others how Paul was responding to his Roman imprisonment. He was not anxious before the government authorities. (4) They had "seen" Paul in action. They knew that he had prayed and praised God during his Philippian imprisonment. They knew from intimate acquaintance that the apostle practiced what he preached.

If believers do these things, they have the guarantee that the God of peace will always be with them. They have the peace of God within them and around them. They have both the presence and protection of peace, because wherever God is, so are His essential attributes.

Study Questions

1. Are some Christian leaders more interested in programs than in people? What constitutes the joy of believers today?

2. When should a sinning Christian be rebuked publicly? Privately?

3. In what areas can women be effective laborers in the gospel? Should women take the place of men? Should they be ordained?

4. Are Christians sometimes vindictive? Why? How can this attitude be changed?

5. Why do believers worry? Should they go to psychiatrists? To Christian psychologists?

6. How are our minds affected by TV? By contemporary music? By magazines and books? Should believers practice censorship?

CHAPTER 14

The Joy of Financial Provision
Philippians 4:10–23

Preview:

Paul commends the Philippians on their renewed support of him financially. He explains that, through the strengthening of the Lord, he is able to be content in prosperity or in humility. His concern, however, is not for the money but for the Philippians to gain blessings from their faithful giving. He closes with heartfelt greetings to all of the brethren, emphasizing that all of our needs are met through the riches of the Lord bestowed on us.

One major cause of anxiety is money—too much of it or too little of it. The rich worry about losing it and the poor worry about getting it. Money in itself is morally neutral; rather, it is the love of money that is the root of all kinds of evil (1 Tim. 6:10).

God has promised to provide us with our needs, not our desires. Christ assured His disciples that the heavenly Father would always supply food, drink, and clothing for His own (Matt. 6:25, 31). God, however, provides through human channels. In this section, Paul rejoices in God's faithfulness to meet his financial needs through the gift sent to him by the church.

The Gift from Philippi (4:10–20)

The church sent Epaphroditus as its messenger to give Paul some financial assistance. His return afforded the apostle an opportunity to thank the church in writing.

Paul's Attitude Toward the Gift (4:10–13)

Paul rejoiced in the Philippians' renewal of interest (4:10). He rejoiced in the Lord greatly when he received their gift. Rejoicing is usually not self-initiated; rather, it is caused by someone or something.[1] Paul rejoiced because God had constrained the Philippians to give.

Furthermore, Paul rejoiced when he saw the believers' personal interest in him. The phrase "your concern for me" literally means "the act of thinking in behalf of me" (Greek, *to huper emon phronein*). He was in their thoughts constantly. Their care for him was "revived" (Greek, *anethalete*). This verb was used of trees and flowers that sprouted, shot up, and blossomed again in the spring after a dormant winter. Paul knew that the Philippians had wanted to give to him before this time but simply had lacked the opportunity to do so. The trip of Epaphroditus to Rome thus gave them the chance to do it.

Paul rejoiced in the lessons of contentment (4:11–12). He did not rejoice over the amount of the gift. He rejoiced more in their thoughtfulness than in their money. He was more grateful for the givers than for the gifts.

Paul then used three verbs to describe his total acceptance of his financial condition. First, he learned to be self-sufficient regardless of whether he had much or little. The Greek verb *emathon* views all of Paul's learning experiences as a whole. It took both time and trials to perfect his inner convictions. The adjective *content* (Greek, *autarkēs*) is a compound word meaning "self" (Greek, *autos*) and "sufficient" (Greek, *arkeō*). It means that Paul learned to manage his financial affairs properly. He controlled the money and did not permit money or the lack of it to decrease the effectiveness of his ministry or the joy of his heart (1 Tim. 6:6, 8).

Second, Paul knew how to get along with humble means as well as how to live in prosperity. He knew how to get along with little and how to get along with much. He did not become depressed when he found himself in want (2 Cor. 11:27). The verb "get along with humble means" (Greek, *tapeinousthai*) means to be humbled. The apostle also knew how to receive gifts and how to use that financial assistance.

Third, Paul was instructed to trust in God regardless of his financial circumstances. The Greek verb *memuēmai* was used of the pagan mystery religions when a person was initiated into a secret society. The apostle thus was initiated into that group of believers who had learned to put their confidence in God, not in gold. Food and money, in either shortage or abundance, did not alter his spirituality.

Paul rejoiced in Christ's enablement (4:13). Paul's statement of confidence ("I can do") did not originate from egotistical pride. The Greek verb *ischuō* refers to possessing enough strength of will to control the feelings and the body. He knew divine strength was made perfect through his human weakness (2 Cor. 12:9). The more dependent on God he became, the stronger he developed.

Paul's strength came from his union with Christ, who had told His disciples that they could do nothing apart from Him (John 15:5). Having enjoyed few material possessions on this earth (Luke 8:3; 9:58), Christ did through Paul what He had achieved Himself.

> Properly, *I have strength in all things,* rather (according to the context) to bear than to do. But the universal extension of the maxim beyond the immediate occasion and context is not inadmissible. It represents the ultimate and ideal consciousness of the Christian. The first thing needful is to throw off mere self-sufficiency, to know our weakness and sin, and accept the salvation of God's free grace in Christ; the next, to find the "strength made perfect in weakness," and in that to be strong.[2]

Paul's Evaluation of the Gift (4:14–20)

At first glance, the Philippians might have thought that Paul was not as grateful to them as he should have been. He had just announced how he could manage on very little support; however, he had not forgotten their human instrumentality. He was thankful to them, and he wanted them to know it. The conjunction *nevertheless* served as the transition between divine sufficiency and human means.

Paul rejoiced over the Philippians' present gift (4:14). To them he said with thanksgiving, "You have done well." The Greek adverb *kalōs* stresses that which is good and beautiful, attractive. Whenever people complete a task and do it well, they can have a sense of personal satisfaction and joy (Gal. 6:4). At the judgment seat, Christ will reward good and faithful servants for doing well (Matt. 25:23).

The explanation of the Philippians' good work is given in the phrase "you have done well to share *with me* in my affliction." In Rome, pressures came at Paul from all directions: the Roman authorities, the Judaizers, the ill-motivated preachers, and the needs of the churches from which he had been absent for almost five years. The verb *share* (Greek, *sugkoinōnēsantes*) means fellow sharers or joint partakers. The Greek term forms the basis for the concept of "fellowship." Paul earlier thanked the church for their fellowship in the gospel (1:5). That involved the sharing of money as well as personal interaction.

Paul rejoiced over the Philippians' past gifts (4:15–16). He remembered two things they had done for him during his second missionary journey about ten years earlier (A.D. 49–52). First, they had written to him about his financial needs after he left their city (4:15). He reminded them of that fact, especially noting what they had done shortly after they were saved ("at the first preaching of the gospel"). Paul had proclaimed the gospel for several years before he came to Philippi, but their city became the foundation for an evangelistic outreach into Europe, starting with the provinces of Macedonia and Achaia. "At the first" therefore refers to the Philippians' active participation in Paul's ministry after they responded in faith. After he departed from Macedonia, the apostle went into Achaia to the cities of Athens and Corinth (Acts 17:14–15). He later informed the church at Corinth about the support given to him by the Philippians and other Macedonian believers (2 Cor. 11:8–9).

Paul never asked for support, but he did not refuse it if it came voluntarily from outside sources. He never took money from the people to whom he was presently ministering. Only the church at Philippi had "shared" (Greek, *ekoinōnēsen*) with him via letter, messengers, and gifts. By this time, other churches were in existence; however, they did not expend the time or effort to discover what his needs were.

Second, the Philippians sent gifts on two separate occasions during the time Paul ministered in Thessalonica (4:16). Paul's next stop after Philippi was Thessalonica (Acts 17:1–9). He again experienced needs, including lack of funds for food and lodging. Their gifts permitted him to give more time to evangelistic outreach, both in the synagogue and among the pagan idol worshipers (1 Thess. 1:9).

Paul rejoiced over the Philippians' future reward (4:17). Paul was criticized for both his refusal to take money from one group and his willingness to accept it from others. When he labored in Philippi, he did not take their money; but when he moved on to Thessalonica and Corinth, he gladly received their support (1 Thess. 2:3–8). He could not understand why his friends would entertain such attacks on his integrity (2 Cor. 11:7).

Paul now denied that he sought their money. The verb *seek* (Greek, *epizētō*) means to desire. He did not seek to add one gift upon another. They had already given to him twice; now he dispelled the notion that he was after a third or fourth gift or even more. Rather, he sought after "profit," or "fruit." He often referred to converts and to the righteous change within believing sinners as fruit (Rom. 1:13; 7:4; Eph. 5:9; Col. 1:6). Fruit, for the believer, is total submission to the indwelling Christ, who will then manifest Himself through the child of God (John 15:1–8). Just as Christ came to seek and to save the lost, so a fruitful or profitable believer will seek the salvation of others.

Paul did not want this profit for himself, but for the Philippians. The mercantile metaphor ("which increases to your account") shows that the

Philippians had made an investment in Paul's ministry that would bring them heavenly dividends. They were laying up treasure in heaven through him. Paul knew that they would be rewarded at the Judgment Seat of Christ for their financial support. Paul's converts were, in effect, their converts, for their gifts enabled him to evangelize more people.

Paul rejoiced over the Philippians' sacrifice to God (4:18). He now looked at how their gift affected him and God. Three verbs are given to describe its impact upon him. First, he received a full payment from them for his total investment of time in their lives. The verb phrase "I have received everything in full" is a business term that speaks of total reimbursement. Second, Paul actually received more than he expected or deserved ("and have an abundance"). The extra money was like a tip, over and above the actual cost. Third, Paul now was in a financial position without any immediate need. The verb phrase "I am amply supplied" indicates that his financial cup had been filled to the brim and that it had remained there up to the time of writing.[3] He did not need any more money from them.

The apostle then described the gift that was sent by the Philippians through their messenger Epaphroditus. He equated it with the sacrifices given to God by the nation Israel. Three aspects are cited. First, it was a "fragrant aroma." Israel presented to God five different offerings: burnt, meal, peace, sin, and trespass (Lev. 1:1—5:19). The first three were sweet-savor offerings, whereas the latter two were not. The first three were voluntary; the latter two were compulsory, offered through confession of sin. The incense of the first three was sweet before God, but the incense of the latter two was not. Thus, their gift to Paul was voluntary, given out of love and gratitude.

Second, the Philippians' gift was an "acceptable sacrifice," a gift freely given from a life totally dedicated to God (Rom. 12:1; 2 Cor. 8:5). Such people have first given themselves as a gift to God.

Third, the Philippians' financial support was "well-pleasing to God." There is a difference between obeying the commandments of God and doing those things that are pleasing in His sight (1 John 3:22). The former are required, but the latter go beyond the call of duty. Paul was pleased with their gift because God was pleased with it.

Paul rejoiced over God's sufficiency (4:19–20). By making the apostle full, the church had created a financial need for itself ("all your needs"). They had poured out of the container of their lives into the vessel of Paul. He informed them that God would fill them back up to the brim. The verbs *am amply supplied* (4:18) and *shall supply* (4:19) come from the same Greek term (*plēroō*). A person will always receive more than what he or she has given. God will always make up the difference (2 Cor. 9:8). People may become impoverished when they give, but God always gives out of His inexhaustible wealth ("according to His riches in glory in Christ Jesus"). There is no end to His abundant provision for the needs of His children. The promise of this verse is restricted to those who create personal needs for themselves by giving to others. Paul gave praise to God for meeting the needs of both the church and himself (4:20). He deserved the glory for that which He had done.

Closing Remarks (4:21–23)

Greetings from Paul. He saluted "every saint in Christ Jesus." He spoke to the entire church as a whole, but he now wanted to be remembered to each individual believer. Each Christian positionally is a saint, set apart from the world unto God by the initial sanctification of the Holy Spirit. Paul began the epistle with greetings to the saints (plural), and he now ends with greetings to each saint (singular).

Greetings from the brethren (4:21). His associates also wanted to greet the church. This group probably included Timothy, Epaphras, Mark, Aristarchus, Demas, and Luke (Philem. 1:23–24).

Greetings from the saints (4:22). The saints in Rome would include the membership of the church in that city (Rom. 16:1–15). The greeting thus went from saints to saints. Both groups were one in Christ. When Paul announced the greetings of the next group, the Philippians probably gasped in amazement. The Romans also wanted to greet them, "especially those of Caesar's household." Through Paul's imprisonment and witness, some servants, soldiers, and perhaps relatives in the emperor's household had been saved. God used the imprisonment to advance the impact of the gospel (1:12). The church originally was saddened by news of Paul's imprisonment; now he wanted them to rejoice with him over what God had accomplished in the lives of his captors.

Benediction. Paul always magnified the grace of God. He wanted the church to experience the daily sustaining grace that all people need (John 1:16). Such grace is for all believers, not just a select few. The theme of the grace of God begins and ends the epistle (1:2).

In closing, Peter O'Brian notes:

> The Epistle to the Philippians is the most intimate of all Paul's letters. The apostle had the warmest of personal relations with this Macedonian congregation. So it is surprising that, contrary to his usual custom, he includes no personal names in these greetings and makes no mention of any individuals. It is possible that special greetings were to be conveyed by Epaphroditus, the bearer of the letter. But perhaps the omis-

sion of all personal salutations and the sending of his greetings to "every saint in Christ Jesus" was deliberate, that is, to prevent any suggestion that he was being partial.[4]

O'Brian concludes:

Paul closes his letter in a regular and consistent fashion, that is, with a benediction. As the opening epistolary greetings or benedictions are quite stylized, so too the . . . ("grace") benediction was a frequent and formally consistent element in Paul's endings. Its uniformity of phraseology, structure, and position are clear when a comparison is made and the sense is the same.

Perhaps, as many suppose, this form of words came into epistolary usage from the blessing pronounced at the conclusion of services of worship. Such a benediction brings the letter to a definitive conclusion. . . . This final benediction picks up the introductory greeting of 1:2, where Paul desires that the Philippians may apprehend more fully the grace of God in which they stand (cf. Rom. 5:2), and assures them that the grace will remain with them. In the opening benedictions, with few exceptions, the apostle speaks of "the grace of God our Father and the Lord Jesus Christ," [while] those which close his letters usually focus on "the grace of the Lord Jesus Christ," which is an expression of the former. The phrase describes not a character or quality of Jesus but something he shows and does. The Lord Jesus who is the source of grace bestows it freely on the congregation at Philippi. It will sustain the community, for it is by grace alone that they will stand.[5]

Study Questions

1. How often should Christians give to the same missionary project? What often hinders such giving?

2. Have modern believers learned the secret of financial contentment? Have they succumbed to the pressures of business success, inflation, and material security?

3. What specific spiritual and financial problems does a wealthy believer encounter? A poor Christian?

4. What contrasts can be made between believers in the United States and those in underdeveloped countries? Between those who grew up in the Depression and the younger generations?

5. Should money management seminars be held in church? In what ways can the church assist its own in proper stewardship?

6. Have you ever written to a Christian college, a mission board, or an individual missionary to determine what their needs are? If not, why not? How can such lines of communication be improved?

7. How do Christians view their gifts of money? Do they really give to God or to the church treasury?

SECTION 2

Completeness in Christ

The Book of Colossians

CHAPTER 15

Background of Colossians

Author

Pauline authorship of Colossians is now rarely questioned. Some critics have subjectively argued that if Paul wrote this letter from Rome and not from Ephesus or Caesarea, then it is a forgery. Most of these objections come from older liberal scholars who wish to destroy the Bible in any way possible. But the strongest evidence supports Paul's authorship under the circumstances described within the letter's pages.

> While there are some who will challenge the claim to Pauline authorship, there is, by and large, a great percentage of Biblical scholars who agree that Colossians is, as it is declared to be (1:1; 4:18), from the hand of Paul. There is sufficient evidence from within the epistle to establish beyond any reasonable doubt that we are considering one of Paul's epistles. Early Christian writers support the reception of the epistle as the genuine work of Paul. One of the earliest direct allusions to the epistle is found in Justin Martyr. Direct quotations are found in Irenaeus and Tertullian, both of whom cite passages from every chapter. The external evidence is strong, thus confirming the unwavering witness from the first, to the genuineness of the epistle.[1]

No other author could pen such glorious and specific words about the person of Christ as the apostle Paul. The book of Ephesians deals with sanctification while Colossians is about "Christ over all." Paul's Christology in Colossians is far advanced over his other epistles. In answering incipient as well as overt heresies, the apostle appeals to the lofty nature of Christ as very

God to answer foolish doctrinal errors. R. C. H. Lenski writes, "To go into the epistle itself, to rethink its inspired thought that is clothed in inspired language, to let the light and the power of this thought fill the soul and mold the life, this is enrichment for time and for eternity."[2]

The City of Colossae

Colossae was situated on a rocky ridge overlooking the valley of the Lycus River that runs through this mountainous district. It was located about one hundred miles east of Ephesus and about eleven miles slightly southeast of Laodicea.

In the fifth century B.C., during the Persian wars, Colossae was an important city, but as its companion cities Laodicea and Hierapolis grew, it declined. However, it did retain some mercantile value because it was one of the stops on the trade route to the East and because glossy black wool was provided by sheepherders in the adjoining hills.

An earthquake destroyed the city during the reign of Nero, but it was quickly rebuilt. Today the ancient site lies in ruins with a modern town, Chronas, located nearby.

Establishment of the Church

The evangelization of Colossae is not specifically mentioned in the book of Acts. Luke recorded that the entire province of Asia heard the gospel during Paul's three years of ministry in Ephesus (Acts 19:10). Most scholars think that the church at Colossae was founded at this time. Paul, however, probably did not go to Colossae and Laodicea himself (2:1).

How then were the churches started? There are two plausible alternatives. The first is that one of Paul's associates, possibly Timothy, went into the region of Laodicea and Colossae during the apostle's stay at Ephesus. Perhaps this is why Timothy's name is included in the greeting (1:1). The second is that residents of Laodicea and Colossae journeyed to Ephesus, were saved directly through Paul's ministry, returned to their hometowns, and started churches there. These could have included Epaphras (1:7–8; 4:12–13), Nympha (4:15), and Philemon (Philem. 1:1–2). Since Paul had led Philemon to Christ (Philem. 1:19) and knew several in Colossae and Laodicea by name (Epaphras, Apphia, Nympha, and Archippus), this view emerges as the more likely possibility. The disciples of these initial converts never had the privilege of seeing Paul, yet they looked to him for apostolic direction. In a sense, he was their spiritual grandfather. This is why Paul's knowledge of their spiritual condition was secondhand (1:4, 8).

The membership of the church at Colossae was composed largely, if not exclusively, of Gentiles (2:13; cf. Rom. 2:24–27; Eph. 2:11). In summary:

> It is impossible to furnish a firm date for the introduction of Christianity to Colossae and its neighbouring cities. There is, however, the possibility that amongst those "of Phrygia" who listened to the apostles on the day of Pentecost, were some from the Lycus valley. If such were the case, the gospel would have been brought into Colossae from the earliest days of the church. Internal evidence precludes any idea that Paul had himself visited Colossae (2:1). Paul had twice been through Phrygia, and yet there is no evidence that he actually came to Colossae.
>
> The assembly at Colossae appeared to have been founded as a result of the evangelistic labours of Epaphras, who himself was a Colossian (4:12). Epaphras stood in intimate relation to the assembly. He had shown Paul their love (1:8), he was a faithful minister of Christ on their behalf (1:7), and it was from this distinguished servant of God that the Colossians had learned the gospel in its original simplicity.[3]

Nature of the Heresy

The false teaching at Colossae consisted of a mixture of Jewish legalism, incipient Gnostic philosophy, and possibly Oriental mysticism. Because of these diverse elements, some scholars have thought that Paul was dealing with two or three different groups of false teachers. However, the characteristics are so interwoven as to suggest one group with multiple errors in their teaching. Whether these teachers were Jewish or Gentile is difficult to determine. But since the content of the heresy is affected neither way, it is safe to identify the error as either Judaistic Gnosticism or Gnostic Judaism.

Many Jews lived in the Colossae area because their ancestors were forced to migrate there under the Seleucid ruler Antiochus III. Their descendants eventually strayed away from Orthodox Judaism and succumbed to the influence of Greek philosophy. The heresy at Colossae did have a strong Jewish ritualistic character, whereas second-century Gnosticism manifested more the philosophical element.

It is also difficult to determine whether these heretics developed within the church membership or attacked the church from without. Paul earlier warned against both sources (Acts 20:29–30). Since the church was young and did have adequate leadership, it would seem that the heresy came as an outside threat.

What was this heresy? It taught that spiritual knowledge was available only to those with superior intellects, thus creating a spiritual caste system.

Faith was treated with contempt. Advanced Gnosticism even taught that salvation was received only by knowledge. Adherents believed they could understand divine mysteries totally unknown and unavailable to the typical Christian. This heresy also taught that all matter was innately evil and that the soul or mind was intrinsically good. This logically led to a denial of the creation of the material world by God and to a denial of the incarnation of Jesus Christ. The latter involved a repudiation of His humanity, His physical death, and His physical resurrection.

To explain the existence of the material world, the heretics taught that a series of angelic emanations created it. According to them, God created an angel who created another angel who in turn created another angel. This continued until the last angel in the series created the world. This angelic cosmogony thus denied God's direct creation and supervision of the world, resulting in some practical theological error. It stressed God's transcendence to the exclusion of His immanence. Since God did not create the world in the past, the heretics argued, He does not work in the world in the present. This ruled out the value of prayer and the possibility of miracles. It also led to a false worship of angels. If the world resulted from angelic emanations, then persons in the world had to work their way back to God through this series. Thus, they would have to know who those angels were and how many there were in order to give each his proper respect. Jesus Christ was reduced by most Gnostics into a creature, perhaps the highest being God created. This was an attack on the Trinity and on the eternal deity of Jesus Christ.

In daily living, this heresy led to asceticism and legalism. If matter is evil, then the body is evil. The heresy taught that to destroy the desires of the body in order to satisfy the needs of the soul, a rigid code of behavior—including circumcision, dietary laws, and observances of feasts—had to be followed.

Time and Place of Writing

During Paul's absence from Asia, the heresy began to infiltrate the area. The leaders of the church were apparently unable to cope with it, so they sent Epaphras to Rome to consult with Paul. Quite possibly, Epaphras was the founder and pastor of the church. When he left, Archippus assumed the pastoral responsibility (1:7; 4:17). Epaphras informed Paul about the faith of the church (1:4–5), their love for Paul (1:8), and the heretical threat.

Unable to go to Colossae because of his imprisonment, Paul penned this epistle and sent it to the church through Tychicus and Onesimus (4:7–9). For some unknown reason, Epaphras was imprisoned along with Paul (Philem. 1:23). Paul assured the church that Epaphras was laboring in his prayer ministry (4:12). Thus, within eight years of the establishment of the church, Paul had to warn this young church against the errors of the heresy (2:8, 16, 20–23).

Purposes

Paul wrote, therefore, to express his prayerful interest in the spiritual development of the Colossian believers (1:1–12), to set forth the sovereign headship of Jesus Christ over creation and the church (1:13–29), to warn against the moral and doctrinal errors of the heresy (2:1–23), to exhort them to holiness (3:1—4:6), to explain the mission of Tychicus and Onesimus (4:7–9), to send greetings from his associates (4:10–15), and to command the exchange of correspondence with the Laodicean church (4:16–18).

> With such a background it is not surprising that the epistle is priceless in its description of the Person and work of Christ. Nowhere else does Paul touch such heights on this theme and it is impossible to read it without realizing that Christ possesses a glory and station which can only move the soul to worship when the tremendous impact of the epistle reaches the mind. The theme of the epistle then is the pre-eminence of Christ.[4]

Distinctive Features

Colossians resembles Ephesians both in content and vocabulary. Here are some contrasts:

Colossians	Ephesians
Completeness in Christ	Oneness in Christ
Mystery of Christ in the body of the believer	Mystery of Jews and Gentiles as one in the body of Christ
Emphasis on Christ as the head of the body	Emphasis on the Church as the body of Christ

Colossians contains a classic passage on the preeminence of Jesus Christ (1:14–22). His descriptive titles are unique: the image of the invisible God, the firstborn of every creature, the head of the body, the beginning, and the firstborn from the dead. He is both the creator and sustainer of the universe. In the natural and the spiritual creations, Christ is sovereign and should have the preeminence.

Colossians contains the most severe warning against unguided human intellect or nonbiblical philosophy (2:8). A genuine love for wisdom should lead to a perfect love for Christ (2:3). However, many systems that exist under the guise of philosophy are really governed by human standards, by humanism, and by antisupernaturalism. They are not driven by an unbiased love of wisdom nor by divine revelation centered in the person of Jesus Christ. Christians need to distinguish between true and false philosophies.

CHAPTER 16

The Giving of Thanks
Colossians 1:1-8

Preview:

Paul sends greetings from himself and Timothy, wishing God's grace and peace upon the "faithful brethren" at Colossae. Although Paul had never been there, he commends the Colossians on their great faith in Jesus Christ and their love for the brethren, which has become known to him through their teacher, Epaphras. Since learning of their faith and love, Paul has kept them in his prayers, continually giving thanks for them to God.

Paul's opening greeting in his letter to the Colossians resembles his greeting to the Philippians (1:1-3).[1]

Paul was in prison and the church had moral and doctrinal problems, but the apostle could still give thanks to God. He had neither pity nor a pessimistic outlook for the believers. He exemplified his instructions to others (1 Thess. 5:18)—that is, he practiced what he preached.

Three areas of emphasis can be gleaned from Paul's expression of thanks. In the Greek text, the entire passage (1:3-8) constitutes one lengthy sentence.

For the Colossians (1:3-4)

Gratefulness is one of the most important virtues in that it responds to kindness and grace imparted in life. And Paul quickly gives thanks to God for the testimony and spirituality of the Colossian church. That thankfulness ascends upward to the Father and to the Son, and it is expressed by ongoing prayers for this body of believers.

The theme of thanksgiving is mentioned in all four chapters (1:3, 12; 2:7; 3:15, 17; 4:2). In this first reference, Paul is the person who renders thanks to God, but in the other passages, the Colossians are exhorted to be thankful.

The Expression of Thanksgiving (1:3)

The plural verb indicates that both Paul and Timothy shared this spiritual conviction. The fact that more than one person was involved gives the expression greater impact (Matt. 18:16).

Its meaning. The Greek verb translated "give thanks" *(eucharistoumen)* is a compound word based on the adverb *well* or *good* *(eu)* and the verb *to give freely* *(charizomai)*. It is also related to the verb *rejoice* *(chairō)*. Thus, in general, those who give thanks are full of joy, expressing appreciation for their benefactor's generosity. Believers who give thanks specifically to God express delight about His gift of grace. The present tense of the verb reveals Paul and Timothy's constant gratitude for the repeated blessings bestowed directly upon them by God or indirectly through the changed lives of converts.

The giving of thanks is a priestly ministry of believers in this church age (Heb. 13:15–16). All people can exercise it.

Its object. In the New Testament, the direction of thanksgiving is almost exclusively to God with but three exceptions in the fifty-three cases (Luke 17:16; Acts 24:3; Rom. 16:4). God is always the source of gracious favors (James 1:17).

The title "God, the Father of our Lord Jesus Christ" is unique to the New Testament. In the Old Testament, God was known as the God of the Hebrew fathers Abraham, Isaac, and Jacob. Here, however, He is seen as the God who has revealed Himself through His incarnate Son and through Christ's redemptive death and resurrection (Rom. 15:6; 2 Cor. 1:3; 11:31; 1 Pet. 1:3).

God is not the God and Father of Jesus Christ in the same sense that He is the God and Father of believing sinners. When Christ was on earth, He addressed God as "Father" (John 17:1), "Holy Father" (John 17:11), and "My Father" (John 5:17). Never in His own prayers did He say "Our Father." An eternal relationship exists between God the Father and God the Son. We saved sinners became children of God when we were birthed into His family by faith in Jesus Christ (John 1:12).

Its occasion. The phrase "praying always for you" does not mean that the apostle was constantly involved in a ministry of prayer, for he also was engaged in teaching, writing, and counseling. It does not necessarily mean that whenever Paul prayed, he always prayed for the Colossians, although that is a possibility. Rather, he always gave thanks for them whenever he prayed for them. His first response, whenever they came into his mind, was not to scold them nor to be disappointed in them, but to be thankful for them.

Human prayer to God and the prospect of divine response argued against the Gnostic heresy that there is no direct contact between God and the human race. The apostle did not express his appreciation to any angelic intermediaries; rather, he had direct access to God's presence (Heb. 4:14–16; 10:19–22).

The Cause of Thanksgiving (1:4)

The cause for the apostolic thanksgiving is given in the participial phrase introduced by the words "since we heard" (Greek, *akousantes*).[2] The plural indicates that both Paul and Timothy were dependent on outside sources for their knowledge of the Colossian situation. The aorist tense reveals that they had heard all of the necessary data before they gave thanks. Undoubtedly, they heard from Epaphras, who had traveled to Rome to give the apostle a first-hand report (1:7–8; 4:12). Paul cites two reasons for their thanksgiving.

Their faith. The Colossians' faith was specific and personal. The phrase literally reads, "the faith of you." Paul's usage of the definite article *the* shows that he referred to a particular action of faith, their conversion experience, at which time they believed in the Lord.[3]

The Colossians' faith rested in Christ Jesus. In the New Testament, three Greek prepositions are used with the verb to manifest the scope of redemptive faith. Sinners put faith in (*eis*) Christ and cause it to remain in (*en*) Him; thus, their faith rests on (*epi*) the Savior. Mere faith cannot save anyone; it must have a valid object. Christ must always be the goal (*eis*), the sphere (*en*), and the foundation (*epi*) of spiritual faith. All three concepts embrace both the initial act of saving faith, which receives the imputed righteousness of God and divine justification, and the continuance of faith, which produces the sanctified life. People are justified by faith in Christ, and they must walk by faith (Rom. 1:16–17; 5:1). Since faith comes only by hearing the proclaimed Word of God, the Colossian believers must have been regenerated through the preaching of Epaphras or one of Paul's associates (Rom. 10:17).

Their love. Faith in God and love for God's children always go together (1 John 3:23). Vertical faith precedes horizontal love, because love is the outworking of faith (Gal. 5:6).

Two observations about the Colossians' love are set forth. First, it was divinely given. The Colossians possessed "the love" (Greek, *tēn agapēn*), that type which is an evidence of regeneration (1 Thess. 4:9; 1 John 3:14). This love transcends mere human relationships, which is seen in the Greek words *philos* ("brotherly love, friendship") and *eros* ("unreasoning passion") types of love, and instead reflects the nature of divine love (1 John 4:8).

Second, this love reached out to "all the saints." Although believers should love the entire world of lost people (John 3:16), Paul commended them for their love extended to all Christians, both those in their church and others throughout the Roman Empire. Such love manifests true discipleship (John 13:34-35). Fervent love stretches out to others; it is not selfish or limited (1 Pet. 1:22). It is a fruit of the Spirit (1 Cor. 13; Gal. 5:22).

Paul Urges Believers to Love One Another

Love one another (Rom. 13:8).

Love your neighbor as yourself (Rom. 13:9).

Follow after love (1 Cor. 14:1).

Prove your love with sincerity (2 Cor. 8:8).

With love serve one another (Gal. 5:13).

Love is the fruit of the Spirit (Gal. 5:22).

Forbear one another with love (Eph. 4:2).

Walk in love as Christ loved us (Eph. 5:2).

Husbands, love your wives (Eph. 5:25).

You are taught by God to love one another (1 Thess. 4:9).

Put on the breastplate of love (1 Thess. 5:8).

For the Gospel (1:5-6)

The triad of faith, love, and hope appears in Paul's epistles (1 Cor. 13:13; 1 Thess. 1:3). It is impossible to have one without the others. What is significant is the omission of wisdom, the quality that the false teachers emphasized more than any other. Paul thanked God for their faith, love, and hope but not for their knowledge.

The Gospel Brings Hope (1:5)

The believers at Colossae were not working merely for earthly gain and glory. They were serving for an "anticipation" that was spiritual and stored in a far, far better place—heaven. This church knew its theology well; they realized that the gospel of the Lord Jesus Christ was true and that it gave far greater dividends than mere earthly rewards.

We are saved by hope (Rom. 8:24–25). Redemptive hope has both an inward and an outward character. It is both subjective and objective.

This hope is in heaven. The objective reality of the future, rather than an eager anticipation, is stressed here. Four features of this hope are enumerated. First, it is definite, as seen by the usage of the article ("the hope"). It is specific, not nebulous. Second, this hope is reserved. The verb construction "laid up" stresses the security of that which has been set aside by God.[4] Peter rejoiced that believers had been born again into a living hope, an inheritance that was reserved in heaven (1 Pet. 1:3–4). Christ promised that He would prepare a place for His own in the Father's house (John 14:1–3). The verb connotes preservation without any possibility of loss. Third, this hope is for believers ("for you"). We sometimes hear reports of people who have lived without any awareness of an inheritance bequeathed to them or of people who have been unable to gain access to a fortune because of legal barriers. Believers, however, know they will receive all that God has promised. Fourth, this hope is in heaven. Literally, the phrase reads "in the heavens." Every believer has been blessed "with every spiritual blessing in the heavenly places in Christ" (Eph. 1:3). A believer's citizenship (Phil. 3:20), city and country (Heb. 11:16; 13:14), treasure (Matt. 6:20), and Savior (Phil. 3:20) are all in heaven. Although the hope involves things, it actually is centered in a person—Christ, "the blessed hope" (Titus 2:13).

This hope will find its realization when believers receive their immortal, incorruptible bodies. This will occur when Christ returns to raise the dead and to change living believers (1 Thess. 4:13–18). This event is called the rapture of the church, an event that is signless, imminent, and that will happen before the seventieth week of Daniel's prophecy begins (Dan. 9:24–27).

This hope is in the gospel. The gospel message is that which joins the hope in the heart with the hope in heaven. Three observations can be made about this gospel. First, it must be proclaimed orally. Before Paul wrote and before the heretics invaded their church, the Colossians had heard the redemptive message and had responded in saving faith ("you previously heard"). What they heard was contained "in the word." Sinners are not saved by studying the heavens or by watching the lives of Christians. They must hear the inscripturated word of divine grace (Matt. 13:23; Rom. 10:14).

Second, the gospel involves "the truth." Christ is that truth (John 14:6). Both His divine-human person and His redemptive death and resurrection must be presented with biblical accuracy and logic. People must be told in all honesty who they are, who Christ is, what He has done, and what they must do about it. Method and message must complement each other (1 Cor. 2:4). Truth must be proclaimed in the right way and for the right reason (Gal. 2:5, 14; 1 Thess. 2:3–6).

Third, the gospel centers in Christ's redemptive death and resurrection (1 Cor. 15:1–4). The word *gospel* literally means "a good message" (Greek, *euaggelion*). It brings good news to guilty, condemned humans in that it declares what God has graciously provided through His Son.

The Gospel Bears Fruit (1:6)

The phrase "which has come" refers to the gospel, not to the hope.[5] The gospel came to the Colossians when it was originally preached to them. Paul makes three observations about the gospel's ability to bear fruit.

In all the world. Just before His ascension, Christ commanded the apostles to preach the gospel throughout the world (Matt. 28:19; Mark 16:15; Acts 1:8). During His earthly ministry, He had restricted their preaching ministry to the Jews (Matt. 10:5–6). However, His rejection by Israel and His prediction of the forthcoming church age (Matt. 16:18) changed that earlier limitation.

Through His death, Christ provided reconciliation for the world (2 Cor. 5:19). He was the propitiation for the sins of the whole world (1 John 2:2). He died for all people: Jews and Gentiles, slaves and free, rich and poor, men and women. Paul did not mean that the gospel had gone out into the entire population of the planet, but that it had brought forth fruit wherever it had gone into the world. The universal application of the benefits of Christ's death thus refuted the exclusive claims of the Judaistic Gnostic heretics.

In you. Paul assured the Colossians that their conversion and their subsequent spiritual growth were the same as that produced by the ministries of all the apostles throughout the Roman Empire. They were not deficient as the false teachers suggested.

A harvest always has a beginning. The time of the initial fruit at Colossae is indicated by a clause that contains two key verbs: "since the day you heard *of it* and understood the grace of God in truth." The believers heard and understood fully the gospel of grace. They comprehended the significance of Christ's death and resurrection. They knew that intellectualism and legalism were not the means of salvation. At the time of their conversion, the Colossians possessed a thorough and accurate saving knowledge (Greek, *epegnōte*) that surpassed that of the boastful Gnostics.[6]

Constantly. The verb "is constantly bearing fruit" (Greek, *estin karpophoroumenon*)[7] stresses the fact that the gospel was still bearing fruit at the time Paul wrote, both in the world and at Colossae. People were continually being saved and growing in the faith. The middle voice of the participle shows that the gospel has innate ability to reproduce itself in the lives of its hearers. Thus, one person is saved after hearing the gospel, and then that person bears witness to another, who in turn becomes a Christian. The gospel also produces the fruit of the Spirit within the believer (Gal. 5:22–23). The gospel is like "trees bearing fruit, with seed in them, after their kind" (Gen. 1:12).

The Lord Jesus reminded the disciples that it was necessary for them to be attached to Him ("abide in Me") in order to bear spiritual fruit (John 15:1–8). The Father is described by Jesus as the vinedresser who trims the vine to increase fruit bearing. Unfruitful branches are taken away, and the other branches are pruned back. Christ was giving a painful but important lesson about how the Father may take His own children through difficulties to bring about spiritual health so that they may better produce spiritual fruit that can be seen and bear witness.

Abiding in Christ is a command and not an option for the child of God (vv. 4–5), and it is extremely essential for the Christian life, in that the Lord says, "Apart from Me you can do nothing" (v. 5b).

For Epaphras (1:7–8)

Epaphras of Colossae should not be confused with Epaphroditus of Philippi. He is mentioned only three times in the Scriptures (1:7; 4:12; Philem. 1:23).

His Titles

A servant. Paul identified Epaphras as "our beloved fellow bond-servant." The word "fellow bond-servant" (Greek, *sundoulou*) literally reads "a joint slave." Christ owns those whom He has redeemed (1 Cor. 6:19–20). Their wills were subject to His. The same title is later used of Tychicus (4:7). The pronoun *our* shows that Paul linked Epaphras to himself and to Timothy. Although Paul was an apostle, he saw himself as a slave and equal to his associates in that relationship. Epaphras was "beloved" (Greek, *agapētou*) by God, the apostle and Timothy, and the church.

A minister. The word *servant* (Greek, *diakonos*) is the basis for the English term *deacon.* The Bible presents deacon-servants in the official, technical sense as assistants to the pastor (Acts 6:1–7; 1 Tim. 3:8–13) and also in the general sense as those committed to service for others (Mark 15:40–41; 1 Cor. 3:5). The derivation of the word is interesting. It is a compound Greek word based on *dia* ("through") and *konis* ("dust"). The imagery suggests a person who quickly moves to perform his tasks and creates a trail of dust by his haste.

The church ("on our behalf") sent Epaphras as its emissary to minister to Paul in Rome. While there, he also labored through intercessory prayer for the believers (4:12). He was faithful in the discharge of his duties. Faithfulness is a key qualification for Christian service (1 Cor. 4:1–2).

His Deeds

The church learned from him. Epaphras probably both evangelized Colossae and edified the believers through his teaching. The verb *learned* (Greek, *emathete*) is the basis of the term *disciple.* Christ charged the apostles to disciple all nations, a process that includes evangelism, baptism, and instruction (Matt. 28:19). Since Epaphras had taught the Colossians the basic doctrine of grace, his integrity was under attack by the heretical philosophers.

He informed Paul. Paul also stated that Epaphras "informed us of your love in the Spirit." The verb *informed* (Greek, *dēlōsas*) was used in the Greek papyri to indicate official legal evidence. This means that Epaphras gave the apostle solid proof of the conversion of the Colossian believers, their subsequent spiritual growth, and their love for Paul. Paul then had no cause to question the validity of their confession. It was as genuine to him as to Epaphras.

Again, the presence of love is seen as an evidence of true spirituality. This was not mere human love developed to its fullest extent; rather, this was "love in the Spirit" (Greek, *agapēn en pneumati*). The Holy Spirit had caused the believers to love God, one another, and the unseen apostle. Their attitude toward the Savior was reflected in their feelings toward Paul. Paul was naturally thankful that he was included in their loving outreach (1:4).

STUDY QUESTIONS

1. Do Christians adequately thank God for other believers? What often prevents the development of this gracious spirit? How can a Christian cultivate this attitude?

2. What kinds of faith are set forth in the Scriptures? What is the difference between a true and a false faith?

3. In what practical ways can saints manifest their love to others? To those they know? To unseen brothers and sisters?

4. What heavenly possessions await the believer? What is the difference between a genuine and a false hope?

5. In what ways has the gospel been robbed of its truth? How can error slip into evangelism? What effect does this have on conversions?

6. Is lack of fruit bearing a sign of hypocrisy? Of spiritual deadness? Can sterile hearts become fertile again?

7. What are the marks of genuine service for Christ? Do believers see themselves as slaves today?

CHAPTER 17

The Worthy Walk
Colossians 1:9-13

Preview:

Because of their faith in Jesus Christ, Paul has been praying for the Colossians to be filled with spiritual wisdom concerning God's will, that they may walk in a worthy manner. He desires that their walk be pleasing to God and that they bear good fruit. To these ends Paul prays that, through increased knowledge and strengthening from God, they will be steadfast, patient, joyous, and thankful.

Believers in Christ may find it difficult to continually place before the Lord the needs of other Christians. When we do pray for others, often our requests have to do with physical or material issues rather than spiritual things. But here in this section, Paul and Timothy continue unceasingly to pray that the Colossian saints be fortified by knowing God's will and be filled with His wisdom and understanding.

Although the Christian life is a race to be run with purpose and patience (1 Cor. 9:24-26; Heb. 12:1), it is normally described as a *walk*. Believers are charged not to walk in sin (Rom. 8:1; 1 Cor. 3:3; 2 Cor. 4:2; 5:7; Eph. 2:2; 4:17; 2 Thess. 3:6; 1 John 1:6). Rather, they are exhorted to walk in holiness (Rom. 6:4; 8:1, 4; 13:13; 14:15; 2 Cor. 5:7; Gal. 5:16; Eph. 2:10; 5:8, 15; Col. 4:5; 1 John 1:7; 3 John 1:3).

The above passages reveal the quality of a worthy walk (Eph. 4:1; Col. 1:10; 1 Thess. 2:12). A worthy walk is consistent with the divine purpose of redemption and is lived out in God's will daily. Its essence is to walk as Christ walked (1 John 2:6).

Foundation of a Worthy Walk (1:9)

Paul's prayer develops around two purpose clauses, both introduced by the connective "that" (1:9–10). The second purpose is a result of the first; therefore, the first must be achieved for the second to occur.[1]

The Object of Human Prayer

Spirituality involves strong interest and effort. Although believers must work out their own salvation (Phil. 2:12), they also need the assistance of others. Here Paul informs the Colossians that he is praying for their moral development.

Cause of the prayer. The opening words "for this reason" refer to the Colossians' love in the Spirit (1:8) but also include their faith in Christ, brotherly love, expectant hope, and fruit bearing (1:4–6). The plural pronoun *we* is emphatic and points to the apostolic team plus Epaphras (4:12–13). Their ministry of intercession began when Epaphras reported to them about the spiritual vitality of the church ("since the day we heard it").

Nature of the prayer. Four observations can be made. First, it was constant ("have not ceased"). They did not pray only once; rather, they started and continued their ministry of intercession. Second, the prayer was intercessory ("for you"). Although Paul was a prisoner in Rome, he was not concerned about himself. Rather, he bore their burdens (Gal. 6:2). Third, his prayer was incorporated within his devotion and worship. The word here used is the general word for prayer, always directed to God (Greek, *proseuchomenoi*). The verb occurs eighty-five times and its noun thirty-seven times. Genuine prayer is exercised under the control of the Holy Spirit and arises from a personal awareness of being one of God's own children (Rom. 8:15; Gal. 4:26). Fourth, the prayer involved a specific request ("to ask"). God has asked His children to make requests of Him (Matt. 7:8). Christians cannot demand that God do something, but they can ask Him for that which He has promised to give if they will make their requests in the right way. The middle voice of the verb (Greek, *aitoumenoi*) shows their strong emotional interest in their prayer.

The Knowledge of God's Will

It is not enough simply to pray for someone else. The petitioner must also ask God to accomplish specific goals in the life of that person. Three features of Paul's goals can be found.

That the Colossians be filled by God. Believers cannot fill themselves, nor can they be filled by other saints. The passive voice (Greek, *plērōthēte*) indicates that this ministry is performed by God through the Holy Spirit. Spiritual truth is imparted to spiritual hearts by the Spirit of God (1 Cor. 2:10–12).

The verb means "to fill out to completion." In this book, the verb is used five times (1:9, 25; 2:10; 4:12, 17) and the noun twice (1:19; 2:9).

That the Colossians be filled with the knowledge of God's will. The heretics emphasized knowledge per se (Greek, *gnōsis*), but the word used here stresses an intensive, thorough knowledge (Greek, *epignōsin*).[2] The plan for the counteroffensive against the onslaught of false teaching was more knowledge, not ignorance nor an appeal to experience. *more knowledge not less*

Paul refers to a specific knowledge, a perception of the divine will. This deals with God's preceptive will for believers as expressed in the following verses (1:10–13). God will always make His will known to His children who want to know it and do it because they love it. Children of God must recognize the truth that the will of God offers the best avenue for their lives even before they know what that will is. God's will is always manifested under the guidance of the Holy Spirit according to the proper interpretation of the Scriptures. God never directs His own to do that which is contrary to the revealed, inscripturated Word. To be filled with such knowledge, believers must empty themselves of their self-will (John 4:34; 6:38). *do you want the truth.*

That the Colossians be filled with wisdom and understanding. The two adjectives, *all* and *spiritual*, qualify both nouns; thus, the phrase means "all spiritual wisdom" and "all spiritual understanding." God's will pertains to all areas of believers' lives: vocational, marital, financial, and social. These areas are spiritual in that the Holy Spirit instructs saints in the spiritual things of the Scriptures which He inspired. Unsaved persons, devoid of the Holy Spirit, cannot perceive these things (1 Cor. 2:9–14).

The two realms, wisdom and understanding, are distinctive yet corollary. The concept of wisdom (Greek, *sophia*) deals with what we should be and do, and the idea of understanding (Greek, *sunesis*) refers to how we can accomplish those goals. The former possibly alludes to what we should believe, and the latter to how we should behave.

The word "wisdom" is found six times in the book (1:9, 28; 2:3, 23; 3:16; 4:5). The term "understanding" occurs twice (1:9; 2:2). Both wisdom and understanding involve critical thinking about the complexities of life and a Spirit-guided solution that manifests biblical content. Such wisdom and understanding will always manifest genuine humility and a greater glorification of God.

Marks of a Worthy Walk (1:10–13)

The second major purpose of the prayer is introduced by a Greek infinitive (*peripatēsai*): "that you may walk." The divine will must be shown in a human walk—the walk of a Christian's life from regeneration to death. The goal of the worthy walk is the pleasure of God. The noun *pleasing* (Greek, *areskeian*) is found only here in the New Testament, although the verb form is used often. Believers please God when they complete their obligations to Him (1 Cor. 7:32; 1 Thess. 2:4; 4:1), to family (1 Cor. 7:33–34), and to others (Rom. 15:2; 1 Cor. 10:33). In so doing, they follow the selfless example of Christ (Rom. 15:3).

The four marks of this pleasing, worthy walk are set forth in four participial phrases.

Fruitfulness (1:10)

The nature of bearing fruit. Bearing spiritual fruit is a human responsibility. The participle "bearing fruit" is in the active voice (Greek, *karpophorountes*). The gospel has innate fruit-bearing properties, but believers must actively yield to the indwelling Holy Spirit in order to produce fruit. The present tense of the participle shows that children of God should constantly produce spiritual fruit, in contrast to the seasonal harvests of the natural creation.

The fruit is the life of Christ in and through believers (John 15:4; Gal. 2:20; Phil. 1:21). It is holy fruit (Rom. 6:22) that begets a distinctive spiritual temperament: love, joy, peace, patience, kindness, goodness, faithfulness, gentleness, and self-control (Gal. 5:22–23). It is the evidence of genuine discipleship and results in the glorification of God (John 15:8).

The realm of bearing fruit. The worthy walk manifests fruit "in every good work." Believers should never make a distinction between the sacred and the secular. They must glorify God in everything they do. The "good work" (Greek, *ergō agathō*) is not the fruit; rather fruit must be produced in the sphere of every good work. Good works correspond to the goodness of God (Mark 10:18) and are innately good (Greek, *agathos*), not just outwardly good in appearance to human observation (Greek, *kalos*). Since no person can do such good, it can be performed only by God working through him or her (Rom. 3:12).

Knowledge of God (1:10)

Knowledge must increase. The participle "increasing" (Greek, *auxanomenoi*) denotes constant growth.[3] Homer A. Kent Jr. observed that the verb form "depicts a fruit tree which yields its fruit and keeps on growing, in contrast to grain which produces its harvest and then dies."[4] Believers must continue to grow in grace (2 Pet. 3:18; same verb), and their capacity for God must grow larger.

Knowledge must be thorough. The goal of increase is unto the full knowledge of God. To become a Christian, a sinner must have a saving knowledge of Christ's person and redemptive work (John 17:3; Phil. 3:8). To become a spiritual Christian, however, one must have a seeking, sanctifying knowledge. The word *knowledge* (Greek, *epignōsei*) implies an intense personal, experiential awareness to which more can be added. The major motivation in Paul's life was to know Christ (Phil. 3:10). All believers should have the same goal (2 Pet. 3:18). This goal can be achieved only through a humble study of God's self-revelation through the Scriptures and in the application of biblical truth to the various facets of life. To know God is to love him. To love Him is to walk with Him and for Him in a worthy fashion.

Strength (1:11)

7 Sanctification

Source of strength. Strength is not gained in a once-for-all crisis experience; rather, it involves a lifelong process. The participle *strengthened* (Greek, *dunamoumenoi*) literally reads "being strengthened." Believers cannot strengthen themselves, but they can be yielded to God, who provides the moral enablement (Eph. 3:16; 6:10; Phil. 4:13). Both the indwelling Christ and Spirit are the source of this needed power. ✳

Sphere of strength. Believers are to be strengthened with all power (Greek, *dunamei*). The words *power* and *strengthened* come from a Greek root that implies ability, power, and innate strength. Christ taught that such inner ability results from being filled with the Holy Spirit (Acts 1:8). God never asks His ✳ children to do anything without first supplying them with the power to do it.

Standard of strength. God strengthens literally "according to His glorious might." The noun *might* (Greek, *kratos*) refers to supernatural strength. Of the twelve times it is used in the New Testament, eleven refer to God and one refers to Satan. The glory of God is the outward expression of who He is. At times it refers to the blinding brightness that radiates from His holy being, but it also expresses the demonstration of His attributes, such as power, grace, truth, mercy, and love (John 1:14; 2:11). God here reveals Himself through ←✳ what He enables believers to do with the ability only He can provide.

Goal of strength. The goal is twofold. The term *steadfastness* (Greek, *hupomonēn*) points to circumstances sent by God, and the word *patience* (Greek, *makrothumian*) refers to the endurance of things imposed by man. The first virtue, "steadfastness," is a compound word meaning "to remain under." People are steadfast when they remain patient under the difficult pressures of life. The second quality, "patience," is literally "wrath that is put far away." Spirit-controlled believers put distance between themselves and this emotion. It enables Christians to tolerate people who try their patience (2 Cor. 6:6). It permits them to forgive and to forbear others in love (3:13). Patient believers do not have quick tempers. The goal of this inner strengthening is humble endurance of trials "with joy." Steadfastness and patience without joy will lead to depression and a defeatist attitude. Joy gives optimism, triumph, and trust. Christians must believe that God is working out His sovereign purpose through the situation (Rom. 8:28; James 1:2).

Thanksgiving (1:12–13)

A worthy walk is a thankful walk (1:3). The heretics charged that there was no direct contact between God and man, but the apostle claimed that believers could give thanks personally and directly to their heavenly Father. Paul gives three reasons, indicated by the three verbal actions, to show why the Father is worthy of thanks. All reveal God's intervention into the time-space universe to act directly in behalf of His own.

God qualified them to be spiritual heirs. The Greek verb *hikanōsanti* looks back at conversion when God enabled a person to have a sufficient, acceptable position in Christ. The believer was not made deserving at that time but was placed into the Son who is deserving. The purpose of the divine qualification was that they might "share in the inheritance of the saints in light." Christians have been allocated a definite part of the eternal riches. They will share in the many abiding places promised by Christ (John 14:2). The inheritance is incorruptible, undefiled, imperishable, and reserved in heaven (1 Pet. 1:4). All regenerated sinners are saints, God's children, thus heirs of God and joint-heirs with Christ (Rom. 8:17; Gal. 4:7). They share equally in what Christ has provided through His redemptive death and resurrection. The Christian's portion is a holy inheritance. God the Father is light (1 John 1:5), God the Son is light (John 1:9), and the holy city will be full of light (Rev. 21:23; 22:5). At conversion, sinners go from darkness to light, from slavery to sanctification, and from poverty to wealth (Acts 26:18).

God delivered them. Paul emphasizes two aspects of the deliverance. First, it was a total, divine rescue. This verb form (Greek, *errusato*) is used only of God in the New Testament. Christ is called "the deliverer" (Rom. 11:26), but in this passage, the stress is on deliverance by the Father. Deliverance was decisively accomplished at the conversion of sinners.

Second, believing sinners have been rescued "from the domain of darkness." With sobering words, John Eadie says:

> The unregenerate state is described as the kingdom of darkness. It is one of spiritual gloom in its government, essence, pursuits, and subjects. In its administration it is named—"the power of Satan," in itself it is darkness—its actions are "works of darkness," Luke xxii. 53; Acts xxvi. 18. . . . This principality is named "darkness" on account of its prevailing ethical element.

Above it the heaven is shrouded in dismal eclipse, around it lies dense and impervious gloom, and before it stretches out the shadow of death.[5]

This expression points to the kingdom of Satan that is marked by sin and moral darkness (Eph. 6:12). The concept of darkness includes an opposition to the light as well as an absence of it. This is a realm of moral rebellion, insubordination, and creaturely independence (John 3:19–20).

God conveyed them into Christ's kingdom. The verb *transferred* (Greek, *metestēsen*) was used of the geographical transfer of people from one country to another. In that sense, a believing sinner has been transported from darkness into light, from the kingdom of Satan into the kingdom of Christ, and from hell into heaven.

God the Father eternally loves God the Son (Matt. 3:17). This is a kingdom marked by love: love of the Father for the Son, love of the Son for the Father, love of both the Father and the Son for the saints, love of Christians for the triune God, and love of believers for one another. This kingdom, ruled by Christ, must be contrasted with the satanic kingdom, dominated by fear, slavery, and darkness.

STUDY QUESTIONS

1. In what ways do believers try to determine the will of God for their lives? Which ways are right? Which are wrong?

2. How does common sense relate to disclosure of the divine will? Do they ever contradict each other? Why?

3. For what reasons do believers walk before the Lord today? Give illustrations of the worthy walk for contemporary living.

4. Why do many believers lack spiritual fruit? Why do some stop producing fruit?

5. How can we know God more fully? What are some of the obstacles to this goal?

6. Why do believers lack joy in endurance? How can patience and longsuffering be cultivated in each life?

7. Do believers praise the Son more than the Father for their salvation? What is the proper biblical balance?

CHAPTER 18

The Exaltation of Christ
Colossians (1:14-18)

Preview:

Paul gives the Colossians a primer on our Lord Jesus Christ. In these few short verses he speaks of Jesus as our redeemer, the creator and sustainer of all things, and the head of the body, which is the Church universal. His focus is the preeminence of Christ. He is first, above all and over all.

The main error of the Judaistic Gnostic heresy centered in its repudiation of the person and redemptive work of Jesus Christ. Through their exaltation of angelic mediators between God and man, the false teachers denied the deity and humanity of the incarnate Son (2:18-19). Through their emphasis on legalism and intellectualism, they denied the efficacy of Christ's substitutionary atonement and physical resurrection (2:13-17). They reduced Christ to a creature, the most powerful and intelligent being within the universe but nonetheless still a creature. He was like God but not the same as God.

In his refutation of this heresy, Paul has here given one of the key Christological passages in the New Testament (cf. John 1:1-18; Phil. 2:5-11; Heb. 1:1-3). It contains positive assertions rather than negative refutations. It clearly sets forth the eternal deity of Jesus Christ, the physical reality of His incarnation, His direct creation of the entire universe, His death and resurrection, and His ontological relationship to the Father.

This detailed exposition about the Son actually develops out of the closing remarks of the apostle's prayer for the Colossians (1:9-13). With the mention of the Son (1:13), Paul begins a series of clauses introduced by the relative pronouns *whom* and *who* (1:14, 15, 18).

The Proof of Preeminence (1:14-18)

Christ's exaltation is set forth in four basic relationships: to sin (1:14), to God (1:15a), to creation (1:15b–17), and to the church (1:18). He thus is preeminent because He is the redeemer, the revealer, the creator, and the head.

In Redemption (1:14)

Its sphere. Christ is the personal sphere of salvation ("in whom"). Eternal life is not an abstract possession; rather, it is a union with the living Savior. Christ came that people might have life, and He Himself is that life (John 10:10; 14:6). Paul wanted to be "found in Him" (Phil. 3:9).

Its possession. The simple verb here, "we have," indicates that redemption is a present possession. Paul is boldly stating a fact.

Its meaning. All believers have literally "the redemption" (Greek, *tēn apolutrōsin*). The usage of the definite article shows that Paul referred to the one and only redemption accomplished by God through Christ (Rom. 3:24). The noun emphasizes the concept of release because of a paid ransom. It is used ten times in the New Testament in this compound form that basically means "to set free from" (Greek, *apo* and *luō*). Freedom from the penalty and effects of sin is the spiritual emphasis (Luke 21:28; Rom. 3:24; 8:23; 1 Cor. 1:30; Eph. 1:7, 14; 4:30; Col. 1:14; Heb. 9:15; 11:35).

In cognate words, Christ gave His life a ransom (Greek, *lutron*) for many (Matt. 20:28; Mark 10:45). He obtained eternal redemption (Greek, *lutrōsis*) for His people (Heb. 9:12) by giving Himself as a ransom (Greek, *antilutron*) for all (1 Tim. 2:6). Other words are also used to depict the full picture of biblical redemption. All unregenerate people are viewed as slaves in the marketplace of sin, but Christ has bought (Greek, *agorazō*) them with the payment of His vicarious death. This purchase price, however, can be either rejected or received (1 Cor. 6:19–20; 2 Peter 2:1). The provision was made for all, but its value is applied only to those who believe. A second word (Greek, *exagorazō*) stresses the removal of the believing sinner out from the dominion of sin (Gal. 3:13; 4:4–5). This concept is used only of the saints.

Its result. The practical result of redemption in the life of the believer is "the forgiveness of sins." Actually, this phrase is in apposition to "the redemption." The noun *forgiveness* (Greek, *aphesin*) comes from a verb, "to send" (Greek, *hiēmi*), and a preposition, "away from" (Greek, *apo*). Thus, the essence of forgiveness is the sending away of sins from a person who has committed those sins (Ps. 103:12). This noun occurs seventeen times in the New Testament but only four times in the epistles (Eph. 1:7; Col. 1:14; Heb. 9:22; 10:18).

The word *sins* (Greek, *hamartiōn*) has a more general meaning than any of its synonyms. It means "to miss the mark," as does an archer whose arrow falls short of the target. All unregenerate people have sinned in thought and deed; thus, they have fallen short of God's righteous essence (Rom. 3:23).

With great poetic grace, John Eadie describes the nature of this redemption:

It is a first and prominent blessing. So soon as faith springs up in the heart the pardon of sin is enjoyed—the results of expiation are conferred. . . . So deep is man's guilt, and so tremendous is the penalty; so agonized is his conscience, and so terrible are his forebodings; so utterly helpless and hopeless is his awful state without Divine interposition, that a free and perfect absolution from the sentence stands out not only as a blessing of indescribable grandeur and necessity, but as the first and welcome offer and characteristic of the gospel of Christ.[1]

The Doctrine of Redemption

Redemption is in Christ Jesus (Rom. 3:24).

Redemption brings believers out from under the curse of the Law (Gal. 3:13; 4:5).

Christians await the final redemption of the body (Rom. 8:23; Eph. 4:30).

Redemption is only through the blood of Christ (Eph. 1:7).

Believers are sealed until the day of redemption (Eph. 1:13).

Christ's redemption purifies a people for Himself (Titus 2:14).

In Revelation (1:15a)

Persons are not known as things are known. Persons must choose to reveal themselves before others can know them fully. If this is true of finite man, it is truer of the infinite God.

God is invisible. He literally is "the God the unseen one" (Greek, *tou theou tou aoratou*). The gods fabricated by the imaginations of sinful humans are totally visible and creaturely. They have mouths, eyes, ears, noses, hands, and feet (Ps. 115:4–7). The psalmist concluded: "Those who make them will become like them" (Ps. 115:8). Paul commented that sinful people changed the glory of God into images of men, birds, and animals (Rom. 1:23).

The true and living God, however, is a spirit being (John 4:24). The essence of deity is spiritual, not material (1 Tim. 6:16). No human, who can be in only one place at one time, has ever viewed the infinite, eternal God who can be everywhere at all times (John 1:18). In the Old Testament period, people saw the invisible God (Heb. 11:27). What they saw, however, were theophanies— appearances of God in visible form for the purpose of communication. When God spoke to humans, He used anthropomorphic expressions (such as hands and eyes) to describe His strength and sight. These divine manifestations were unique and temporary. God can never be limited by space and time. Even though the glory of God filled the temple as an indication of divine presence, Solomon confessed that all the heavens could not contain Him (1 Kin. 8:27).

Christ is the image. Christ is the image of the invisible God in that He both represents and manifests God to the world. What is God like? Look at Jesus Christ and you will see what God is like (John 14:9). Since there is an intrapersonal oneness and equality within the triune divine Being, the essence of the Father can be seen in the Son. Through Christ, people can see God in action (John 1:18). The Son has literally exegeted (NASB, "explained") the Father.

The word *image* (Greek, *eikōn*) was used of the head of the ruler minted on a coin (Matt. 22:20). It also was used to describe the idol of the Antichrist (Rev. 13:14) and to refer to the parental likeness in a child. In each case, the image always pointed to that upon which it was based.

Adam was made in the image and likeness of God (Gen. 1:26). People today are still the image and glory of God (1 Cor. 11:7; cf. Gen. 9:6; Col. 3:10; James 3:9). Truth about God can be learned from an objective, biblical study of humans. Since humans are living personalities, one can conclude that God also is personal, possessing intelligence, emotions, and volition. Since humans have an innate sense of moral oughtness (a conscience), God also must be a moral being. Humans, however, are only *like* God; they are not the same as God. Humans are made in the image of God.

On the other hand, Christ "is" (Greek, *estin*) the image of God (2 Cor. 4:4). He did not become the image of God at His incarnation; rather, He is the eternal image of the eternal, invisible Father. Humans are a finite image, but Christ is the perfect, infinite image. This eternal relationship became visible through the incarnation and the subsequent manifestation in Christ's life, miracles, and words. Only God could reveal God.

W. E. Vine says this about image:

The word *eikōn*, image, involves the double idea of representation and manifestation; it does not denote mere likeness or resemblance. When in Hebrews 10:1 it says "a shadow of the good things to come, not the very image of the things," it means "not the essential and substantial form of them." Man as he was created was a visible representation of God (1 Cor. 11:7), a being corresponding to the original. Regenerate persons are moral representations of God's character (see 3:10, below); in their glorified state they will not merely resemble Christ, they will adequately represent what He is both in His spiritual body and His moral character (Rom. 8:29; 1 Cor. 15:49). That Christ is "the image of God" (2 Cor. 4:4) means that He is essentially and absolutely the perfect expression and representation of God the Father.[2]

Vine sums up:

That [Christ] is the "image of the invisible God," gives the additional thought that He is the visible representation and manifestation of God to created beings, and the likeness expressed in this manifestation is involved in the essential relations in the Godhead, and is therefore unique and perfect: "he that hath seen me hath seen the Father" (John 14:9).[3]

In Creation (1:15b–17)

Since the false teachers stressed an angelic cosmogony, it was essential for Paul to set forth the proper doctrine of creation. Christ is identified as the direct Creator-God in two ways: His title and His work.

Christ's title. Christ is "the first-born of all creation" (Greek, *prōtotokos pasēs ktiseōs*). The title connotes both priority and sovereignty: He existed before the world was created and He is the ruler over that creation. His voluntary subordination to the Father and subsequent incarnation did not abrogate this innate authority.

Some have suggested that this phrase teaches that Christ Himself was a creature, the first created by God and through whom God created all other things.[4] This heresy, however, is contradicted by the context. The passage does not say that Christ *became* a creature or that He was the first creature to be made. If that had been the intent of the apostle, he would have used a different word: "first-created" (Greek, *prōtotokos*). Rather, Paul asserts that Christ existed before creation and that He created (1:16–17). If he were a "thing," how could He exist before He came into existence?

In its basic meaning, *prōtotokos,* meant "the first one born" in a family. In Middle Eastern culture, the eldest son, by right of being born first, received the birthright, which entitled him to a double inheritance and family leadership upon the death of the father. The idea of supremacy soon overshadowed the concept of temporary priority. God thus established Israel as His "first-born," the sovereign nation, even though many other nations existed before Israel

(Ex. 4:22). God planned to elevate the Son of David, the Messiah as His "first-born, the highest of the kings of the earth" (Ps. 89:27). Because Christ is who He is, one day every created being will bow before Him and acknowledge His sovereign deity (Phil. 2:10–11).

W. Robertson Nicoll writes:

> With this verse the great Christological passage of the Epistle begins. Its aim is to refute the false doctrine, according to which angelic mediators usurped the place and functions of the Son to nature and grace. He, and He alone, is the Creator, Redeemer and Sovereign of all beings of the universe, including these angelic powers. The passage does not deal with the eternal relations of the Son to the Father, but with the Son's relations to the universe and the Church. It is not of the pre-existent Son that Paul begins to speak, but of the Son who now possesses the kingdom, and in whom we have our deliverance.[5]

Christ's work (1:16–17). Christ's preeminence as the creator is indicated in five key statements. First, He is the *sphere* of creation. The phrase "by Him" literally reads "in Him" (Greek, *en autō*). The heretics taught that the creation centered in a series of angelic beings, whereas the apostle affirmed that it centered in one person. Both the plan to create and the power to create resided in Him. He was the originator, both the architect and the builder. Creation was within His domain.

The object of creation was "all things" (Greek, *ta panta*). This concept embraces the totality of the created universe in both time and space. All things, collectively and individually, came from Christ. From within His will and might proceeded the complex universe, although He must not be identified with it. He still remains both transcendent and immanent.

The scope of the creation is then made specific in three areas. First, it reaches every locality—all things in heaven and on earth. The former includes the stars, the planets, and all other astronomical phenomena, whereas the latter points to both living and inanimate objects on planet Earth. Second, it envelops all kinds—all things visible and invisible. The false teachers espoused the erroneous principle of dualism—that material things were innately evil and that immaterial things were intrinsically good. They denied that God directly created the physical world. But the two worlds—seen and unseen by the senses, natural and supernatural—were both created by Christ. Third, it incorporates all ranks—thrones, dominions, rulers, and authorities. These four classifications are used elsewhere to describe the world of angels, both holy and evil spirit beings (Eph. 1:21; 3:10). In the Gnostic series of angelic emanations, a superior being created an inferior creature, and the latter in turn produced yet another lesser one. Christ, however, created all angelic beings instantaneously and directly.

Second, Christ is the *agent* or *means* of creation. All three Persons of the triune God actively participated in the work of creation (Gen. 1:1-2; John 1:3). If a distinction of work assignment can be discovered, then the Father was the source of creation, the Son its agent, and the Spirit its preserver (Job 34:14-15; 1 Cor. 8:6). The same preposition, "by" (Greek, *dia*), is elsewhere used of Christ's creative agency (John 1:3; Heb. 1:2).

Third, Christ is the *purpose* or *goal* of creation. All things are literally "unto Him" (Greek, *eis auton*). Creation has meaning only when it points to Christ. People should praise Him when they view the minute complexities of life through a microscope or the vastness of the universe through a telescope. Glory should be attributed to Him, not to a series of angelic emanations, to an impersonal Mother Nature, or to an atheistic principle of evolution.

The change in tenses of the two verbs for creation should be noted. The first (Greek, *ektisthē*) looks back to the creative act, whereas the second (Greek, *ektistai*) views creation as it presently stands. The contemporary universe is not the result of an ongoing creation process; rather, it is the permanent result of a past creative act.[6]

Fourth, Christ is *prior* to all creation. The verb is (Greek, *esti*) indicates Christ's eternal existence, an attribute of deity. Mere preexistence could have been set forth with the verb *was*. However, the text states that Christ *is* before all things, not that He *was* before all things. This verb structure can refer only to God (John 8:58; 17:5). It also proves that Christ was not a thing, a created person.

Fifth, Christ is the *sustainer* of creation. The verb "hold together" (Greek, *sunestēken*) means "to stand or consist, to cohere." His work of creation finds permanency in His work of preservation, which began during the creation week and continues into the present.[7] He rested on the seventh day from His creative activity, but He did not cease His direct control of the universe (Gen. 2:1-3; John 5:17). He always is "upholding all things by the word of His power" (Heb. 1:3).

R. C. H. Lenski well concludes:

Two additional statements complete the immense thought so far expressed: "and he is before all things whatever . . . , and all the things that exist . . . have their permanence in connection with him," in connection with whom they were created in the first place. Creation and preservation naturally go together. The latter is highly pertinent here. No created being in the universe is independent of Christ. All are "through him and for him" so that "he is before them," and all of them have their continuous existence only "in connection with him."[8]

In Headship (1:18)

The ruler of creation is also the sovereign of redemption. The focus of Christ's preeminence now switches from the old natural creation to the new spiritual creation. The Creator now becomes the Savior. Three titles are given to describe this exalted position.

Christ is the head. The terms *body* and *church* are in apposition to each other and describe the same entity. Christ predicted that He would build His Church (Matt. 16:18). He then informed His disciples that He would have to be crucified and be resurrected in order to lay the foundation for the Church (Matt. 16:21). The Father officially established Christ as the head of the body, the Church, after His ascension into heaven (Eph. 1:20–23). From the exalted position, Christ sent the Holy Spirit into the world as He had promised and prayed (John 14:16; 15:26; Acts 1:5). It is by the baptism in the Holy Spirit that believing sinners are united with each other and with Christ to form the one true Church (1 Cor. 12:12–13; Eph. 4:4–6). The body of Christ, the true Church, therefore constitutes the entire group of saved people from the Day of Pentecost (Acts 2:1–4) to the Rapture, the time when Christ returns to take His people into His presence before the Day of the Lord (1 Thess. 4:13–18).

As "the head" (Greek, *hē kephalē*) of the Church, Christ has functional authority over His people. The Church forms His body, His Church, and His sheep (John 21:17). The Church thus draws its sustenance and direction from Him (Eph. 4:15–16).

Christ is the beginning. The term *beginning* (Greek, *archē*) is a singular form related to a plural word translated earlier as "rulers" (Greek, *archai*; 1:16). It has multiple usages because its word stem *(arch)* is the basis of two concepts: "to rule" *(archō)* and "to begin" *(archomai)*. It often refers to the start of something (Matt. 19:4; Mark 1:1), but it can also point to political power (Luke 12:11; 20:20) and to supernatural rule (Rom. 8:38; Eph. 3:10).

This title for Christ is found only here and in the book of Revelation. In that closing canonical book, He is depicted as "the Beginning and the ending" (Rev. 1:8; 21:6; 22:13) and as "the Beginning of the creation of God" (Rev. 3:14). Using this latter phrase, some have argued that Christ was the first creature to be created by God; however, if that thesis were true, how could He be both the beginning and the ending, the first and the last creature to be made?

Christ is "the beginning" in that He originated both the natural and the spiritual creations. He created the worlds and He redeemed the Church; thus, only He qualifies to be the ruling head in both areas.

Christ is the firstborn. Christ is "the first-born from the dead" (Greek, *prōtotokos ek tōn nekrōn*). He is the authoritative head of the Church in that He brought life out of death (Rev. 1:18). During His earthly ministry, Christ raised at least three persons out of physical death: the daughter of Jairus (Matt. 9:18-26), the widow's son at Nain (Luke 7:11-18), and Lazarus (John 11:38-44). Through delegated authority, the apostles also raised the dead in their preaching journey (Matt. 10:8). These resurrections, however, were restorations to normal physical life. All of these people later died again. On the other hand, Christ was the first to come out of death in an immortal, incorruptible body. His resurrection established Him in His rightful position as the supreme ruler of the realm of the dead. Through His death and resurrection, Christ destroyed Satan, who heretofore had the power to keep people in the realm of death (Heb. 2:14).

The phrase "the dead" literally means "the dead ones" (Greek, *tōn nekrōn*). It refers to people, not to a place or to the principle of death. At His death, Christ went into paradise, the place of comfort within Sheol or Hades, the realm of departed human spirits (Luke 16:19-31; 23:43; Acts 2:25-31). When He arose, He left that realm and united Himself to a resurrected body. He alone has the authority over death and hell (Rev. 1:18).

As the firstborn, Christ will call all people out of death to stand in judgment before Him (John 5:28-29). He has the authority to permit believers to spend eternity in the holy city and to consign the unsaved to everlasting torment in the lake of fire.

The Declaration of Preeminence (1:18)

As God, before and after creation, Christ possessed an innate sovereignty. By His incarnation, death, resurrection, and ascension, He obtained a new type of preeminence. He had the former as God, but He gained the latter as the God-man.

The verb "might come" literally means "might become" (Greek, *genētai*). It was used of things coming to exist out of nothing (John 1:3) and also of the incarnation (John 1:14). Thus, Christ became after His resurrection what He was not before His incarnation.

This is the only place in the New Testament where the phrase "first place in everything" (Greek, *en pasin autos prōteuōn*) occurs. The Greek word *prōteuōn* is also found in a compound form *(philoprōteuōn)* of Diotrephes, an arrogant church leader (3 John 1:9). The word is actually a participle meaning "to have first place." Coupled with the main verb, it denotes a permanent position of priority and authority. As the Creator-Redeemer who has both a divine nature and a human nature united within His single person, Christ has become pre-eminent over the realms of men and angels, both good and evil, throughout eternity (Phil. 2:9–11).

STUDY QUESTIONS

1. How shallow is the believer's comprehension of the concept of biblical redemption? Is there a scarcity of doctrinal preaching today?

2. How can human forgiveness express divine forgiveness? What are the similarities and differences?

3. How can the doctrines about the Trinity and the deity of Christ be successfully presented to evangelical churches? How can those concepts be defended against attacks? What groups do not accept these two basic doctrines today?

4. Can Christ receive any glory if believers accept the idea of theistic evolution? In what ways are evolution and biblical creationism contradictory?

5. How can we distinguish between God's ordinary activity in the preservation of the universe and His extraordinary activity through miracles?

6. What is the difference between the universal church and the local church? How can the headship of Christ be applied to the operations of the local church? Of a family?

7. In what practical ways can Christ be given the preeminence in all things within the life of each Christian?

CHAPTER 19

The Work of God and Man
Colossians 1:19-29

Preview:

Paul first speaks of the work of Christ as the Father's good pleasure. Christ's cross brought peace and reconciliation between the Father and believers, removing them from the imprisonment of unforgiven sin. Paul then speaks of himself and his role as minister to the Church, having been given the stewardship of the gospel. He proclaimed that which had been a mystery in time past, Christ in them, the hope of glory.

God and humans are colaborers in redemptive ministry (1 Cor. 3:9). People need the enablement of God, and God has chosen to work through them. In outreach to the world, the Holy Spirit and believers must witness together as a team (John 15:26-27; 16:7-11).

In this section, Paul stresses both human effort and divine enablement in the works of evangelism and discipleship (1:29). The apostle is the minister who preaches (1:23, 25, 28), but God reconciles and makes known (1:21, 27). Both God and Paul want to present each believer perfect before Christ (1:22, 28).

The Pleasure of the Father (1:19-23)

The causal connective *for* (Greek, *hoti*) shows that the basis for the preeminence of the Son was the pleasure of the Father. It was the Father "good pleasure" (Greek, *eudokēsen*) that these things happen. His pleasure is synonymous with His will and predetermined plan.

For Christ (1:19–20)

The Father's plan involved two aspects for the Son. The first pertained to fullness *in* Him and the second to reconciliation *by* Him. The former refers to His incarnate person, whereas the latter points to His redemptive work.

Fullness. Three truths concerning the Son are enumerated here. First, the fullness of God dwells *in* Him—not around, upon, or under Him, but *in* Him. No creature, man or angel, could qualify as the tabernacle for the divine fullness.

Second, the verb *dwell* (Greek, *katoikēsai*) points to the event of the incarnation.[1] God the Son in His total deity came to dwell within a human body (2:9). As God, the Son possessed the complete fullness of the divine essence by eternal, innate right. The Son was, is, and forever shall be God, equal to the Father within the ontological Trinity. In the plan of God, which involved the subordination of the Son in order to provide redemption, there was no diminishing of the divine attributes when God the Son took to Himself a perfect and complete humanity. God cannot be less than what He is, and the Son's total submission to the Father did not change that unalterable truth.

Third, the phrase "all the fullness" (Greek, *pan to plērōma*) refers to the total essence of deity. In classical Gnosticism, the concept referred to the total number of aeons or emanations that formed the bridge between God and man. As the eternal Son, Christ had all of the divine fullness, and when He became man, He manifested all of that essential fullness in official, redemptive acts (John 1:14, 16).

Reconciliation. Five aspects of reconciliation are set forth. First, the meaning of "to reconcile" (Greek, *apokatallaxai*) is "to change completely." Before the entrance of sin, God and humans experienced unbroken fellowship. However, when Adam and Eve sinned, that communion was broken. People turned away from God. In reconciliation, the barriers are removed so that people can return to God. Scripture never says that God is reconciled or that both God and humans are reconciled. Reconciliation always comes from God and is directed toward humans (2 Cor. 5:18–20). It is provisional in that humans must willfully accept its condition of repentant faith.

Second, the means of reconciliation is Christ. The phrase "through Him" (Greek, *di' autou*) is used twice in the verse to emphasize that point.

Third, the goal is "to Himself" (Greek, *eis auton*). God chose to bring people back to Himself for His glory.

Fourth, the basis of reconciliation is the cross. People rebelled and have waged war against God ever since. People erected the barrier, and Christ knocked it down (Eph. 2:14). Christ's peace extends to all saved people, both

Jews and Gentiles (Eph. 2:17). This provision of peace through reconciliation was made when people were enemies of God (Rom. 5:10). Spiritual peace was gained "through the blood of His cross." Christ had to die; He had to die as a sacrifice; and He had to die on a cross. Blood had to be shed (Lev. 17:11; Heb. 9:22) in a prescribed way at a definite place (Gal. 3:13). The value of the death, however, is inseparably connected to the intrinsic worth of the dying person, the Creator-Redeemer in whom the fullness of God dwelt.

Fifth, the object of reconciliation was the universe ("all things"), the entire created world, both earth and heaven. The universe became unclean through angelic and human sin (Job 15:15; 25:5). Even the plants and animals suffered damage because of human sin (Gen. 3:17–18; Rom. 8:19–22). But Christ died to purify both heaven and earth (Heb. 9:23). The benefits of His death will be manifested to this total domain in the millennium and throughout the eternal state.

Paul's Doctrine of Reconciliation

Believers have the ministry of reconciliation of the world to God (2 Cor. 5:18).

Christ reconciled the world to Himself (2 Cor. 5:19).

On behalf of Christ, be reconciled to God (2 Cor. 5:20).

Believers were reconciled to God through the death of Christ (Rom. 5:10).

Believers received reconciliation through Christ (Rom. 5:11).

Jews and Gentiles are reconciled in the body of Christ (Eph. 2:16).

Christ reconciled believers in His body through death (Col. 1:22).

For Believers (1:21–23)

Paul now changed the emphasis of reconciliation from the general ("all things") to the particular ("and you"). As representative of all the redeemed, the Colossian believers were reminded to contemplate the spiritual work of God in its triple perspective: past, present, and future.

Their past. A contrast is made between the Colossians' pagan past ("formerly") and their Christian past ("yet . . . now reconciled [aorist tense, past action with continuing results]"). The former refers to their lost spiritual position, whereas the latter refers to the time when they were saved and entered into a position of acceptance before God.

Five concepts describe the Colossians' unregenerate condition. First, they were all equally under the penalty and power of sin (Rom. 3:9). The pronoun *you* (Greek, *humas*) included all of the Colossian believers, both corporately and individually, both Jew and Gentile. In their practice of sin, they undoubtedly differed, but not in their position. They all were totally depraved.

Second, the Colossians were alienated from God. Their alienation continued from their conception to their conversion and manifested their position of spiritual estrangement in Adam (Rom. 5:12–21). The Gentile unsaved are aliens both from the commonwealth of Israel (Eph. 2:12) and from the life of God (Eph. 4:18).

Third, the Colossians were hostile. It is one thing to be estranged from someone; it is another thing to act in a hostile manner toward that one. They actively opposed God and willfully broke His moral law.

Fourth, the Colossians had mental enmity. Here the word *mind* (Greek, *dianoia*) focuses on their thoughts and decisions. Intelligence is part of the image of God in humans and is therefore good. People were created to think God's thoughts after Him. The unsaved, however, do not "see fit to acknowledge God any longer" (Rom. 1:28). Their thinking has become both humanistic and antisupernaturalistic because their minds have been blinded by the ultimate enemy, Satan (2 Cor. 4:4). Their carnal mind is at enmity with God (Rom. 8:7).

Fifth, this mental enmity manifests itself by evil deeds. Thoughts and actions go together. With a reprobate mind, the unsaved "do those things which are not proper" (Rom. 1:28).

In spite of these negative traits, God reconciled the Colossians. The verbal action looks back to the time when they were saved by faith in Christ. The propitiatory sacrifice took place "in His fleshly body through death." The Judaistic Gnostic heresy claimed that material entities were innately evil and that immaterial concepts were intrinsically good. That false dichotomy is negated by the fact that Christ provided salvation in a physical body of skin, bone, and blood. He abolished the enmity in His flesh (Eph. 2:15) and through a physical death on a materialistic cross (Phil. 2:8).

Their future. The purpose behind the pleasure of the Father and the reconciliation of the Son was to present saved sinners in heaven for all eternity. The verb *present* means "to stand beside" (Greek, *parastēsai*). In that future day, believers will stand beside each other, dressed in the righteousness of Christ before the presence of almighty God. The aorist verbal tense points to that time when the entire body of Christ, the true Church, will be presented. This will occur at the rapture of the Church when resurrected Christians and living believers will be caught up into heaven to meet the Savior (Eph. 5:25–27; 1 Thess. 4:13–18).

The manner of presentation involves three aspects. First, all believers will be presented as "holy" (Greek, *hagious*). This will be the climax of the divine work of sanctification. All redeemed are positionally set apart in Christ today; thus, they are saints. They are also striving to be holy in their daily experiences, but at the rapture of the Church, they will be forever set apart from the effects of sin. Moreover, all believers will be "blameless" (Greek, *amōmous*), without spot or blemish (Eph. 5:27). Blamelessness is the opposite of imputation in that it denotes the total removal of sin and guilt from the believing sinner (Eph. 1:4). And finally, all believers will be "beyond reproach" (Greek, *anegklētous*). This compound word literally means "not to be called in." It is a legal term. No charge of condemnation nor sentence of eternal death can ever be brought against believers in the court of divine justice (Rom. 8:33–34). These three truths are the possession of each Christian today. God's faithfulness guarantees that this acceptable standing will endure until the day of Christ (1 Cor. 1:8).

What is God's role in reconciliation? John MacArthur writes:

From His holy perspective, His just wrath against sin must be appeased. Far from being the harmless, tolerant grandfather that many today imagine Him to be, God "takes vengeance on His adversaries, and He reserves wrath for His enemies" (Nah. 1:2). "A His wrath the earth quakes, and the nations cannot endure His indignation" (Jer. 10:10). The one who refuses to obey the Son will find that "the wrath of God comes upon the sons of disobedience" (Eph. 5:6). Man and God could never be reconciled unless God's wrath was appeased. The provision for that took place through Christ's sacrifice. "Much more then, having now been justified by His blood, we shall be saved from the wrath of God through Him" (Rom. 5:9). It is "Jesus who delivers us from the wrath to come" (1 Thess. 1:10). He bore the full fury of God's wrath against our sins (cf. 2 Cor. 5:21; 1 Pet. 2:24). After all, "God has not destined us for wrath, but for obtaining salvation through our Lord Jesus Christ" (1 Thess. 5:9).[2]

Their present. Doctrinal integrity is a sign of genuine reconciliation. Continuance in the faith is a necessary prerequisite to presentation in heaven (2 John 1:9). The conditional particle ("if") seems to imply that persons could lose their salvation if they failed to continue in the faith. Paul, however, taught just the opposite. He assumed that the Colossians were continuing in the faith. This conditional clause can be translated: "If indeed you continue in the faith, and I believe that you are doing so."[3] Reconciled sinners show evidence of divine work in their lives by proper doctrinal belief. Any denial of the deity and redemptive work of Christ, subsequent to the profession of saving faith, would demonstrate that the sinners did not genuinely accept Christ with essential understanding (Matt. 13:23).

The phrase "the faith" refers to that body of biblical truth that is essential to the doctrine of salvation, not to one's personal faith (Jude 1:3). The issue is doctrinal accuracy, not gross sins such as immorality or murder.

The fact that the Colossians remained in the faith is seen in three ways. First, they were "established" (Greek, *tethemeliōmenoi*). They had built a permanent spiritual foundation on the person and work of Christ, as expounded by the apostles and prophets (1 Cor. 3:11; Eph. 2:20). Second, they were "steadfast" (Greek, *hedraioi*). This adjective denotes a strong superstructure strengthened by the ministry of the indwelling Holy Spirit (Eph. 2:21–22). Third, the Colossians were not being "moved away from the hope of the gospel." The heretics tried to weaken their doctrinal convictions about the person and work of Jesus Christ, but the foundation and the walls of their faith did not develop any cracks. Spiritual growth and the production of godly fruit are the best safeguards against the attacks of false teachers (Eph. 4:14–15; 2 Pet. 1:10).

The Purpose of the Apostle (1:23–29)

The mention of the gospel serves as a transition from the work of God in the believers to the work of God through a believer, namely, Paul. Paul makes three brief observations about the gospel. First, the Colossians heard it from Epaphras or one of Paul's other associates. Second, the same gospel was preached to every creature under heaven. This idiom refers to the inhabited Roman world. It does not imply that every living person had heard the gospel, but that the same gospel that was preached to the Colossians was also preached elsewhere, in all countries and to all classes of people. On the other hand, the heresy at Colossae was a local phenomenon. Third, Paul became a minister of that gospel by divine selection and enablement (1 Tim. 1:11–12). His ministry is now set forth in three areas.

Minister of the Gospel (1:23)

Paul was an apostle, yet he was also a minister. He makes this claim twice (1:23, 25). The word *minister* (Greek, *diakonos*), also translated as "deacon," has both a technical and a general meaning. The former refers to an official position in the local church (1 Tim. 3:8–13). The latter can refer to the service ministry of angels (Heb. 1:14), women (Matt. 8:15), Christ (Matt. 20:28), and of preachers (1 Cor. 3:5). As a minister of the gospel, Paul was concerned about the doctrinal facts and truths he preached.

Minister of the Church (1:24-27)

Paul was interested in evangelizing people and edifying them (1 Cor. 9:19-23). He had three major concerns.

To suffer for the church. At the time Paul wrote this letter, he was a prisoner in Rome (4:3, 18). Despite this difficulty, he rejoiced in his sufferings for the local church at Colossae ("for your sake"). He saw himself as its representative as he stood before pagan authorities because of false Jewish accusations. He was a prisoner because he preached the gospel of grace to uncircumcised Gentiles and incurred the wrath of Jewish religious leaders for doing so. He resisted both Jewish legalism and worldly philosophy, and he rejoiced that he could do so. His sufferings were many and extreme (2 Cor. 11:23—12:10) as he defended the integrity of the gospel (Phil. 1:7).

Paul also suffered for the universal church. He filled up "on behalf of His body (which is the church) in filling up that which is lacking in Christ's afflictions." Paul was Christ's substitute. Christ suffered to save the church, and now Paul suffered to spare it. The redemptive work was finished at the cross, so Paul could add nothing to that accomplishment. The word *afflictions* (Greek, *thlipseōn*) is never used to describe the sufferings of Christ on the cross. Christ had informed Paul that Paul would suffer for Him (Acts 9:16). Paul counted it a privilege to suffer for his Savior (Acts 9:4). He underwent great tribulation in the defense of the spiritual oneness of both Jew and Gentile in Christ.

To serve the church. Paul had three relationships to the church. First, he was its minister. He evangelized sinners, established local churches, trained their leaders, prayed for them, visited them, sent associates to them, and wrote letters to them. He did everything he could for the church's spiritual welfare, and he required no direct financial assistance for his labor.

Second, Paul was the church's steward. He conducted his ministry "according to the stewardship from God bestowed on me for your benefit." The word *dispensation* (Greek, *oikonomian*) literally means "house law." Every private home has distinctive family rules. Every nation has laws that pertain to what happens within its borders. In like manner, God has administered His creative-redemptive program in different ways within the various ages of biblical history. He dealt with Adam differently after sin occurred than before his fall. After the Mosaic law was given, the people of Israel had more responsibilities before God than prior to that event. The crucifixion and resurrection of Christ likewise have changed the means of divine government in this age. These various periods can be called dispensations in that God revealed more truth and held people responsible to act according to this new revelation. In this present age, God has produced a new entity, the church, out of believing Jews and Gentiles. The church age extends from the Crucifixion, Resurrection, Ascension, and the Day of Pentecost to the Rapture before the Great Tribulation. God imparted more truth about the church age to Paul, especially as it pertained to the salvation and spiritual position of the Gentiles (Rom. 15:16; Gal. 2:7–9).

Third, Paul became the minister to "fully carry out the preaching of the word of God." In a primary sense, he attempted to preach the truth of Gentile salvation by grace through faith throughout the known world (Rom. 15:14–21). In a secondary sense, he inscripturated the revelation of distinctive church truth.

To reveal the church. Paul revealed five concepts about the church. First, it is a "mystery" (Greek, *mustērion*). This word is based on an ancient term that conveyed the idea of shutting the mouth. The biblical usage carries the sense that what was once silent is now vocal. Scriptural mysteries are divine truths once unknown and unspoken by people in past ages but now proclaimed and understood by spiritual believers (1 Cor. 2:7; 15:51). In this passage the term is used in apposition to the word of God (1:25), the concept of Gentile salvation within the true church.

Second, the essence of the church was "hidden from the *past* ages and generations" (cf. Eph. 3:5). Ages (Greek, *aiōnōn*) refer to time periods, whereas generations (Greek, *geneōn*) refer to the people who lived in those days. Paul is speaking of both Jews and Gentiles, both the saved and the lost.

Third, this mystery "has now been manifested to His saints." The adverb *now* (Greek, *nun*) contemplates the present church dispensation with special application to the apostolic period when the New Testament writings came into being (Eph. 3:3–5).

Fourth, the essence of the church was the object of divine revelation. God willed to create the church and to delay its revelation until the gospel was given—the apostolic period (Eph. 3:9). The "riches of the glory of this mystery" envelop the total significance of Christ's incarnation, crucifixion, resurrection, ascension, and the descent of the Holy Spirit.

Fifth, the mystery was "Christ in you, the hope of glory." The Old Testament both depicted and predicted Gentile salvation through faith in the redeeming God of Israel, but it never revealed that Jews and Gentiles would become spiritually one in Christ and that Christ would dwell in both (Eph. 3:6). Christ predicted this spiritual union (John 14:20).

The Gnostic heretics constantly bragged about their spiritual knowledge that was inaccessible to the majority; however, all saints in the church age can know what was heretofore unknown to the best minds of the past. The best mystery is a revealed mystery. It is not what we know that counts, but who we are and whom we have, namely, Christ.

Paul's Use of the Word Mystery	
The mystery:	Christ in you, the hope of glory (Col. 1:27)
The mystery:	A partial hardening of Israel until the fullness of the Gentiles has come in (Rom. 11:25)
The mystery:	The gospel to all nations (Rom. 16:25)
The mystery:	The gospel, God's wisdom (1 Cor. 2:7)
The mystery:	We shall not all sleep, but we shall all be changed (15:51)
The mystery:	All things summed up in Christ (Eph. 1:9)
The mystery:	Of Christ, Gentiles made fellow heirs through the gospel (Eph. 3:3–9)
The mystery:	Of lawlessness (2 Thess. 2:7)
The mystery:	Of the faith (1 Tim. 3:9)
The mystery:	Of godliness (1 Tim. 3:16)

Minister of Christ (1:28–29)

Paul belonged to Christ, and he knew and lived that truth. He often identified himself as an apostle or a minister. In that service, he wanted to accomplish three goals.

To preach Christ. Paul proclaimed a message that centered in a person ("We proclaim Him"). The present tense of the verb indicates the constant activity of the apostolic team. To preach the Word properly is to expound the person and redemptive work of the Savior (2 Tim. 4:2). The Scriptures testify of Him (Luke 24:44–45; John 5:39; Rev. 19:10).

Paul's declaration had both a negative and a positive aspect. He was "admonishing every man" to watch for false teachers who would invade the church from outside and rise up within its ranks (Acts 20:29–31; Phil. 3:1–2). And he was "teaching every man" what to believe and how to live. Didactic preaching is part of the discipleship program (Matt. 28:18–20). Paul warned and taught "with all wisdom." Such wisdom is redemptive and spiritual in character and is found in Christ as revealed in history and in the Scriptures (2:3).

The object of Paul's ministry was every believer. The triple usage of the phrase "every man" shows that no believer, regardless of sex, race, or social status, is excluded from the teaching ministry of the Holy Spirit though spiritual men and women. On the other hand, the heretics practiced an intellectual exclusivism.

To present believers to Christ. The apostle wanted to "present every man complete in Christ." Four concepts are found in this purpose clause. First, the agent of presentation is man, whereas an earlier presentation was made by God (1:22). Paul wanted the believers to be doctrinally and morally pure and correct at the time of the Rapture when Christ would summon them into His presence (2 Cor. 11:2). Second, the object of presentation is again every believer. Paul was concerned for the entire church congregation. Third, the goal of Paul's presentation is every person's completion in Christ. Although in spiritual standing, all believers are as perfect or complete as they can be (2:10), they are not yet complete in their moral practice or doctrinal understanding. The word *complete* (Greek, *teleion*) speaks of the end or goal of a process. The heretics used the term to describe one who had been fully initiated into the mystery cults in contrast to a novice within their movement. Fourth, the sphere of Paul's presentation is "in Christ Jesus." No ministry that ignores a true biblical Christology is worthy to be called a Christian ministry.

To labor by Christ's enablement. Paul labored (Greek, *kopiō*) in the ministry. This word stresses physical and mental exhaustion, weariness and toil. He put forth more effort than any other apostle (1 Cor. 15:10). He even toiled at making tents in order to support his ministry (1 Thess. 2:9). He knew that his labor was not in vain (1 Cor. 15:58). Furthermore, Paul agonized or strove (Greek, *agōnizomenos*). This metaphor from the sport of wrestling indicates the opposition Paul faced in the pursuit of his task. In a weak, tired body, he still had to fight against satanic onslaughts (Eph. 6:12). His endurance came only through divine enablement ("according to His power"). God actually did the work in and through Paul ("which mightily works within me"). Paul did not originate the work and then ask God to relieve him when he grew tired. His ministry was a divine-human endeavor. Paul surrendered his availability to God's ability. In so doing, he paradoxically grew stronger as he became weaker (2 Cor. 4:16; 12:10).

STUDY QUESTIONS

1. How can people who deny the deity of Christ actually appear to be evangelical? How can their true doctrinal position be detected?

2. Is the blood of Christ still emphasized in preaching and singing today? Are there any acceptable words that can be substituted for "blood"?

3. In what ways do the unsaved manifest mental hostility toward God? How can it be seen in their lives?

4. Why do many groups insist that believers can lose their salvation? What passages or concepts do they use?

5. Do evangelicals emphasize the local church today at the expense of the universal Church? Is the opposite true? How can balance be maintained?

6. What other New Testament mysteries were hidden from past ages? What does progressive revelation mean to you?

7. Are some Christians overworked? Are others lazy? What can be done to achieve the biblical standard? What is that standard?

CHAPTER 20

The Means of Perfection
Colossians 2:1-8

Preview:

Having never actually visited some of the newly established Christian churches was a concern for Paul. Here he expresses his desire to encourage those who are now "knit together in love." He wants to be assured that they have a firm understanding of who Christ is, that false teachers may not come along and mislead them. Paul exhorts them to walk confidently in the Lord, being firmly rooted in Him, not swayed through "philosophy and empty deception."

God has given gifted leaders to equip the saints to do the work of the ministry so that the church is edified (Eph. 4:12–13). All believers need outside help in their determination to achieve spiritual perfection. This pursuit is obligatory (Matt. 5:48).

Paul's Teaching (2:1-3)

Biblical teaching should always be warm and personal. It should never become cold, academic, and professional. It must be done with the heart as well as the head. Teachers must not only love what they are teaching, but whom they are teaching. Paul taught with his total being (1 Thess. 2:8).

Concern in Teaching (2:1)

Statement of concern. Believers should be informed that other Christians are interested in their spiritual welfare. Paul shared his concern for the Colossians through the content of his letter and the testimonies of Tychicus and Onesimus (4:7–9).

Paul describes his concern as a "struggle" (Greek, *agōna*). Transliterated as "agony," this is the noun form of the verb "striving" (1:29). What was general is now particular—he was concerned for all believers, and he was concerned for each believer. Thus, Paul's concern was "great" (Greek, *hēlikon*). This word, used only twice in the New Testament (2:1; James 3:5), stresses magnitude. A raging forest fire that can devastate thousands of acres can be started from a tiny spark. The report of the presence of heresy at Colossae caused Paul to have great inner distress about the local church. Furthermore, Paul's concern was constant. The present verb ("I have") points out continuity of interest. Even after Paul's associates left with the letter, his concern persisted and he continued to wage spiritual battles through intercessory prayer and vicarious sufferings (1:24).

Areas of concern. Paul cites three groups of people. First, Paul had concern for the believers at Colossae ("for you"). Earlier he had described them as saints and faithful brethren (1:2).

Second, Paul had concern for "those who are at Laodicea," a city about forty miles southeast of Philadelphia (in ancient Lydia) on the road to Colossae. It too was situated on the Lycus River, about eleven miles west of Colossae. With Colossae and Hierapolis, it formed a unique tri-city area. The apostle John later recognized the local congregation as one of the seven churches of Asia (Rev. 1:4, 11; 3:14–22). Started as the direct result of Paul's evangelistic efforts in Ephesus (Acts 19:1–10), it became a wealthy, fiercely self-sufficient church. Paul's associates probably traveled to Laodicea and won converts there. Because of its proximity to Colossae, Laodicea probably was invaded by the heretical teachers too. This partially explains why Paul commanded the Colossians to share his letter with the Laodiceans (4:16). The church met in the house of Nympha (4:15).

Third, Paul also had concern for "all those who have not personally seen my face." This phrase referred to other believers in that region, including those at Hierapolis (4:13). He was interested in the lives of all Asian converts, both known and unknown to him. He apparently had not visited Colossae or Laodicea.

Purpose for Teaching (2:2)

Although verse 2 states one main purpose, four separate goals can be detected. These four build upon one another.

To encourage. The Greek verb *paraklēthōsin* literally means "to be called beside." An encourager, therefore, is one who is called to stand beside another to comfort and help that one. This encouragement can involve either consolation for the sorrowing or comfort for the weak and perplexed. The Holy Spirit is the divine Comforter who encourages both through the Scriptures and caring, involved believers. Thus, Paul sent Tychicus to comfort their hearts (4:7–8). The heart refers to the total inner being of a person, with special attention to thoughts and feelings (Prov. 23:7).

To unite. The legalistic, intellectual error had caused schism within the congregation. The believers were fragmented in their evaluation of the new teaching and in their relationship to the heretics. Paul wanted them to be "knit together in love." The Greek verb *sumbibasthentes* reflects a medical metaphor. It means "to join or unite together." Since believers are members of the spiritual body of Christ, they should not be out of joint. They should always be in submission to Christ, the head of the Church (2:19). Organizational unity and conformity without love, however, are like lifeless bones joined together in a skeleton. The Colossians had to be knit together "in love." Love for God and for one another is the blood stream of the body, the Church. It is the bond of perfection that holds everything in place (3:14).

To assure. Paul wanted the Colossians to attain "to all the wealth that comes from the full assurance of understanding." The essence of spiritual understanding (Greek, *suneseōs*) is the Spirit-guided ability to perceive the redemptive purpose of God in the Scriptures and to relate it to the complexities of contemporary life. He is able to integrate the sacred and the secular into a united whole. Such understanding will produce an unmovable conviction of the heart. For example, this "full assurance" (Greek, *plērophorias*) characterized Abraham's faith in the power and promise of God to give him a son (Rom. 4:21). In Paul's day, however, the heretics had caused the Colossian believers to question their doctrinal foundations. They were forced to reexamine their understanding of the person and creative-redemptive work of Jesus Christ. The apostle wanted them to know beyond a shadow of doubt that they were in the truth.

To inform. Paul's final goal was for the believers to know "God's mystery, *that is,* Christ *Himself.*" This mystery centers in the union between Christ and the body of believers within the church (1:26–27; Eph. 5:30, 32). The sense of "knowledge" (Greek, *epignōsin*) is a thorough comprehension of what God is doing today and how that relates to His program for the ages. It implies a full theological, dispensational, and Christological approach to life.

Content of Teaching (2:3)

Wisdom is in Christ. Genuine wisdom is centered in a person ("in whom"), not in facts written on paper. That person is Jesus Christ. All truth, specified as wisdom and knowledge, resides in Christ. He is its center and circumference.

Spiritual wisdom is spiritual wealth. The English term *thesaurus* is based on the Greek word translated as "treasures" (Greek, *thēsauroi*). The Gnostic teachers claimed that knowledge (Greek, *gnōseōs*) rested in them. Christ, however, is the real depository of true knowledge and wisdom. If knowledge refers to the understanding of each particular truth, then wisdom (*sophia*) sees the relationship between the truths (1 Cor. 13:9).

Wisdom is hid. The predicate adjective *hidden* (Greek, *apokruphoi*) is related to the verb *to hide* (Greek, *apokruptō*; 1:26). Just as the world did not know Christ when He lived on the earth, so sinful humans cannot understand the real meaning of life or the redemptive program recorded in the Scriptures (John 1:10). It is hidden to those who are wise in their own sight (Matt. 11:25), to pagan government authorities (1 Cor. 2:6–8), and to the lost of all ages. Yet such wisdom has been revealed to those who see themselves as spiritually ignorant babes (Matt. 11:25), to the saints of this church age (1:26).

Since this treasure is in Christ, and Christ is in each believer, each child of God has full access to this treasure. By inference, the heretical concept of a spiritual caste system is refuted. The believer, however, must actively study the Word of God to grow in grace and in knowledge of Christ (2 Pet. 3:18). The key to the treasure is yieldedness and purity of heart.

Paul's Warning (2:4–8)

The words "I say this" form a transition between the two sections. They refer to the previous instruction (2:1–3) and anticipate the four warnings that follow (2:4, 8, 16, 18).

Means of Error (2:4)

Just as one germ can infect the entire body and one drop of poison can pollute a cup of pure water, one false teacher ("no one") can corrupt a church. The apostle was far more concerned with the methods of deceit than with the identity of the deceiver. The principle, not the person, was the key.

False teachers deceive. The verb *delude* (Greek, *paralogizētai*) literally means "to reason or to speak beside." To delude involves faulty logic not based on the authoritative Word of God. It uses erroneous interpretations, giving meanings and making applications other than those that are normally accepted. Paul warned against building on a foundation that was placed beside Christ rather than on proper doctrinal comprehension of His person and redemptive work (1 Cor. 3:11). The illogical reasoning of the heretics rested on faulty premises and presuppositions, such as the denial of the Trinity, the repudiation of the Incarnation, and the perception of matter as evil.

False teachers persuade. False teachers attempt to delude with "persuasive argument." These two words are actually the translation of a single Greek term *(pithanologia)* that depicts a type of speech that is designed to entice others. In the papyri, the term was used of thieves who attempted to retain their booty by facile speech. It is what a crafty salesman uses to convince a person to buy something that he or she really does not want. It is deceit carefully packaged and presented.

Paul deplored such deceitful tactics (1 Cor. 2:4). He did persuade people to accept Christ, but he did not use rational and emotional appeals that were devoid of scriptural content or spiritual import.

Protection Against Error (2:5–7)

Believers must be alert. They should watch out for the enemy, but they should also build their defenses (Neh. 4:18).

Unity. Unity may be genuine or superficial. Paul praised the Colossians for their genuine spiritual oneness. Epaphras reported that the church had advanced even though the threat of heresy was real. Paul accepted this testimony as absolutely true and responded as if he had actually been in the city himself: "For even though I am absent in body, nevertheless I am with you in spirit." He rejoiced over the report, reckoning himself to be a present observer. It is always an encouragement to Christians when others tell them that they are noticed and appreciated.

Paul described the Colossians' unity in two ways. First, they had "discipline" (Greek, *taxin*). In the military world, orderly soldiers have no breaches in their ranks. They are in their assigned places and perform their assigned duties. In the Jewish world, the term was used of the priestly orders (Heb. 5:6; 7:11). Each priest carried out his own responsibilities in order that the goal of the entire priesthood might be fulfilled. Disorderly persons, on the other hand, disobey the clear commands given to them (2 Thess. 3:6–11).

The Colossian believers had "stability" (Greek, *stereōma*).[1] The focus of this word is on corporate strength. This noun is found only here, but its adjective form is used elsewhere (2 Tim. 2:19; Heb. 5:12; 1 Pet. 5:9). The verb referred to ankle bones being made strong (Acts 3:7, 16) and to the establishment of churches in the faith (Acts 16:5). In warfare it depicted the strength of a united front.

Walk. Paul earlier prayed that the Colossians might have a worthy walk (1:10–12). Now he issues a clear command to walk in Christ. The present tense of the verb (Greek, *peripateite*) stresses the daily walk of spiritual development. Six features of this walk are given. First, they were to walk in faith ("as you therefore have received Christ Jesus the Lord"). They received Christ by faith; therefore, they should walk by faith (Rom. 1:17). The verb *received* (Greek, *parelabete*) refers to the time when Epaphras or others evangelized and taught them. They received a person, not a philosophy.

Second, Paul's readers were to walk in Christ ("in Him"). As fish swim in water, so believers must walk in Christ. He must be their spiritual environment. Believers can do nothing apart from Christ (John 15:5).

Third, the believers were to be "rooted" (Greek, *errizōmenoi*). At conversion, believers actually put their roots down deep into Him. Now they should continue to draw their life and sustenance from Him.[2] He must be the rich soil and nutrient base out of which they grow into fruitful Christians. The passive voice of the participle indicates that God placed believers into Christ by baptism in the Holy Spirit (1 Cor. 12:13).

The Spiritual Walk of the Believer

Walk in newness of life (Rom. 6:4).

Do not walk according to the flesh (Rom. 8:4).

Walk by faith, not by sight (2 Cor. 5:7).

Walk by the Spirit (Gal. 5:16).

Walk no longer as the Gentiles (Eph. 4:17).

Walk in love (Eph. 5:2).

Walk as children of light (Eph. 5:8).

Be careful how you walk (Eph. 5:15).

Walk in a manner worthy of the Lord (Col. 1:10).

Walk and please God (1 Thess. 4:1).

Fourth, Christ's followers should be "built up in Him." At conversion, all believing sinners are built upon the foundation of Christ laid by the apostles and prophets (Eph. 2:20). The emphasis of regeneration is on the proper foundation; however, the focus of spiritual growth is on the superstructure. Believers have a choice to build spiritual lives of success to the glory of God or carnal lives of failure to the shame of self (1 Cor. 3:10–12). All lives will be judged at the Judgment Seat of Christ, an event that takes place after the church is raptured into heaven (1 Cor. 3:13–15; 2 Cor. 5:10).

Fifth, the believers were to be "established in the faith." It is not enough to place brick upon brick in a wall; such bricks must be properly anchored and cemented to each other to provide strength and stability. For Christians, firmness and stability is formed "in the faith." This phrase includes the whole body of doctrinal truth that had been revealed through the apostles (Jude 1:3). Persons cannot obtain this stability through their own inner faith, experience, or feelings. Although God can teach believers directly from their own inductive Bible study, He normally instructs through gifted teachers ("as you were instructed"). The Colossians had been taught by Epaphras (1:7). If a believer is to be taught in the faith, the teacher must know what that faith is (2 Tim. 2:2). In fact, the pastor-teacher should have been taught by someone else (Titus 1:9).

Sixth, these Christians were to have a thankful walk. They were to abound in the faith with thanksgiving. Instruction in biblical doctrine should produce inner joy and gratitude. The more believers learn about God and His redemptive program, the more they should love Him for what He has done for them.

Description of Error (2:8)

The command "See to it" shows that all believers should be on constant alert for the inroads of error and those who spread false teaching (Acts 20:29–31).

The goal of error. Heretics wanted to take the Colossians "captive" (Greek, *sulagōgōn*). This compound verb means to carry away (Greek, *agō*) booty (Greek, *sulē*). The force of the threat was not so much to rob Christians of something as to kidnap them. False teachers, therefore, were like slave traders. They wanted to steal believers away from their spiritual family and sell them as slaves into false doctrine.

The features of error. The preposition *through* shows the means by which heretics would attempt to capture the believers. Five features of their methodology are enumerated. For one thing, they would use philosophy (Greek, *philosophia*). The term basically means a love of wisdom. Paul was not against philosophy per se; rather, he opposed a specific type of philosophy. The Greek text reads "*the* philosophy." A mere love of wisdom for the sake of wisdom is wrong. This type of philosophy is humanistic and manifests the wisdom of the world. A genuine philosophy is a love of wisdom that has its source and meaning in Christ (2:3).

Second, the heretics would employ "empty deception" (Greek, *kenēs apatēs*). Philosophy stresses what is taught; deceit depicts how and why it is taught. These tactics constitute two aspects of the same error. What is taught is empty in that it contains no substance to edify. It is void of genuine spiritual truth, power, and hope.

Third, worldly philosophy is "according to the tradition of men." Traditions (Greek, *paradosin*) can be either good (2 Thess. 2:15; 3:6) or bad (Mark 7:3). Since the heretical traditions at Colossae originated with men and elevated a legalistic approach to God, they were innately evil.

Fourth, this methodology is "according to the elementary principles of the world." The Greek word *stoicheia* was used of anything that appeared in a row or a series; thus, it came to refer to the letters of the alphabet, to the basic notes of music, and to the fundamental components of the material universe (2 Pet. 3:10–12). In the context of heresy, Paul used it to describe legalistic observances, both Jewish and pagan (2:16–17, 20–22; Gal. 4:3, 9). In the heresy at Colossae, it probably denoted the initial requirements of new converts. Such legal conformity was the first step toward the ultimate denial of all that was accomplished at the cross.

Fifth, the methodology is "rather than according to Christ." A true Christian philosophy centers in Christ and seeks to understand more fully His incarnate person and His redemptive death and resurrection.

On the word *philosophy*, R. C. H. Lenski writes:

It is speculation, devoid of facts, and thus deceives. "Philosophy" is here used in the general sense according to which we to this day call any speculative scheme a philosophy. Paul's use of the word does not justify the idea that the Colossian Judaizers had obtained their speculation from the universities of Alexandria or from some notable "philosopher" in the technical sense of the term. These Judaizers are not what we call men of learning, men of standing in the world because of their philosophical study. The whole epistle presents them as being ordinary men. They are like so many modern errorists who invent a specious scheme of reasoning and base their religious notions on it.[3]

STUDY QUESTIONS

1. How can believers encourage and comfort one another? When should this occur?

2. How can unity be achieved in the midst of denominational diversity? What is the common basis for genuine unity?

3. What enticing words can be seen today in various sects and cults? How does brainwashing fit into this?

4. In what ways do Christians walk in a disorderly manner? How can true spiritual compliance be achieved?

5. How can believers indeed walk by faith? Why is there a tendency to walk by sight?

6. What false philosophies are prevalent today? How can their deceitfulness be detected?

7. How has legalism infiltrated evangelicalism? Give examples. How can this be corrected?

CHAPTER 21

The Identification with Christ
Colossians 2:9-15

Preview:

After affirming Christ's power through identifying Him as deity, Paul turns to confirm our identification with Christ through His completed work. He explains in detail the change that occurs in all believers: our completion, our spiritual circumcision, our symbolic burial and resurrection with Him through baptism, and the total forgiveness of our sins—all through His work on the cross.

The meaning of identification with Christ is simple: Christ is in the Christian, and the Christian is in Christ (1:14, 27-28). A proper understanding of this identification will promote the triumphant life of godliness and will protect believers against pagan intellectualism and oppressive legalism. In this section, Paul further delineates the advantages of being in Christ.

In Christ's Person (2:9-10)

The connective ("for") indicates the reason why believers should beware of a philosophy that is not according to Christ (2:8). He alone is the standard by which all religious claims must be judged.

The Fullness of God in Christ (2:9)

Its meaning. Paul earlier declared that the Father was pleased that all the fullness of deity should dwell in Christ (1:19). Now he repeats the same truth with a significant addition, "all the fulness of Deity dwells in bodily form."

The inclusive phrase "all the fulness" (Greek, *pan to plērōma*) denotes all that God is in His divine essence. It envelops the totality of the divine attributes. The Son is neither the Father nor the Spirit, but all three Persons within the Trinitarian Being are equally divine. This deity can never be diminished or lost. God can never be less than what He is (Mal. 3:10; James 1:17). The explicit nature of the divine fullness is further claimed by the qualifying words *all* and *the*.

Furthermore, Christ possesses the "fulness of Deity" (Greek, *tes theotētos*). This noun, found only here in the New Testament, is based on the Greek word for "God" *(theos)*. Another word *(theiotēs)* is translated as "Godhead" (Rom. 1:20), but there is a key, subtle theological difference. Nature (Rom. 1:20) reveals God as He acts, but Christ revealed God as He is (John 1:1, 18). Since God is a personal being, He cannot be known personally through things. The natural creation can show that God exists and that He is intelligent and powerful. Only Christ could manifest that God is loving, merciful, and forgiving. A person can learn about God through nature but can only know God through the incarnate Son (John 14:9).

Its location. The sphere of divine fullness is seen in two ways. First, it is in Him. The emphatic position of the prepositional phrase "in Him" reinforces the concept that only in Christ could the essence of deity dwell.[1] Second, the divine fullness is in Christ bodily (Greek, *sōmatikōs*). As God the eternal Son, Christ always possessed the fullness of the Godhead. In refutation of the heretical teaching that matter was intrinsically evil, Paul asserted that Christ was still God, in the fullest sense of that word, even after the Incarnation. There was no loss or corruption of the divine essence when the eternal Son took to Himself a full and complete humanity. In fact, the crucifixion, resurrection, and subsequent exaltation of Christ did not alter the hypostatic union. Although a surrender and a restoration of divine glory occurred at the Incarnation and Resurrection respectively (John 17:5), this truth did not affect the innate possession of deity by the Son of God.

Its permanence. When Paul wrote this epistle, Christ had been in the third heaven for almost thirty years. The usage of the present tense of the verb *dwells* (Greek, *katoikei*) thus points out two facts about Christ. First, He had a material body that could be seen and touched. It was a resurrected, immortal, incorruptible, materialistic body. The Incarnation presupposes a permanent union between the divine and human natures in Christ. He did not surrender His deity at His incarnation, and He did not give up His humanity at His resurrection.

Second, this verb (Greek, *katoikeō*) denotes permanent residing in contrast to a temporary sojourn (Greek, *paroikeō*; Heb. 11:9). As God the Son, Christ shared equally in the essence of deity. When He became man, this fullness came to indwell a human nature and presently abides in His divine-human person.

Marvin Vincent well writes:

The fullness of the Godhead dwells in Him *in a bodily way, clothed with a body.* This means that it dwells in Him as one having a human body. This could not be true of His pre-incarnate state, when He was "in the form of God," for the human body was *taken on* by Him in the fullness of time, when "He *became* in the likeness of men" (Philip. ii. 7), when the Word *became* flesh. The fullness of the Godhead dwelt in His person from His birth to His ascension. He carried His human body with Him into heaven, and in His glorified body now and ever dwells the fullness of the Godhead.[2]

The Completeness of the Believer in Christ (2:10)

The simple connective ("and") serves to join the ideas that the fullness of God is in Christ and the believer is complete in Christ. The two key words of this section, *fulness* (Greek, *plērōma*) and *complete* (Greek, *peplērōmenoi*), both come from the same Greek verbal stem (*plēroō*). Both Christ and the Christian have fullness but for different reasons.

Its meaning. All believers are complete in Christ. The concept behind this verb construction is that they become complete in the Savior at conversion and that they presently stand in a position of total spiritual completeness before God.[3] In fact, the main emphasis is on the continuity of their acceptable stance. The passive voice of the verb shows that God completed believers through the ministry of the Holy Spirit, who applied the positional benefits of Christ's redemptive work to them. The heretics promoted a spiritual caste system whereby an adherent could become more complete as he achieved certain goals. But Paul emphasized that a total completeness is the possession of all believers.

The word *completeness* was used of a ship totally fitted and ready for a voyage. Adam, the first man, lost his moral, mental, and spiritual completeness at his fall in the Garden of Eden, but the regenerate person has regained it in Christ. All believers have received fullness and grace from Christ (John 1:16). This fullness has been specially applied to "the church, which is His body, the fulness of him who fills all in all" (Eph. 1:23).

Its location. Completeness is only in Christ. Paul identifies Him as "the head over all rule and authority." Since Christ created all celestial beings, they are all subject to His sovereign rule (1:15–16). The heretics claimed that an angelic host ruled over the world of humans, but in fact believers share in Christ's headship over the created universe through their completeness in the

Savior. Such completeness gives Christians direct and personal access to the Father. They do not have to work their way back through angelic intermediaries and legal conformity as the Gnostics taught.

In Christ's Power (2:11–15)

The emphasis in the first part of this section was on who Christ is, but in the second half, it is on what He has done. Believers thus can identify themselves with His redemptive work as well as with His redeeming person. Five areas of work are set forth.

Circumcision (2:11)

The fact. In Christ, the believers "were circumcised" (Greek, *perietmēthēte*). The word means "to cut around." The physical rite was first practiced when Abraham circumcised Ishmael, his household servants, and himself in direct obedience to God's command (Gen. 17:9–14, 23–27). From that point on, all physical descendants of Abraham were circumcised at the age of eight days to show faith in the fulfillment of the promises contained in the Abrahamic covenant (Gen. 17:1–10). In time, the rite developed into a distinctive racial barrier between Jew and Gentile (3:11). The Gentiles became known as the "Uncircumcision," whereas the Jews identified themselves as the "Circumcision" (Eph. 2:11).

Some of the Jews who professed Christianity believed that physical circumcision was essential to salvation and tried to force that rite on converted Gentiles (Acts 15:1; Gal. 6:12). At Colossae, the heretics sought to impose circumcision as an initiatory rite to their brand of Christianity. All believers, however, were circumcised spiritually when they were converted. Positional circumcision, not physical, is what is important (Phil. 3:3).

The type. What saves is "a circumcision made without hands." The Jews unfortunately equated outward conformity with inward reality, but Paul dispelled that faulty logic (Rom. 2:28–29). Even the Old Testament prophet cried out for Israel to repent and to circumcise their hearts (Deut. 10:16; 30:6; Jer. 4:4; 9:26). Stephen declared that the circumcised Jews were obstinate and uncircumcised in their hearts (Acts 7:51).

The result. Inner, spiritual circumcision results in "the removal of the body of the flesh." This action occurs at conversion and removes the guilt, penalty, and pollution of the sin principle with its sinful thoughts and deeds. It does not eradicate the sin nature, but it does strip away the power of the sin nature so that believers do not need to obey its dictates anymore. It is equivalent to laying aside "the old self with its *evil* practices" (3:9).

The means. Spiritual circumcision is made possible by the circumcision of Christ. This statement does not mean that the believer was in Christ when the infant Jesus was physically circumcised when He was eight days old (Luke 2:21). Rather, Christ is the one who circumcises the inner person. He performs this spiritual ministry at the conversion of sinners when He applies the benefits of His death and resurrection.

Baptism (2:12)

The initiatory rite into Judaism is circumcision, but the introductory ordinance of organized Christianity is water baptism (Matt. 28:18–20; Acts 2:41). Water baptism, however, is only an outward sign of an inner work of divine grace. Unfortunately, many professing Christians have put their confidence in this external sign as the means of their salvation.

Several types of baptism are mentioned in the New Testament: Judaistic ceremonial cleansings (Heb. 6:2), the baptism of repentance by John the Baptist that anticipated the establishment of the kingdom (Matt. 3:2), the personal baptism of Jesus Christ (Matt. 3:13–17), the baptism of suffering at the cross (Matt. 20:22–23), the baptism in the Holy Spirit (1 Cor. 12:13), and Christian water baptism in which believers identify themselves with Christ in His death, burial, and resurrection.

Which baptism is expounded in this verse? There is no indication that the believer was in Christ when Christ was baptized in the Jordan River. The converts of John the Baptist later submitted to Christian baptism (Acts 19:1–7). Since spiritual circumcision, without human hands, was just explained (2:11), this must be spiritual baptism, the one baptism that unites believers with one another in the body of Christ, the true church, and with Christ, the living Head (Eph. 4:5). Ceremonies performed by people can never achieve eternal redemption. This is one of the reasons why Paul attacked the legalistic heresy.

Baptism involves burial. Believers were buried with Christ in baptism. Burial presupposes death. When Jesus Christ died on the cross and was buried in the tomb, all believers were spiritually identified with Him in those acts. The phrase "in baptism" literally reads "in the baptism." The definite article ("the") points to the one true baptism in the Holy Spirit that all believers received at their conversion (Rom. 6:3–5; 1 Cor. 12:13; Eph. 4:5).

Since believers are in Christ, God reckons the death and resurrection of Christ to be that of the children of God. Just as sin and death do not have dominion over Him, neither do they have dominion over Christians. Believers need to believe this truth and to apply this positional reality to their practical experience (Rom. 6:11).

Baptism involves resurrection. All believers were also raised with Christ. In the judicial sense, this occurred at the actual physical resurrection of Christ, but it is personally and spiritually realized at regeneration.

Although water baptism by immersion best pictures the procedure of death, burial, and resurrection, it is not the means to secure that form of identification with Christ. Being raised with Christ comes through saving faith, that "faith in the working of God, who raised Him from the dead." To experience deliverance from both physical and spiritual death, a person must believe that God has raised Christ from the dead and that He will deliver believing sinners from eternal, spiritual death.

Quickening (2:13)

The need for quickening. The emphasis here is on the spiritual plight of the Colossian believers just before the time of their conversion ("And when you were dead"); the present participle shows that their condition was constant and unchanging. They were dead (Greek, *nekrous*). They had no spiritual life and were alienated from the life of God (Eph. 4:18). Christ came into the world to give life to those who were dead (John 10:10).

The Colossians had been dead in two realms. First, they were dead in their "trangressions" (Greek, *paraptōmasi*). This compound word is based on the verb *to fall (piptō)* and the preposition *beside (para)*. It denotes deliberate acts of sin in which a person chooses to deviate from the path of righteousness. Though they had no knowledge of the Mosaic law, pagan Gentiles nevertheless still had a sense of moral oughtness in their consciences. Yet they violated that moral compass (Rom. 2:14–15).

Second, they were dead in "the uncircumcision of [their] flesh." This unique term (Greek, *akrobustia*), which literally meant the foreskin of the penis, was a designation for the pagan Gentile world. They were uncircumcised both racially and redemptively (Eph. 2:11–12). Their trespasses and their racial status separated them from both God and His covenant people, Israel. They were indeed dead.

Its means. All believing sinners have been "made . . . alive together with Him." Positionally, when God raised Christ from the physical dead, He also raised spiritually believing sinners. In personal experience, the truth becomes actual at the time of saving faith (Eph. 2:5–6). Sinners are made alive through the Holy Spirit, who convicts them through the Word of God and energizes them to believe unto life everlasting.

Its result. There can be no spiritual life apart from forgiveness. The verbal action of forgiveness (Greek, *charisamenos*) stems from the grace (Greek, *charis*) of God. It is totally undeserved and is apart from human merit. Sinners cannot even earn the right to be forgiven. They receive forgiveness solely as a gracious gift from a merciful God.

The scope of forgiveness is all trespasses. In providing reconciliation, God did not impute the trespasses of sinners to them (2 Cor. 5:19). That barrier was removed at the cross, but actual forgiveness occurs at the time of personal conversion.

Removal of the Law (2:14)

The Law is holy, and the commandments are holy, just, and good (Rom. 7:12). The Mosaic law was the specific revelation of the moral law of God to Israel (Rom. 9:4). It was good, because any revelation from a good God must necessarily also be good (James 1:17). The Law, however, was not given to be the instrument of salvation, because no person was capable of keeping it (Gal. 3:21). Through the Law, God intended to stimulate within people a consciousness of sin and guilt whereby convicted sinners would turn to the gracious provision of God for redemption.

Character of the Law. Paul makes three observations. First, the Law was "the certificate of debt consisting of decrees." The first word (Greek, *cheirographon*) is found in the papyri and indicates a certificate of debt on which the signature of the debtor was inscribed. When the debt was canceled, a large "X" was placed over the document. In a similar vein, the ordinances of the Law written by God through Moses declare the debt of sinful humans to God. They have come under its curse because they have not kept all of the laws all of the time (Gal. 3:10; James 2:10). Second, the Law was "against us." It offered no hope or encouragement. It demanded judgment without mercy (Heb. 10:26–28). Finally, the Law was "hostile to us." The Law was the prosecuting attorney, judge, jury, and executioner of the sinner.

Action of Christ. In His death and resurrection, Christ dealt with the Law in three ways. First, he wiped it out (Greek, *exaleipsas*). He erased it. With a cry of triumph, Jesus exclaimed, "It is finished!" (John 19:30). The payment was made, and it was both full and final. Christ also took the Law out of the way. The perfect tense of the verb (Greek, *ērken*) indicates the permanence of the removal. Thus, believers should have no fear that the penalty for a broken law will later be exacted from them. To create the Church, Christ had to remove two barriers: sin, which separated sinners from God, and the Law, which formed a fence between Jews and Gentiles. His death accomplished this double result (Eph. 2:14–15). Third, Christ "nailed [the certificate of debt] to the cross." Pilate placed a superscription on the cross to show the crime for which Christ was crucified (John 19:19). In Christ's atonement, however, He canceled the debt of humankind to the Law. His death covered all trespasses—past, present, and future.

As Paul declares this bond to be against *us,* including both Jews and Gentiles, the reference, while primarily to the Mosaic law, is to be taken in a wider sense, as including the moral law of God in general, which applied to the Gentiles as much as to the Jews. See Rom. iii. 19. The law is frequently conceived by Paul with this wider reference, as a principle which has its chief representative in the Mosaic law, but the applications of which are much wider. See on Rom. ii. 12. This law is conceived here as *a bond, a bill of debt,* standing against those who have not received Christ. As the form of error at Colossae was largely Judaic, insisting on the Jewish ceremonial law, the phrase is probably colored by this fact.[4]

Triumph over Powers (2:15)

The heretics incorrectly elevated the role of angels in creation and redemption. Paul demonstrated that the cross directly affected the activity of angels. There is disagreement over whether these angels are good or evil. If they are good, then the death of Christ ended the mediation of these angels in the giving of the Law (Acts 7:53; Gal. 3:19; Heb. 2:2). If they are evil, then He triumphed over Satan and the fallen angels through His death, resurrection, and ascension (Gen. 3:15). Since both concepts are true, it is difficult to determine which view is in mind here. The second position is the common choice of most evangelicals.

Christ disarmed them. He disarmed "the rulers and authorities." These two areas of supernatural authority can refer to the entire angelic world, both good and evil, or to either one in particular (1:16; 2:10; Eph. 6:12). The verb *disarmed* (Greek, *apekdusamenos*) means "to put off away from." It often is translated "laid aside" (3:9). The metaphor refers to a person who strips off his clothes. If these are evil angels, then Christ stripped from them their evil power. He bruised the head of Satan (Gen. 3:15) and destroyed this angelic ruler who had the power to keep people in the realm of death (Heb. 2:14). During Christ's earthly ministry, He manifested His absolute power over evil angels when He cast out demons (Luke 11:20–22). Satan is a defeated foe; nevertheless, he can still do terrible spiritual damage (1 Pet. 5:8). His ultimate doom in the lake of fire was secured at the cross (Matt. 25:41; Rev. 20:10).

Christ displayed them. Next, He "made a public display of them." The Greek verb *edeigmatisen* means "to display, publish, or proclaim." At the cross, Satan as the prince of this world was cast out (John 12:31). Satan was as lightning fallen from heaven to earth (Luke 10:18). In His descent into and ascent out of Hades, Christ gained the keys of death and Hades (Rev. 1:18). He proclaimed to the evil spirits in Hades (Tartarus, KJV) that their multiple attempts to destroy the redemptive line from Adam to the promised Messiah had failed (1 Pet. 3:19; 2 Pet. 2:4).

Christ triumphed over them. The imagery behind the verb *triumphed* (*thriambeusas*) is taken from the processions of ancient Roman emperors and generals who led the captives taken in battle and exposed them to the gaze of a cheering public. Believers are part of the victorious army, enjoying the triumphant march as they follow their spiritual King (2 Cor. 2:14).

STUDY QUESTIONS

1. What are the qualities of true humanity? How did Christ manifest these in His earthly existence? Since the Resurrection?

2. What is involved in positional completeness? How does this truth support the doctrine of eternal security?

3. In what ways do the cults use regulations to help their adherents gain perfection? How can cult members be rescued from this conformity?

4. In what ways do contemporary Christians identify outward rites with inner reality?

5. What are the various views of water baptism? Spiritual baptism? How are those views different? How are they the same?

6. What part should the Mosaic law have in the lives of believers today? Are Christians basically legalistic?

7. In what ways can believers claim victory over Satan because of the cross? Why are so many people living defeated lives?

CHAPTER 22

The Contrast in Doctrine
Colossians 2:16–3:4

Preview:

Many false teachers were confusing the Colossians by trying to add human works to the gospel messaage as a necessity for salvation. To build up the Colossians in their faith, Paul exposes some of the aberrant views and requirements espoused by these false teachers. He reminds the believers that their faith is in Christ and their salvation is complete in Him. He teaches them that their salvation is a spiritual matter not served by their earthly activities. While the actions proposed and demonstrated by these false teachers may appear pious and holy, they are really of no value. Believers are to set their minds "on the things above, not on the things that are on earth."

God gave Israel criteria by which they could determine whether a prophet was genuine or false (Deut. 18:15–22). Christ also set forth such guidelines (Matt. 7:15–20), as did John (1 John 4:1). In this section of Colossians, Paul challenges his readers to evaluate their beliefs. Using this theme, he concludes the first half of the epistle and establishes the transition to the second half (3:5—4:6), which deals specifically with practical Christian living.

The Practice of False Doctrine (2:16–23)

Paul earlier warned against the deceitful, Gnostic philosophy that was humanistic, legalistic, and non-Christian (2:8). Now he refutes three specific areas of false practice within the heresy that threatened the church.

Legalism (2:16–17)

Many Jewish believers continued to circumcise their children and to be zeal-ous for the Law (Acts 21:20–24). They recognized that believing Gentiles did not need to observe these practices (Acts 15:28–29; 21:25). The Gnostic Judaizers, however, tried to impose Mosaic legalism on the Colossians as the means of spiritual perfection. When that which was optional became manda-tory, Paul had to act. He commanded the church to stop the procedure of judgment ("let no one act as your judge"). The present tense of the imperative (Greek, *krinetō*) indicates that the heretics and their converts constantly had been criticizing the lack of legal conformity within the church. This issue was far severer than differences of opinion within the areas of Christian liberty (Rom. 14:1–15; 1 Cor. 8:1–13).

Areas of legalism. Five areas are listed. First, the phrase "to food" (Greek, *en brōsei*) encompasses the entire area of eating. It denotes Jewish dietary regula-tions with their distinction between clean and unclean foods (Lev. 11; Acts 10:14). The Pharisees extended the restrictions by requiring people to bathe and to wash their hands before eating (Mark 7:1–23). Since Christ's death and resurrection, all foods reflect divine provision and should be received with thanksgiving (Acts 10:15; 1 Cor. 10:25–26; 1 Tim. 4:3–5). The heretics may have taught that certain foods helped the mind to develop a spiritual sensi-tivity, whereas others prevented that goal.

Second, the area of "drink" (Greek, *posei*) probably included the prohibi-tion of wine and strong drink. Levites and Nazirites observed this restriction (Lev. 10:9; Num. 6:3). Liquids could not be stored in unclean vessels (Lev. 11:34–36).

Third, the "festival" was literally a "feast" (Greek, *heortēs*). The three major feasts in the Jewish calendar were Passover, Pentecost, and Tabernacles (Ex. 23:14–18). At those times, all Jewish males were to worship God at Jerusalem through the sacrificial system.

Fourth, the "new moon" marked the observance of the lunar calendar (Num. 10:10). It was a day of rest, worship, fellowship, and eating. Paul else-where criticized this form of legalism (Gal. 4:10).

Fifth, the "Sabbath day" pointed to Saturday, the day of weekly rest in which Israel remembered the divine work of creation and their covenant rela-tionship with God (Ex. 20:8–11; 31:12–18). Christians, however, should remember the work of spiritual creation by gathering in the local church on Sunday, the day on which Christ rose from the dead (Acts 20:7; 1 Cor. 16:2).

Weakness of legalism. The Mosaic law, with its moral and ceremonial regu-lations, was "a *mere* shadow of what is to come." A shadow does not exist in and of itself. It is caused by a material object or person. It has reality only in that it points to the substance that formed it.

In like fashion, the Law was given to produce a sense of moral guilt and to drive convicted sinners to put their faith in the gracious provision of God, namely, Christ (Gal. 3:24). The sacrificial calendar produced pictures or types of what Christ would accomplish in His death and resurrection (Heb. 9:13–14; 10:1). He is the Passover lamb for believers (1 Cor. 5:7) and the open veil into the very presence of God (Heb. 10:19–20). In real life, one embraces the body, not the shadow.

Angel Worship (2:18–19)

Paul warned, "Let no one keep defrauding you of your prize." These nine words actually translate three Greek terms *(medeis humas katabrabeuetō)*. The verb *katabrabeueto* is related to two words: "prize" (Greek, *brabeion*; 1 Cor. 9:24; Phil. 3:14) and "umpire" (Greek, *brabeuō*; Col. 3:15, "rule"). Because of the double relationship, the warning allows for two different interpretations. First, believers could lose their reward at the Judgment Seat of Christ if they fail to maintain their doctrinal and moral steadfastness. Second, believers should stop anyone from giving an official judgment against their rejection of legalism (Rom. 14:12–13). The second seems more plausible in this context.

Angel worship promotes self. Four participial phrases describe the false teacher who tried to force error on the Colossians.[1] First, he was marked by "delighting in self-abasement and the worship of the angels." Genuine humility, produced by the Spirit of God, is commendable (Eph. 4:2; Phil. 2:3), but this heretic took delight in his humility. If it was false self-abasement, he did it for external appearance; if it was genuine, he may have sincerely believed that he was unworthy to go directly to God. This premise would thus form the basis for his respect of the angels. The emphasis of this worship is on ceremonial rites and conformity. Although the false teacher's humility was impressive to others, it achieved erroneous results.

Second, the false teacher intruded into a forbidden area. The participle "taking his stand" (Greek, *embateuōn*) was used of an initiate in the mystery religions who performed introductory rites. The area of intrusion is debatable. He moved into either the realm of the invisible ("into those things which he has not seen") or the domain of the visible ("into those things which he has seen").[2] The reason for the textual difference may lie in the supposition that the false teachers claimed to have special visions and revelations that they alone witnessed. In any case, they elevated extrabiblical content and based their authoritative teaching on what they personally had experienced.

Third, the false teacher was "inflated without cause by his fleshly mind." He felt superior because of what he thought he knew and could reason. Believers should grow in spiritual knowledge as they are taught by God through His Word, but a false biblical intellectualism is empty or vain (Greek, *eikē*). The imagery behind "inflated" (Greek, *phusioumenos*) is that of a pair of bellows (Greek, *phusa*) that are used to blow up or inflate (Greek, *phusioō*). Such knowledge apart from love is self-destructive (1 Cor. 4:6, 18; 8:1). His knowledge was produced by the sinful human flesh rather than by the Spirit of God.

Fourth, the false teacher did not elevate Christ, the Head of the church. The present participle "not holding" (Greek, *ou kratōn*) shows that he was continually not elevating the Savior. In fact, all of the four verbal descriptions show a constant pattern of false belief and behavior. Although this false teacher had gained some preeminence in the church, he was actually unsaved (Matt. 7:15).

Angel worship demotes Christ. The Holy Spirit came to glorify Christ (John 16:14). Paul gloried in the cross of the Savior (Gal. 6:14). In the church, Christ should have all the preeminence (1:18). The distinctive feature of all heretical sects within professing Christendom, however, is a total or partial denial of the divine-human person of Christ and His redemptive death and bodily resurrection.

The intellectual, legalistic teaching at Colossae likewise did not properly esteem Christ. In its worship of angels, it denied to Christ four areas of emphasis. First, He alone is the Head of the body, the church (1:18). There can be only one head from which the body can receive life and direction. A hierarcy of angels and a Gnostic caste system constitute many heads.

Second, Christ nourishes the body. This spiritual food and strength come from the Word of God as it is ministered by gifted teachers under the control of the Holy Spirit (Eph. 4:11–16). The participle "being supplied" (Greek, *epichorēgoumenon*) means "to furnish supplies for a musical chorus." In ancient times, a benefactor would pay for the singers and the dancers at a festival. In time the word came to mean "to provide generously." In medical terminology, it was used of the joints and ligaments that joined two bones together (Eph. 4:16). As a person nourishes his or her physical body, so Christ ministers to His spiritual body, the church (Eph. 5:29).

Third, Christ unites the church. The participle "knit together" (Greek, *sumbibazomenon*) was used earlier (2:2) and elsewhere by Paul (Eph. 4:16). The joints and ligaments are the means of unity as well as the means of sustenance. In a similar manner, Christ came to build *one* church (Eph. 4:4–6).

Fourth, Christ increases the church ("grows with a growth which is from God"). Christ, not humans, is the builder. As believers elevate and love Christ, they will love and edify one another (Eph. 4:16).

Asceticism (2:20-23)

Asceticism and legalism are partners in humanistic religion. Asceticism promotes self-denial, the deliberate rejection of material comforts in order to develop spiritual sensitivity. It usually leads to fasting, celibacy, and the monastic life. Initially it gives the impression of total dedication, but it actually is contrary to grace living and to the practice of a believer's position in Christ.

Its ignorance. Professing Christians who practice asceticism are ignorant of three basic facts. First, believers have died positionally in Christ. Paul did not doubt the salvation experience of the Colossian believers; rather, he assumed it as the basis of his argument. This first-class conditional clause can be translated: "If therefore you died with Christ, and you have. . . ."[3] It could even be rendered: "Since you died with Christ." At conversion, believing sinners are baptized in the Holy Spirit into Christ (1 Cor. 12:13). The result is a positional, judicial identification with Christ in His actual death on the cross. Believers died with Christ and in Christ when Christ satisfied the righteous demands for the broken law of God. This fundamental truth must be known and appropriated in order to live a victorious life over sin (Rom. 6:1-10).

Second, believers have thus been separated from "the elementary principles of the world." Death brings separation and freedom from prior obligation (Rom. 7:1-6). These legalistic regulations originate within the world of lost humanity and represent their attempt to gain favor before God (2:8; Gal. 4:3). They are powerless to provide redemption, and they cannot supply a spiritual inheritance (Gal. 4:9).

Third, believers do not need to yield to legalism. The question supports that conclusion drawn from the assumed reality of the condition: "Why, as if you were living in the world, do you submit yourself to decrees . . . ?" Believers are still in the world, but they are no longer of the world (John 15:19). They should use, not abuse, the world (1 Cor. 7:31). They should resist human dogmas that stem from a worldly system of self-righteousness and that are brought into the church under the guise of submissive humility.

Its description. Legalists and ascetics always emphasize the negative. They assert that spirituality is measured by an absence of prescribed sins rather than by the presence of positive virtues. Three examples of their prohibitions are given. First, "do not handle" (Greek, *mē hapsē*). Since the third imperative also deals with the sense of touch, this command may stress sexual abstinence for those who were married and the prevention of marriage for those who were single. The false teachers doubtless charged that physical marital privilege had to be forfeited in order to gain a sensitivity to the spiritual marriage of believers to Christ. Paul later advised Timothy to watch for apostates who prohibited marriage (1 Tim. 4:3).

Second, "do not taste" (Greek, *mēde geusē*). This command encouraged fasting and a prescribed diet. Avoiding specific foods was deemed necessary for the preparation of visions and for promoting a desire for the food of the soul (Dan. 10:2–3). Quite often such asceticism leads to vegetarianism. Certain foods are looked upon as essential for the development of the mind and the elimination of bodily poisons. However, all foods, both meats and vegetables, can be eaten by believers today if they are received with thanksgiving (1 Tim. 4:3–5).

Third, "do not touch" (Greek, *mēde thigēs*). A person must touch before he or she can taste. This legalistic command prohibited even the mere handling of a forbidden food. Legalists are afraid of even an occasional contact with an item whose usage is forbidden to them.

Its weakness. Legalists look on asceticism as a spiritual discipline and strength, but actually it is a weakness and an obstacle to true Christian living. Four aspects of its weakness are discussed here. First, it permits the material to dominate the spiritual. The forbidden things are those that perish with the using. God created sex, food, and drink, as well as the desires to have them. Sin occurs through their abuse, not by their proper use. Believers must not permit these temporal drives to control their lives. They must control them through prayer and submission to the sovereignty of Christ (1 Cor. 6:12–13). Likewise, they must not view certain foods that are morally neutral to be either satanic or evil (1 Cor. 8:8).

Second, asceticism originates with humans ("in accordance with the commandments and teachings of men"). Christ never imposed asceticism on believers. He taught that dietary restrictions push aside the divine commandment in favor of a human tradition (Mark 7:6–15). The distinction between "commandments" (Greek, *entalmata*) and "teachings" (Greek, *didaskalias*) is subtle. The former may refer to the actual command and the latter to its explanation and application. Also, the former may point to that which is written and the latter to that which is spoken.

Third, asceticism is hypocritical. It has an impressive reputation. The world is usually awed by the lifestyles of ascetics. Their commandments and doctrine have "to be sure, the appearance of wisdom." The term *appearance* (Greek, *logon*) normally translates as "word" and connotes the idea of a verbal report. To the adherents, the regulations are rational and logical. This false religious intellectualism becomes even more deceptive because it operates in a threefold domain. It functions in "self-made religion" (Greek, *ethelothrēskeia*) that originated within the human will and not from divine revelation, and it is marked by "self-abasement" and "severe treatment of the body." The verbal noun (Greek, *apheidia*) comes from a term that means "to spare" (Greek, *pheidomai*); thus, the word connotes an unsparing severity manifested in the denial of sleep, self-imposed beatings, and fasting.

Fourth, asceticism cannot overcome the power of the sin nature ("no value against fleshly indulgence"). Asceticism actually becomes an enemy to the Spirit-controlled life. The more legalistic one becomes, the more powerful is the grip of the sin nature. Regulations cannot restrain sensual indulgence. The cure for the sins of the flesh is submission to the Holy Spirit, not conformity to a list of man-made laws.

Believers Have "Died" with Christ

Christ died for all (2 Cor. 5:15).

In Christ, believers died to the Law (Gal. 2:19).

Believers are buried with Christ in spiritual baptism (Col. 2:12).

When believers were formerly dead in their sins, Christ made them alive in Him (Col. 2:13).

Believers have died but have been raised with Christ (Col. 3:1).

Believers have died, and their lives are hidden with Christ (Col. 3:3).

When Christ is revealed, believers will be revealed with Him (Col. 3:4).

"If we died with Him, we shall also live with Him" (2 Tim. 2:11).

The Principles of True Doctrine (3:1–4)

Genuine teachers not only inform their people about what is wrong; they also guide them into what is right. The two major divisions of this section are developed around two commands: "Seek" and "Set."

Seek Heavenly Things (3:1)

Paul's use of the present imperative in this verse stresses constant, daily seeking (Greek, *zēteite*). Christian perfection is a goal that demands diligent pursuit. The horizon of spiritual attainment grows broader as believers advance higher and further into the will of God.

Paul assumed that the Colossians were identified positionally with Christ. The first-class conditional clause can be rendered: "If then you were raised with Christ, and you have been." Through positional identification, all believers have died with Christ, have been buried with Him, have been raised with

Him, and have been seated with Him in God's presence (2:12, 20; 3:1; Rom. 6:3–5; Eph. 2:5–6). In the redemptive program, God always sees converted sinners in Christ; therefore, whatever Christ has done is also done in believers. This divine reckoning becomes real in the lives of sinners at the time of their regeneration, but they must appropriate this truth daily in order to live a normal, victorious Christian life. They must "keep seeking the things above." If they are not heavenly minded, they will never be any earthly good. The "things above" (Greek, *ta anō*) are in contrast to the "things that are on earth" (Greek, *ta epi tēs gēs*), the legalistic, ascetic practices of the heretics. The proper objects of seeking include God's presence, the holy city, and the total possession of "every spiritual blessing in the heavenly places in Christ" (Eph. 1:3). The process of seeking incorporates the revealed will of God for one's life, the essence of all that one should become in Christ (Phil. 3:14).

Believers should seek "where Christ is, seated at the right hand of God." They should seek Him as the Magi did. They should seek Him in whom all of the truths of their positional acceptance are found. The fact that Christ was exalted and is constantly sitting at the Father's right hand shows that His redemptive work was finished and accepted (Phil. 2:9; Heb. 1:3; 10:12).

Think Heavenly Things (3:2-4)

Whereas the first command ("seek") dealt with the will and active pursuit, the second imperative refers to the mind. This is comparable to a marathon runner who is thinking about the race as he attempts to finish it. Seeking and thinking should occur simultaneously.

Positively, believers should think "on the things above" (Greek, *ta anō*). This phrase is greatly emphasized in the Greek text because it occurs both first in the sentence and before the verb. It points out spiritual realities that have their source in God. It does not refer to future events exclusively, such as life after death and the eternal state, although it includes those truths as they affect present behavior (1 John 3:1–3).

Negatively, believers should not think "on the things that are on earth." In the context, the primary interpretation and application are to the legalistic and ascetic regulations imposed by the false teachers. In a secondary manner, they include all earthly involvements that retard genuine spiritual development. Yielded Christians make no distinction between the sacred and the secular. To them, everything—including personal, family, and social responsibilities (3:5—4:6)—should be done for God's glory (3:17; 1 Cor. 10:31). However, they must differentiate between that which is beneficial and that which is detrimental to their spiritual health (Phil. 1:9–10).

Five reasons are given for heavenly thinking. First, the believer died in

Christ. The verb "you have died" (Greek, *apethanete;* cf. 2:20) looks back to the cross. The child of God died positionally in Christ at the moment of salvation. This reality has separated the believer forever from any obligation to a worldly legalism. As a wife is loosed from marital law through the death of her husband, so a believer becomes "[dead] to the Law through the body of Christ" (Rom. 7:4).

Second, the life of the believer "is hidden with Christ in God." The perfect tense verb (Greek, *kekruptai*) stresses the resultant state of safety and secrecy that believers presently possess because they trusted Jesus Christ as their Savior in the past. It is hidden to the lost because no unsaved person can understand the mystical identification of the believer with Christ. This truth is part of the revealed mystery (1:26–27). It fulfills the prediction of Christ that He would be in the believer and that the believer would be in Him (John 14:20).

Third, Christ is the very life of the believer ("Christ, who is our life"). He is the way, the truth, and the life (John 14:6). When a person has Christ, he has life (1 John 5:12). He is the spiritual bread from heaven that people must partake of by faith, in the same manner that they receive physical food for sustenance (John 6:51). As the living vine, He gives spiritual nourishment to the branches, those who have trusted Him (John 15:1–5).

Fourth, Christ shall appear (Greek, *phanerōthē*) from heaven. From that standpoint, it becomes logical for believers to look up rather than to look down or around. The temporal "when" (Greek, *hotan*) is better translated as "whenever." The fact of Christ's return is certain, but its time is indefinite. The coming of Christ and the rapture of the church are imminent. He could come today. Since believers do not know when that great event will occur, they must be constantly watching.

Fifth, the glorification of the believer will occur in heaven. Believers died with Christ, rose with Christ, and ascended with Christ. They have that positional oneness in Christ. In that future day, they will also appear with Christ. Whenever Christ returns, the real position of believers, hidden to the world, will be made known. The "glory" comes from the total transformation of the person as evidenced in the immortal, incorruptible body, not from outward conformity to earthly laws (Rom. 8:18).

William Hendricksen well states:

Though the world will never be able to see the closeness of the inner relationship between believers and their Lord, the outward expession of this inner relationship, *the glory*, will one day become clear to all: **When Christ (who is) our life is manifested, then you also will be manifested with him in glory.** "Christ (who is) our life." This cannot mean identity. To say that our life is "the extension" of Christ's life is ambiguous. Christ and we are not the same in *essence*, as are the Father and the Son. The life of Christ—hence, Christ himself—is, however, the Source and Pattern of our life. Moreover, through the Holy Spirit and Spirit-given faith, Christ is most closely united with us, and we with him.[4]

STUDY QUESTIONS

1. In what erroneous ways do believers judge other believers today? What legalistic practices have replaced conformity to the Mosaic law?

2. What types of Christ can be seen in the Jewish sacrificial system? How did Christ fulfill those types in His life and ministry?

3. In what ways (e.g., moral or doctrinal) can believers lose their rewards? How can they prevent this from happening?

4. What church practices fail to exalt Christ as the Head of the church? What church practices are acceptable? Why?

5. How can a person distinguish between true and false humility? How does humility relate to spiritual boldness and aggressiveness?

6. How can a believer help himself to seek and to think heavenly things? What earthly things can hold him back?

7. What positional truths will become realities at the return of Christ? How should they affect present behavior?

CHAPTER 23

The Change in Behavior
Colossians (3:5-17)

Preview:

To help them in their Christian walk, Paul gives the Colossians a couple of detailed lists regarding how they are to live. These lists cover their physical actions, their emotions, and their desires. He is particularly concerned about their treatment of one another, emphasizing that, in Christ, they are all the same. There are to be no racial, social, or cultural barriers. After the list of "don'ts" comes a list of "do's, climaxing in the ultimate commandment: "Do all in the name of the Lord Jesus."

A change in position must be manifested in a change of practice. Paul demonstrated clearly that the identification of the believer with Christ in His death, resurrection, and ascension had set him free from the pressures of legalism, asceticism, and false intellectualism. This new standing should result in heavenly seeking and thinking.

The transition to the new section can be seen in the logical connective "therefore" (Greek, *oun*). The general principles of a pursuit for holiness are now spelled out in specific patterns of behavior. Proper Christian living involves both putting aside negative behaviors (3:5–11) and putting on positive behaviors (3:12–17). The former involves the elimination of the past sins of the old unsaved life and the latter describes the development of righteous character within the new life.

The Old Life (3:5–11)

Believers must willingly and actively overcome the desires of their sin nature. Paul appealed for this type of obedience by the use of three direct imperatives (3:5, 8, 9). The first deals with sexual sins (3:5–7), the second with personal attitudes (3:8), and the third with sin aimed at fellow believers (3:9–11).

Mortify (3:5–7)

Believers have died in Christ, but they are still alive in the world; therefore, they must actuate their position. They must "consider . . . as dead" (Greek, *nekrōsate*) the old life. The imperative stresses determination and decisive action.[1] The verb means to render as dead, to regard as impotent. Believers cannot eradicate the sin nature, but they can treat it as a morally impotent force in their life (Rom. 6:1).

The objects of spiritual mortification are the "members of your earthly body." The will of the believer must respond negatively to the impulses of the sin nature to use the physical parts of the human body for illicit purposes (1 Cor. 6:13–20).

List of sins. Five sins are mentioned. Fornication (Greek, *porneian*) is a general word for immorality both within and without the marital union.[2] The root meaning of the word is based on two verbs (Greek, *peraō* and *pernēmi*) that convey the idea of selling bodies, both male and female, sometimes for lustful purposes. The word *porneia* is specifically used of prostitution (James 2:25; Rev. 17:1, 5).

Impurity (Greek, *akatharsian*) is moral impurity in all forms. It is marked by a filthy mind, full of sensually suggestive thoughts and humor (Eph. 5:3–4). It reads illicit sex even into the most wholesome situations. Marked by perverted fantasies, it is expressed today through pornographic literature and movies. Caused by the lusts of the heart, it leads to the dishonor of bodies (Rom. 1:24).

Passion (Greek, *pathos*) is erotic love, depraved affection, uncontrollable desire. It uses another for one's own selfish, sensual gratification. It may be either heterosexual or homosexual in character (Rom. 1:26; 1 Thess. 4:5).

Evil desire (Greek, *epithumian kakēn*) is wicked or bad lust. Physical desires are divinely given and intrinsically good, but they become evil when they are controlled by the sin nature and are executed for evil ends.

A specific type of greed (Greek, *tēn pleonexian*) manifests the essence of idolatry.[3] The word means "to have more." When Israel worshiped idols, she committed spiritual adultery because she wanted more than what her spiritual husband, God, gave her. In like manner, a person who commits adultery commits spiritual idolatry. In both cases, the exclusiveness of love and commitment to one is forsaken for another. Paul warned against defrauding [same word] one's partner in the marriage relationship (1 Thess. 4:6).

The Greek word for "greed" *(pleonexian)* is a compound form whose root meaning suggests a desire to have more. It has a much wider significance than in English equivalent. . . . Some interpreters think the context supports the view that greed for sex is the meaning here. But it may be better to retain the more usual meaning and understand it as a ruthless desire for, and a seeking after, material things. This attitude is identified with "idolatry" because it puts self-interest and *things* in the place of God.[4]

Judgment for sins. Four truths can be gleaned. First, people bring divine judgment upon themselves. The causal phrase ("on account of these things") gives the reason why they should be judged. People will reap what they have sown (Gal. 6:7).

Second, the holiness of God and His righteous displeasure over sin are expressed in the phrase "the wrath of God." With God, such anger is judicial rather than temperamental. It is balanced within His holy being by mercy, compassion, and love. God cannot condone sin (Hab. 1:12–13). When God sees sin in action, He is repulsed by it and is constrained to judge it. He cannot be indifferent nor eternally long-suffering.

Third, the divine wrath "will come" (Greek, *erchetai*).[5] The wrath of God presently abides on all who have not trusted Christ (John 3:36); thus, they can be designated as the children of wrath (Eph. 2:3). Unless they are saved, this judicial wrath will be transformed into the actual wrath of God. It is just as certain and imminent as the return of Christ or physical death. The physical expression of divine wrath will occur during the Great Tribulation (Rev. 6:17), and its eternal manifestation will be in the lake of fire.

Life in sins. Paul makes two statements about the past life of believers. First, they once walked with those who had practiced such sins. The Greek verb *periepatēsate* characterizes the entirety of their unsaved life.[6] They walked as world conformists, energized by Satan (Eph. 2:2). Second, believers once lived in such sin. The imperfect tense of the Greek verb *ezēte* stresses the daily continuity of their sinful practice when they used to live in the world of immoral people and deeds.

Put Off (3:8)

The transition to the second command can be seen in the contrast between the past ("once") and the present ("now"). Believers must not only put to death sinful actions, but they must also put off sinful attitudes.

The command. The imagery behind the imperative is that of clothing. Before new garments of practical righteousness can be put on, the old rags of past sinful practice must be discarded. The verb here, "put aside" (Greek, *apothesthe*), calls for decisive, immediate resolution.[7] The presence of the personal pronoun *you* (Greek, *humeis*) reinforces the sense of urgency and responsibility. Just as a runner must lay aside (same word) every weight to run a successful race (Heb. 12:1), so a believer must put off the garments of sin in order to live a successful Christian life.

The sins. Five sins are listed as examples, although the command would definitely include all immoral attitudes ("all these"). First, *anger* (Greek, *orgēn*) is the same word used for the wrath of God (3:6). Anger, in itself, is a proper emotion if it is controlled by the Holy Spirit and is exercised for holy reasons (Eph. 4:26). In the unsaved person and in the carnal believer, it is the inward attitude of the sinful flesh; thus, it is innately wrong. Second, *wrath* (Greek, *thumon*) is closely associated with anger. In fact, it is white-hot anger. It is uncontrolled rage expressed through outbursts of temper. Anger is kept in, whereas wrath is let out. Third, *malice* (Greek, *kakian*) is a general term for moral badness. It envelops personal animosity and malicious gossip. It emphasizes the principle of sin, whereas wickedness (Greek, *ponēria*) points out the practice of sin (1 Cor. 5:8). One who acts with malice does wrong, whereas one who acts with wickedness does wrong with pleasure (Rom. 1:18, 32). Fourth, *slander* can be directed toward both God and man. The term comes from two words (Greek, *blaptō* and *phēmē*) that mean, respectively, to injure someone and a rumor or saying. It includes both abusive words and slander (James 3:9–10). Fifth, *abusive speech* (Greek, *aischrologian*) denotes disgraceful speech. Such words should produce shame for both the speaker and the willing listener. It is low, obscene, and dirty talk. It is full of swearing and sexual innuendo (Eph. 5:4). Such sins as these grieve the Holy Spirit and should be put off immediately (Eph. 4:30–31).

Do Not Lie (3:9–11)

The first two commands stressed a crisis decision, a determined resolution to put away the sinful practices of the past. The present imperative ("Do not lie") points out daily interpersonal relationships within the church. It denotes two basic ideas: Stop lying if you have been doing it; and continually do not lie to one another. To lie is to tell a deliberate untruth, to create a wrong impression by revealing a partial truth, and to distort the facts by exaggeration. Lying must be replaced by the telling of truth before complete victory can be attained (Eph. 4:25). The reason for this verbal transformation is the fact that believers are brothers, sisters, and fellow members of the body of Christ, the true church.

Part of the old life. The four words "since you laid aside" are the translation of one Greek aorist participle *(apekdusamenoi)* that explains why believers should stop lying. At conversion, believing sinners positionally put off their old life. They passed from death to life, from being in Adam to being in Christ (John 5:24; Rom. 5:12–21). In their daily life, however, they must appropriate their spiritual identification with Christ and put off the actual practice of sin.

The past unsaved life is described as "the old self with its *evil* practices." This phrase includes both the position and the practice of sin. When people are genuinely saved, they desire to be delivered not only from the penalty of their lost position before God, but also from the power of the sin nature that causes them to practice sin. The redemptive work of Christ provides this double aspect of salvation.

Contrary to the new life. At regeneration, believers not only put off the old position, they also put on a new standing before God. Or, in terms of the clothing metaphor, they did not put the new over the old. Believers now have only one position before God, although they have two natures: the old sin nature and the new nature centered in the indwelling life of God. The new position guarantees heaven, and submission to the new nature brings spiritual victory (Gal. 5:16).

The new life is described in two ways. First, it has positional newness (3:10). It is "new" (Greek, *neon*) in contrast to that which is "old" (Greek, *palaion;* v. 9). It is not the old made new or the old reformed. The new has no connection whatsoever with the old. New life did not exist in the life of the person until regeneration occurred.

In a literal translation, this new life "is being renewed" (Greek, *anakainoumenon*).[8] This verbal action denotes the process of progressive sanctification whereby the Holy Spirit is transforming the believer into Christlikeness (Rom. 12:2; 2 Cor. 3:18). The believer does not renew himself, but the Holy Spirit does it as He works within him daily. The goal of renewal is knowledge (Greek, *eis epignōsin*). It indicates a full, comprehensive, personal knowledge. Like Paul, we should want to know Christ in a deeper, more intimate way (Phil. 3:10). Thus, to know Him is to become like Him.

The standard of renewal is "the image of the One who created him." God created man in His own image (Gen. 1:26, 28). Humans were originally constituted in true knowledge, righteousness, and holiness (Eph. 4:24). Through the first sin committed in the primeval garden, humans lost the moral expression of that innate image, although they still retained the image itself (Gen. 9:6; James 3:9). Through regeneration and sanctification, the moral expression can gradually be restored to the life. Since Christ is the image of God (1:15), the standard of spiritual excellence is Christ Himself.

Second, the new life has positional oneness (3:11). The adverb ("in which") refers to the new man, the spiritual position of every believer regardless of race, sex, culture, or social status (Gal. 3:28). All believers are one in Christ. Christ is everything to the child of God, and He abides in every Christian ("Christ is all and in all"). The first usage of "all" (Greek, *ta panta*) is neuter gender and looks at all the spiritual riches a believer possesses in Christ (Eph. 1:3–14). He alone provides salvation; thus, there is no need for angelic mediation (1:14–23). He provides satisfaction; thus, there is no need for humanistic philosophy (1:26—2:8). He provides sanctification; thus, there is no need for legalism and asceticism (2:9—3:17). The second usage of "all" (Greek, *pasin*) is masculine and points to the various classes of humankind just mentioned in the verse.

Four divisions of humanity are given here, although there are others (for example, gender: male and female). The concept of race is indicated by the couplet "Greek and Jew." All non-Jews, including those of both Greek and Roman nationality, are classified as Greek. The division of religion is seen in the contrast "circumcised and uncircumcised." The former embraces Judaism with its pure Jewish adherents and Gentile proselytes; the latter points to the pagan world (Rom. 2:25–29; 1 Cor. 7:18–19). Culture is indicated by "barbarian, Scythian." The first term refers to those who were ignorant of the culture and language of the Greeks and Romans in that day (Rom. 1:14). The Scythian was the lowest type of barbarian, a very crude person, such as the nomads who roamed the areas around the Black and Caspian seas. "Slave and freeman" point to social status. The Roman world of the first century was almost equally divided between slaves and freemen. In actual life, these classifications remain. In Christ, however, they are erased. There is no spiritual advantage or disadvantage in any of them (Gal. 6:15).

The essence of it is that the Christian has had a radical, life-changing experience in which he has put off the old self with its practices (that is, habits or characteristic actions) and has put on the new self. The metaphor again is one of clothing. The "old self" (that is, the old, unregenerate self; RSV, "old nature") is like a dirty, worn-out garment that is stripped from the body and thrown away. The "new self" (that is, the new, regenerate self; RSV, "new nature") is like a new suit of clothing that one puts on and wears. The picturesque language gives vivid expression to a great truth, but one must be careful not to press the imagery too far, for we are painfully aware that the old nature is ever with us.[9]

The New Life (3:12–17)

The new life has already been introduced as "Christ" (3:4) and "the new self" (3:10). In this section, Paul set forth the new patterns of behavior that should manifest the new position. They are seen in a series of imperatives.

The Expression of the New Life (3:12–14)

The command ("put on") calls for a firm determination to practice what had already been done positionally (3:10).[10] It continues the imagery of clothing—removal of the old and putting on of the new.

Description of believers. Here Paul describes believers three ways. First, they are the "chosen of God." God sovereignly chose each one to have a position of acceptance before Him (Eph. 1:4). As the elect, they believed in Christ when they were convicted by the Holy Spirit and drawn to the Son by the Father (John 6:44; 16:7–11; Titus 1:1). As the justified elect, they can never be condemned spiritually (Rom. 8:33). Second, believers are "holy" (Greek, *hagioi*). The same word was used earlier of them and translated as "saints" (1:2). They had been permanently set apart from the world unto God for His unique possession. Third, believers are "beloved" (Greek, *ēgapēmenoi*). This verbal adjective indicates that God had fixed His love on them both at the cross and at their conversion and that they would remain the eternal objects of His love (Rom. 8:38–39).[11]

> The elect are "holy," consecrated to God in thought and life; and "beloved," accepted and sustained in their consecration by His love. Both epithets being to them as conformed to the image of Christ . . . ; for He is "the Holy One of God" (Mark i. 24; Luke iv. 34), who "sanctifies Himself for us, that we also may be sanctified in truth" (John xvii. 19); and He is also the "Beloved" the "Son of God's love" (chap. i. 13; Matt. iii. 17; Eph. i. 16), and we are accepted in Him. The two epithets here seem intended to prepare for the two-fold exhortation following. They are "beloved," therefore they should love one another (verses 12–15); they are holy, therefore they should thank God and live to His glory (verses 16, 17).[12]

List of virtues. Eight virtues are delineated within four general categories. The first two show believers' treatment of others; the next two, their estimation of themselves; the next three, their reaction to ill treatment; and the final one, the all-pervasive principle of true discipleship.

The expression *"heart of compassion"* (Greek, *splagchna oiktirmou*) literally refers to the inner organs of the body; thus, it implies softness and vulnerability. By extension, the phrase denotes deep feelings of concern for the needs of others. God is merciful (Lam. 3:22), Christ manifested compassion when He performed miracles, and believers should become emotionally involved with others.

Kindness (Greek, *chrēstototēta*) is grace in action. It is a sweetness of disposition, a desire for the good of others. It is part of the fruit of the Spirit (Gal. 5:22). God manifests acts of kindness toward sinners (Rom. 2:4; Eph. 2:7; Titus 3:4).

Humility (Greek, *tapeinophrosunēn*) is that positive quality that causes people to see themselves as objects of divine grace. They recognize that they have no right to assert themselves. This proper attitude before God can be seen in their service toward others (Phil. 2:3). It manifests the mind of Christ (Phil. 2:5). It is the genuine expression of humility in contrast to the false, self-imposed humility of the heretics (2:18, 23).

Gentleness (Greek, *prautēta*) is marked by courtesy and a spirit of quiet submission. It is not psychological timidity or weakness; rather, it is power under control. An ox within a yoke is gentle, able to be turned in any direction by the will of its master. It is the opposite of insubordination. Moses, Christ, and Paul all were gentle (Num. 12:3; Matt. 11:29; 1 Cor. 4:21).

Patience is literally "wrath that is put far away" (Greek, *makrothumia*). One work of the flesh manifests a wrath that is near and inside (3:8; Gal. 5:20). Spirit-controlled believers, however, put distance between themselves and this wrath (Gal. 5:22–23), enabling them to put up with people who try their patience (2 Cor. 6:6). They do not have quick tempers.

"Bearing with one another" means that believers tolerate others when they are irritating. It seeks redemptive ends (Rom. 2:4; 3:25).

The virtue of *forgiving one another* is the climax of these others. Its meaning is the gracious removal of sin and the gracious treatment of the sinner who is unworthy to receive it. The Greek verb *charizomenoi* is based on the Greek term for "grace" *(charis)*. Its scope is one another. Its need is conditioned upon the complaint (Greek, *momphēn*) that a believer has against another. Its standard is divine forgiveness. Vertical forgiveness should result in horizontal forgiveness. Since Christ has forgiven believers of so much, they should forgive one another of so little. His forgiveness is for time and eternity; ours is only for time. His forgiveness embraced both the quality and the quantity of sins.

Love (Greek, *agapēn*) holds all of the other virtues in place. The imagery is that of the oriental girdle that is placed over all the other pieces of clothing. Thus, love is the girdle that holds the other spiritual qualities, the clothing of the new man, in place. This love is distinctively Christian (literally "the love"; Greek, *tēn agapēn*). It is the type of love that has its source in God and is divinely implanted within the children of God (1 John 3:14; 4:8). Furthermore this love is "the perfect bond of unity." As the bond (Greek, *sundesmos*), it is that which binds together practical righteousness. No believer has achieved spiritual maturity until all of his works of holiness are thoroughly saturated by love. Without such love, the good deeds are nothing (1 Cor. 13).

Albert Barnes comments:

> The bond of perfection; the thing which will unite all other things, and make them complete. . . . The idea seems to be that love will bind all the other graces fast together, and render the whole system complete. Without love, though there might be other graces and virtues, there would be a want of harmony and compactness in our Christian graces, and this was necessary to unite and complete the whole. There is great beauty in the expression, and it contains most important truth.[13]

The Controls of the New Life (3:15–17)

The practical application of the new position is further introduced in a series of four imperatives. They form the guidelines for the new life.

Peace. Three qualities of this peace are expressed. First, it is divine. Its character stems from its source, the triune God: the Father (Phil. 4:7), the Son (John 14:27), and the Holy Spirit (Gal. 5:22). In the midst of circumstances that cause anxiety, it protects the hearts and minds of believers (Phil. 4:7). It is that inner calmness that rests on the assurance that God is too good to be unkind and too wise to make mistakes. The peace *of* God must be contrasted with the peace *with* God that is the result of a justified position (Rom. 5:1).

Second, it is a ruling peace ("rule in your hearts"). The verb (Greek, *brabeuetō*) means "to act as an umpire." Divine peace should constantly regulate all activities of the believer. Peace should always overrule dissension. The domain of rule is the inner man ("hearts").

Third, it is a peace of unity. The prepositional phrase "to which" refers back to the divine peace.[14] All believers were divinely called in one body to a position of peace before God and to a practice of peace within the true Church. Peace and unity go together (Eph. 2:14–15).

Thanksgiving. Paul earlier prayed that gratitude might mark the believers' lives (1:12). Thankful people acknowledge the working of the sovereign will of God in their lives and circumstances (1 Thess. 5:18).

Word of Christ. The command has three key features. First, the word of Christ may refer to the word that Christ actually spoke on earth and to that which He revealed directly to the apostles (John 14:26; 15:7). It may, however, point out the Scriptures that expound on Him and His redemptive work. Second, the imperative "dwell" (Greek, *enoikeitō*) literally means "to be at home in." It is one thing for believers to be in the Word; it is another for the Word to be in them, to have free access to all parts of their lives. Third, the Word must dwell richly to be totally effective. It must be highly prized and appreciated. Believers must recognize that they are spiritual paupers apart from it.

The consequences of the rich indwelling of the Word are indicated in the three participles teaching, admonishing, and singing. Believers will teach others in all wisdom[15]—wisdom that is centered in Christ (2:3). Teaching stresses the positive instruction of truth.

Believers also will admonish one another. The essence of admonition is warning and correction. The two ministries are to be conducted by three means. Psalms are the Old Testament psalms sung to musical accompaniment. Believers compose hymns of praise to the glory of God. Some hymns may have been incorporated into the inscripturated text (1 Tim. 1:15; 4:9). Spiritual songs embrace all other forms of biblical truth that promote an emotional and lyrical response within children of God.

Believers will be singing songs that manifest thanks for the grace of God that has been given to them (1 Cor. 10:30). They must express verbally what is a reality in their hearts. Songs cannot be cold, lifeless, or without meaning. Technical artistry is not a requirement for this ministry of edification. It must be done to the Lord rather than to entertain or impress others.

Glory of God. Three features are involved in this command. First, the scope of activity is inclusive ("whatever you do in word and deed"). Second, activities should be done under the complete authority and approval of Jesus Christ ("do all in the name of the Lord Jesus"). He is the Head of the Church and its ultimate Judge. The name of Christ stands for all that He is and all that He has done. Christians therefore should act in total conformity to their living Lord. Third, believers should always be thankful that God is their Father and that they have the unique privilege and responsibility of living for Him. They must constantly acknowledge that they do not deserve to have anything either in this life or the next. After all, they are just sinners saved by grace.

Barnes rightly concludes:

> Through him; or in his name. All our actions are to be accompanied with thanksgiving. . . . We are to engage in every duty, not only in the name of Christ, but with thankfulness for strength and reason; for the privilege of acting so that we may honour him; and with a grateful remembrance of the mercy of God that gave us such a Saviour to be an example and guide. He is most likely to do his duty well who goes to it with a heart overflowing with gratitude to God for his mercies, and he who is likely to perform his duties with the most cheerful fidelity is he who has the deepest sense of the divine goodness in providing a Saviour for his lost and ruined soul.[16]

STUDY QUESTIONS

1. Why do some believers commit condemned sins such as fornication? How can these sins be prevented?

2. Are some sins worse than others? Defend your answer.

3. How do Christians lie to one another? Is this the most common sin within the Church?

4. What causes dissension and denominationalism? How can spiritual unity be achieved when so many differences exist today?

5. Is there a feeling of superiority within the Church today? Relate your answer to education, finances, and race.

6. In what ways can Christians irritate one another? How should forbearance and forgiveness be manifested?

7. How do we give glory to God in our business life? Family life? Social life?

CHAPTER 24

The Responsibilities of Believers
Colossians 3:18–4:6

Preview:
After having dealt with general Christian behavior, Paul now turns toward family relations between believers. He gives instructions to wives, husbands, children, and slaves and masters, reminding them all that they are to realize their position before the Lord and their responsibility to Him. Starting from this perspective will always yield fruitful interpersonal relationships. Paul ends with instructions on prayer and on living the Christian life before unbelievers.

Corporate positional oneness does not abrogate individual responsibility and function. Racial, social, and gender distinctions remain even though people have equality in Christ. In this new section of his letter, Paul sought to apply the general principles of Christian behavior to specific life situations.

In the Home (3:18–4:1)

God created the original home when He brought Adam and Eve together. The home existed before the church, and it continues to function as the foundation of local congregations. The purpose of the church, therefore, is to complement the family and to honor the unique responsibilities of each member of the household. There must not be any contradiction in function; there must not be any role reversal. In other words, it is not possible for a male to be the authoritative head of the family and for a female to be the authoritative head of the local church. The responsibilities specified for family members must carry over into the church, which is the extension of the family.

In this section, the duties of six family members are set forth. These duties are stated in three pairs of sentences. In each pair, the subordinate person is addressed first.

Wives (3:18)

The term used in the address (Greek, *hai gunaikes*) can refer either to a female in contrast to a male (Matt. 9:20) or to a wife (Matt. 5:28). In this context, it points to the latter.

The command. The imperative (Greek, *hupotassesthe*) can be translated in two possible ways: "submit yourselves" or "be subject to."[1] In either case, the present tense stresses constant, daily submission. A wife is to be in order (*tassō*) under (*hupo*) the directions of her husband.

The submission of the wife to the husband, both in the family and in the church, is functional. It is intended to help believers carry out the divine purpose for the family. It does not imply personal inferiority or dictatorial rule. Within the Trinitarian oneness of the divine Being, there is an equality of the three Persons, but there is also a functional order to execute the creative-redemptive program (1 Cor. 11:3). In like manner, the husband and wife are personal equals, but the wife is subordinate for functional purposes.

The headship of the man is based on the order of creation (1 Tim. 2:13) and the judgment imposed on the woman for her deception in the temptation (Gen. 3:16; 1 Tim. 2:14). Until the establishment of the eternal state, this order must be observed on earth in the family and in the church. Submission involves both love and obedience (Titus 2:4–5). It should mark the godly wife even if her husband is not saved (1 Pet. 3:1–6).

The reason. The reason for such submission is "as [it] is fitting in the Lord." Subordination befits Christian women. God established the authority of family function when He created Adam and Eve. Neither the entrance of sin into the human race nor the experience of personal salvation has changed this basic principle. It is not a cultural anomaly that can be altered in different countries and ages.

Husbands (3:19)

The term used in the address (Greek, *hoi andres*) can refer either to the male in contrast to a female (Matt. 15:38) or to a husband (Matt. 1:19). In this context, it points to the latter. Paul issues two commands to the husbands.

Love. The directive (Greek, *agapate*) calls for continuous love, at all times and in all situations.[2] The husband should love his wife even as Christ loved the Church and gave Himself for it (Eph. 5:25). Christ's love is a sacrificial love, a giving love, an altruistic love, a holy and redemptive love. It is a nourishing and cherishing love, a love that makes its object feel valuable and wanted (Eph. 5:26–27). Such love forgives, sanctifies, and cleanses.

Do not be bitter. Whenever love weakens, bitterness sets in. The negative command warns against this threat to a strong biblical marriage. Bitterness is the opposite of sweetness (Rev. 8:11; 10:9). The imperative (Greek, *pikrainesthe*) stresses the constant prevention of this sour attitude. A bitter husband will become a harsh, unscrupulous dictator. Such a person looks on his wife simply as a servant, an object to satisfy his petty whims. A loving husband understands and appreciates his wife (1 Pet. 3:7) and seeks to meet her needs. He treats her with respect.

Children (3:20)

The word *children* (Greek, *ta tekna*) embraces those who are still dependent on their parents for their daily physical needs. They have not yet married, nor have they reached that designated time when their parents view them as legal adults (Gal. 4:1–2). A young man was regarded as a child until he became a man in the official sense with all the privileges and responsibilities pertaining thereto.

The command. The command has three features. First, a child must obey constantly.[3] The imperative (Greek, *hupakouete*) literally means to hear (*akouō*) under (*hupo*). Obedient children put themselves under the authority of their parents, listen to parental directives, and do as they are told without complaint and rebellion. Second, obedience must be toward both parents. This fact implies that both parents agree about what is expected of their children. If a father and mother give contradictory commands, it is impossible for the child to comply with the divine imperative. Each parent can give a separate charge, but he or she must do so with the full support of the other. The context implies that these are saved parents (3:21). Third, obedience extends to "all things," including all aspects of daily life—work, play, church, and social activities.

The reason. The obedience of children is "well-pleasing" to the Lord. Whatever children do, they should do for the glory of the Lord (3:17). Submission to parental authority is a sign of submission to God. The fifth of the Ten Commandments recognizes the divine authority of parental rule (Ex. 20:12; Eph. 6:1–3). The child who obeys acknowledges that chain of command.

Parents (3:21)

The direct address, "Fathers" (Greek, *hoi pateres*), could refer to the male parent only, but it more likely applies to both the father and the mother (Heb. 11:23). The father is the authoritative head of the family, but the mother also guides the home (1 Tim. 5:14).

The command. The negative command actually constitutes a warning: "Do not exasperate your children."[4] The imperative (Greek, *erethizete*) means to excite or to stimulate. Some provocation can be good and necessary (2 Cor. 9:2). The usual result of bad provocation, however, is strife, a work of the sinful flesh and a display of carnality (1 Cor. 3:3; Gal. 5:20). Since like begets like, a bitter parent will produce a bitter, strife-filled child. Bad provocation makes unreasonable demands on children, humiliates them, and manifests no loving understanding of their unique personhood. It is marked by constant nagging. The remedy is a positive approach of spiritual nurture and admonition (Eph. 6:4). Godly parents must teach and warn, but they must be sure they are communicating God's will and not their own petty convictions.

Paul's Words to the Family

Husbands

Love your wives, just as Christ loved the church (Eph. 5:25).

Love your wives as your own bodies (Eph. 5:28).

Cleave to your wife (Eph. 5:31).

Love your wife as yourself (Eph. 5:33).

Do not provoke your children to anger (Eph. 6:4).

Bring your children up in the discipline and instruction of the Lord (Eph. 6:4).

Wives

Be subject to your husbands (Eph. 5:22).

Respect your husbands (Eph. 5:33).

Love your husbands (Titus 2:4).

Love your children (Titus 2:4).

Children

Obey your parents (Eph. 6:1).

Honor your father and mother (Eph. 6:2).

The reason. Children should not lose heart (become discouraged). The Greek term *athumōsin* literally means "no wrath." Its stem contains the same word that was translated as wrath, an emotional sin that should be put off (3:8). Wrong provocation can quench any vital emotional expression within a child. Emotions must not be eliminated; rather, they must be guided and sanctified. A discouraged child will become sullen and listless, lacking a desire to become what God wants him or her to be.

Slaves (3:22–25)

More content is given to the responsibilities of slaves than to the combined responsibilities of husbands, wives, parents, and children. One reason was the return to Colossae of Onesimus, the runaway slave who was now a believer (4:9). Another is the fact that many Christians were slaves, a class that constituted almost half the population of the Roman Empire. These people were not freemen who were household workers. They were owned as chattel property, to be bought and sold. People became slaves by being born of slave parents, through financial loss, or by military conquest.

The commands. Two are given. First, slaves must obey their human masters. The imperative (Greek, *hupakouete;* cf. v. 22) stresses constant, daily obedience that extends to all things, both pleasant and unpleasant. Obedience must be rendered to owners and foremen ("your masters on earth") whether saved or unsaved. The spiritual condition of the owner was to have no effect on the quality of the slave's work.

Mere obedience, however, is insufficient. Its manner is just as important. Work must not be done "with external service, as those who merely please men" (Eph. 6:5–8). Rather than working only when being watched and doing only enough to satisfy the minimum demands of one's master, slaves are to obey "with sincerity of heart, fearing the Lord." The noun *sincerity* (Greek, *haplotēti*) literally means "without a fold." It denotes that everything is seen and that no misdeed or faulty motive is hidden by duplicity. With a full understanding that God sees both actions and attitudes even when earthly masters aren't present, godly slaves will perform their tasks to the best of their ability to be a good testimony for Christ.

Second, slaves must work for God. The imperative "do" (Greek, *ergazesthe*) denotes faithful toil and labor.[5] This covers all of one's assigned responsibilities ("whatever you do"). Furthermore, all this work must be done with enthusiasm. The adverb *heartily* translates a prepositional phrase that literally reads "out of soul" (Greek, *ek psuchēs*). And work should not be performed merely for humans. Thus, labor is a sacred service even when it is executed in the context of first-century slavery. It is doing the will of God with good human will (Eph. 6:6–7).

The reasons. The participle *knowing* introduces two reasons for the slaves' obedience and work. First, faithful service will receive a divine reward (3:24). If slaves serve Christ in menial tasks, the Savior will reward them at the judgment seat in heaven (2 Cor. 5:10). In earthly life, slaves received no wages or inheritance, but in the spiritual life, Christian slaves are entitled to all the blessings of their heavenly inheritance that Christ has provided. Rewards, however, are not given to make up for inequities on earth. All Christians, regardless of their status, must labor with clean hands and hearts in order to be honored in that future day of examination.

Second, poor service will be judged.[6] To do "wrong" (Greek, *adikōn*) is to do that which does not conform to the righteous character and standards of a just God. Such wrongdoing involves doing less than one's best, doing the minimum rather than the maximum, doing to impress, and doing it apart from the heart. Slaves can fool their earthly masters, but they cannot deceive God.

Before God, there is no partiality. At the judgment seat, slaves will not receive preferential treatment because they had a difficult life on earth. The judgment in that day will be of a believer's faithfulness and spirituality, not of racial distinctions or social deprivation. God will treat all believers alike: slaves and masters, men and women, Jews and Gentiles, rich and poor. Slaves who do wrong will suffer the same judgment as masters who do wrong.

Paul's Rules for Master/Slave Relations

Slaves, be obedient to your masters (Eph. 6:5).

Slaves, act as slaves of Christ (Eph. 6:6).

Slaves, render service as to the Lord (Eph. 6:7).

Masters, do not threaten your slaves, because God is the Master in heaven (Eph. 6:9).

Masters, grant justice and fairness (Col. 4:1).

Masters, remember you have a Master in heaven (Col. 4:1).

Masters (4:1)

In this section (3:22—4:1), the Greek term is translated in the plural as "masters" *(hoi kurioi)* and in the singular as both "master" and "lord" *(kurios)*. The former refers to the earthly owners of slaves (3:22; 4:1) and the latter to the Lord Jesus Christ (3:23, 24; 4:1). The masters referred to in this address are definitely believers.

The command. Masters are charged to give two things to their slaves. First, masters should render what is just (Greek, *to dikaion*). If a master refuses to do this, he does wrong (Greek, *adikōn*; 3:25) and will be judged by God for this sin. A just recompense is legally and morally right. It corresponds to the righteous character of God.

Second, masters should give what is fair (Greek, *tēn isotēta*). Various interpretations of this concept have been suggested. (1) It implies the emancipation of the slaves. (2) Masters should carry out their responsibilities to their slaves equally as well as the slaves serve the masters (Eph. 6:7–9). (3) Masters should treat their slaves the same way God has treated them.[7] (4) It denotes the equality of spiritual brotherhood. (5) It may indicate that a master should not give one slave more and another less for doing the same job with comparable excellence. In this sense, he should not show partiality.

The reason. All Christians, including both slaves and masters, know that they have a heavenly master, the Lord Jesus Christ. Masters will one day give an account to Him for how they have treated others. In the performance of their duties, they must also practice the principles of the new man. They must recognize that they are also spiritual slaves to Christ and that they must willingly serve the needs of others. Although Paul never clearly condemned the institution of slavery, he did set forth principles that would eventually lead to its elimination, at least by dedicated believers.

In the World (4:2–6)

The major didactic section ends with these closing admonitions to all segments of the congregation. Regardless of family or social status, all believers have responsibilities toward all people. These responsibilities must not be neglected in the execution of household duties.

Prayer (4:2–4)

Prayer is the very breath of spirituality. Its absence indicates deadness and coldness. Two of its motivations are concern for self and intercession for others. It is not wrong to pray for oneself; in fact, Christ even prayed for Himself before He prayed for others (John 17). In this section, the apostle wanted the believers to pray for themselves and then for him.

For self. Three elements constitute this command. First, "devote yourselves to prayer." The imperative (Greek, *proskartereite*) means to devote one's time, attention, and strength to a task. This diligence in prayer was seen in the apostles (Acts 1:14; 6:4), the first three thousand converts (Acts 2:41–42), and the Roman believers (Rom. 12:12). Christians must pray without ceasing (1 Thess. 5:17). Prayer is part of their offensive and defensive armor in spiritual battle with the forces of evil (Eph. 6:18). Second, believers should be vigilant in their prayer life. They should watch and pray to avoid spiritual defeat (Matt. 26:41). Watchfulness involves mental alertness and spiritual vigilance, a sensitive awareness that one is in danger (1 Pet. 5:8). Third, believers should pray with thanksgiving. They should express gratitude to the God of peace for the peace that God gives to protect their hearts and minds (Phil. 4:6). Thanksgiving acknowledges submission to God's will (1 Thess. 5:18).

For Paul. Jesus Christ never asked anyone to pray for Him. Paul, however, knew that he needed the intercession of others even though he was a mature, spiritual believer. Paul requested such prayer from the church when it was engaged in prayer and intercession for others ("praying at the same time for us as well").

Paul made two requests. First, he desired an opportunity for witness. He was a missionary evangelist, first and foremost. He included his associates ("for us"). Prayer does not open doors, but God who answers prayers does. When He opens a door for service, no one can shut it; when He closes a door, no one can open it (Rev. 3:7–8). Apparently the Colossians prayed and God answered, because members of Caesar's military guard and household became believers through Paul's proclamation of God's Word (Eph. 6:19–20; Phil. 1:13; 4:22). Paul's spiritual depth can be seen in the fact that he desired an opportunity for witness rather than release from his imprisonment. He was more concerned for others than for himself.

Paul's ultimate purpose was "to speak forth the mystery of Christ" (cf. 1:26–27; 2:2). The truth that both Jew and Gentile become one in Christ through saving faith formed the content of his message. In essence, Christ was the mystery—who He was, what He did at the cross, and what He was doing through His body, the Church. The cause of Paul's imprisonment was his refusal to preach a Judaistic gospel, complete with circumcision and legalism ("for which I have also been imprisoned"). His Jewish opponents constantly accused him (Acts 21:28; 28:22).

Second, Paul desired an effective witness (4:4). It is one thing for God to open a door of service; it is another for a believer to enter it. God had earlier encouraged Paul about his future ministry in Rome (Acts 23:11). God had manifested the hidden mystery to Paul shortly after his conversion, but now he had the privilege and responsibility to make it clear to both sinners and believers. He had no options; he was under obligation to preach (1 Cor. 9:16).

Paul's Imprisonment References in Colossians

"I rejoice in my sufferings" (1:24).

"In my flesh I do my share on behalf of His body (which is the church)" (1:24).

"I labor, striving according to His power" (1:29).

"I want you to know how great a struggle I have" (2:1).

"Devote yourselves to prayer . . . that we may speak forth the mystery of Christ, for which I have also been imprisoned" (4:2–3).

"I have sent Tychicus . . . that you may know about our circumstances" (4:8).

"[Tychicus and Onesimus] will inform you about the whole situation here" (4:9).

"Remember my imprisonment" (4:18).

Witness (4:5–6)

Unsaved people watch and listen; therefore, Christians must be consistent in what they do and say. Lest they be called hypocrites, they must have a holy balance between life and lip. Paul encouraged them to exercise this double witness faithfully.

Conduct yourselves (walk). Conduct that pleases God has four features. First, it must be consistent. The imperative (Greek, *peripateite*) views the Christian life in its total aspects and application.[8] Second, believers are to conduct themselves with wisdom. Spiritual wisdom begins with a genuine fear of God and ends with the exaltation of Christ (2:3; Prov. 1:7). It must be in total conformity to God's will as revealed in the Scriptures (1:9–10). The heretics boasted about their love of wisdom, but genuine wisdom is seen in a godly life under the control of the Holy Spirit. Third, Christians are to reach the unsaved who are outside of Christ and the true Church. The unsaved are hopeless and without God in the world (Eph. 2:12). If they remain unsaved, they will be outside the holy city, the habitation of the redeemed, for all eternity (Rev. 22:15). Fourth, urgency is indicated by the phrase "making the most of the opportunity." All have the same amount of time; the clock is no respecter of persons. The child of God, however, must buy out (Greek, *exagorazomenoi*) opportunities to reach the lost with an effective witness.

John Ellicott notes:

In the parallel passage (Eph. v. 15) we have "walk strictly, not as fools, but as wise," and the limitation "toward them that are without" is omitted, although it is added that "the days are evil." The context, as will be seen by reference, is different, and the idea also somewhat different. There the "strictness" and "wisdom" are to guard against excess or recklessness within; here the "wisdom" is to watch against external dangers and make full use of external opportunities.[9]

Speech. The tongue is the most difficult member of the body to control (James 3:1–10). It can produce either blessing or cursing. The concept of speech (Greek, *logos*) includes both the content and the manner of oral expression. Four characteristics of proper speech for the believer are stated. First, it must be consistent ("always"). At all times and under all situations, it should be the same.

Second, believers must speak with grace. In the face of open hostility, believers must address the unsaved in a way the latter does not deserve. Christians must manifest winsomeness.

Third, believers' speech must be seasoned with salt. Salt enhances flavor and makes food appetizing. Too much or too little makes the food unpalatable. Salt also retards corruption. Christians must give an oral witness in such a way that they show disapproval of sin on the one hand and graciously seek to win sinners on the other. In essence, they must hate the sin and love the sinner at the same time.

Fourth, believer' speech must manifest a sensitivity and awareness to the needs of each individual. Christians cannot use the same evangelistic technique each time, although the content of the redemptive message must never be altered. They must know how to answer every person. This knowledge can be gained only through spiritual and mental preparation and a humble submission to the Holy Spirit (1 Pet. 3:15).

STUDY QUESTIONS

1. Why are wives afraid to submit to their husbands? How can wives contribute effectively to family leadership?

2. How can a husband show that he loves his wife? How can he become more sensitive to her needs?

3. To what extent should saved children obey their unsaved parents? When do they cease being children?

4. How can parents discourage their children? Discuss these principles, and give practical suggestions for avoiding this fault.

5. How can the slave-master relationship be transferred into the modern world of employee-employer? How should Christians conduct their businesses?

6. How strong is evangelical prayer life today? How strong is your prayer life? How can it be improved?

7. How can believers redeem opportunities for witness? At work? At school? On vacation?

CHAPTER 25

The Blessings of Friends
Colossians 4:7–18

Preview:

Instead of adding many pages to his letter describing his condition in prison, Paul tells the Colossians that he will be sending messengers, Tychicus and Onesimus, to them with this information. He gives loving reports on many Christian people who are helping him personally and in the work of the gospel while he is in prison, then ends with specific greetings and instructions regarding the distribution of his letters, encouraging one last brother, Archippus, to fulfill his ministry.

Friends encourage and stand by each other in difficult days (Prov. 17:17; 27:6, 10, 17). A person who has friends is rich indeed. In this closing section, Paul mentioned eleven personal acquaintances who had been a blessing to him.

His Representatives (4:7–9)

Paul sent two representatives to the church at Colossae. The first was the bearer of the epistle and the second was returning to his master, Philemon.

Tychicus (4:7–8)

His life. The name Tychicus means "fortuitous" or "fortunate." He is mentioned five times in the New Testament. A native of the Roman province of Asia, Tychicus accompanied Paul into that region at the end of the apostle's third journey (Acts 20:4). He was with the apostle during his first Roman imprisonment (Eph. 6:21) and was given the responsibility of delivering three of Paul's prison epistles (Ephesians, Colossians, and Philemon).[1] Subsequently, Tychicus traveled with the apostle after Paul's acquittal and probably went to Crete as the replacement for Titus (Titus 3:12). He later reappeared in Rome when Paul was imprisoned there a second time. Paul then sent Tychicus to Ephesus shortly before his martyrdom (2 Tim. 4:12).

His character. Tychicus was a beloved spiritual brother both to Paul and the members of the Colossian church. All loved him. He was also a faithful servant who acted as Paul's apostolic representative several times and executed his responsibilities well. Paul could count on him without question. Tychicus was a fellow bond-servant in the Lord as well. Paul, Timothy, and Tychicus were joined together in loving service to their heavenly Master, the Lord Jesus Christ.

His purpose. Paul sent Tychicus for two reasons. First, he was to inform the church about the circumstances surrounding the apostle's imprisonment ("that you may know about our circumstances"). In its concern, the church had sent Epaphras to Rome to get firsthand information, but he too became imprisoned (Philem. 1:23). Tychicus thus made known how God had used the imprisonment to advance the gospel (Phil. 1:12).

Second, Tychicus was to encourage them. The church was undoubtedly anxious about the imprisonments of Paul and Epaphras, about the confusion that the heresy had produced, and about the future vitality of the church. Encouragement and comfort come from concerned, involved friends and from a thorough knowledge of the facts.

Onesimus (4:9)

His life. The name Onesimus occurs only twice in the biblical record (4:9; Philem. 1:10). He was an unsaved slave of a Christian master, Philemon. After Onesimus had wronged his master, he ran away to Rome, where he encountered Paul in prison. Through the witness of the apostle, Onesimus became a believer. Subsequently, Paul sent him back to Philemon under the custody of Tychicus.

His character. Paul described Onesimus four ways. (1) He was a brother in Christ, a brother to all including Paul and Philemon. They were all birthed into the family of God through faith in Christ (John 1:12). (2) He was faithful. At Rome he was known for his life of faith and for his faithful service to the apostle. In domestic duties, he ministered to Paul and proved to be very profitable (Philem. 1:10–11, 13). (3) He was beloved by Paul, the associates, and the Roman church. Now the apostle wanted both Philemon and the Colossian church to love him as well. (4) He was from Colossae ("who is one of you"). This phrase denotes more than just his geographical origin. In Paul's viewpoint, Onesimus was now part of the family of God at Colossae (cf. 4:12).

His purpose. Both Tychicus and Onesimus informed the church about Paul's situation in Rome. In that sense, they were equal apostolic representatives.

His Associates (4:10-14)

Paul mentions seven associates in verses 10–14. With the exception of Barnabas, six were associated with Paul in his imprisonment and limited ministry at Rome. They are identified first as his "fellow workers for the kingdom of God." All were born again by faith in Jesus Christ, and thus they had entered the spiritual realm of the kingdom of God (1:13; John 3:3–5). In addition, they worked with each other and with Paul to bring others into the same salvation experience.

Paul also identifies these associates as an "encouragement" to him in the difficulties of his confinement. The Greek word for "encouragement" *(parēgoria)* has been transliterated into the English as *paregoric,* a medicine that brings relief from pain. They undoubtedly performed this ministry of caring by their mere presence and conversation, by their willingness to stand with him in the pagan court, by their financial help, and by their evangelistic outreach in Rome.

Jewish Workers (4:10-11)

Spiritual oneness in Christ can be seen in the fact that Jewish and Gentile believers worked beside Paul and that both groups wanted to greet the Colossian church. The first three were "from the circumcision" (Greek, *hoi ontes ek peritomēs*). They were Jewish, circumcised when they were infants, raised in legalistic Judaism, and had been saved. Their background and conversion corresponded to that of Paul (Phil. 3:4–6).

Aristarchus. The name Aristarchus means "ruler of the dinner." He was a Jew who lived in Thessalonica (Acts 20:4; 27:2). He may have been converted to Christ during Paul's evangelistic work in that city during the second missionary journey (Acts 17:1–10). He first appears in the biblical record as a traveling companion of Paul during the apostle's ministry in Ephesus on his third journey (Acts 19:29). At that time Aristarchus and Gaius were almost martyred by the pagan silversmiths who had dragged the pair into the amphitheater before an angry mob. Along with others, he moved with Paul into Macedonia, Achaia, back to Macedonia, and on to Asia at the end of the third apostolic journey (Acts 20:4). The Bible is silent as to whether he traveled with Paul to Jerusalem; however, he was with the apostle in Rome (4:10;

Philem. 1:24). Aristarchus is further identified here as Paul's fellow prisoner. This descriptive title may mean that he actually was under house arrest in Rome with the apostle or that he had been in jail at some time in the past for his faith in Christ (Rom. 16:7).

Mark. His given name was John, and his Latin surname was Mark. His mother was Mary, a resident of Jerusalem and a relative of Barnabas. Mark was either a cousin or a nephew to Barnabas (Greek, *ho anepsios*).[2] The family apparently had some wealth (Acts 4:37; 12:12). He may have been the young man who followed Jesus after His arrest in Gethsemane and who later fled naked (Mark 14:51–52).[3]

Mark's home was the site for the prayer meeting in which the believers requested the release of Peter (Acts 12:12–17). He may have been a direct convert of Peter, because that apostle later identified Mark as his spiritual son (1 Pet. 5:13).

Mark's active ministry began when he accompanied Paul and Barnabas in the early stages of the first missionary journey (Acts 12:25; 13:1–13); however, he returned to Jerusalem without completing the trip. At the beginning of the second journey, Paul and Barnabas disagreed over the advisability of giving Mark a second opportunity (Acts 15:36–41). The Bible is then silent about his activities during the next ten years. The differences between Mark and Paul must have been resolved, because Mark was with Paul during Paul's first Roman imprisonment (4:10; Philem. 1:24). Much later, during Paul's second Roman imprisonment, he asked Timothy to bring Mark because the latter was profitable to the ministry (2 Tim. 4:11). Mark thus had matured in both faith and service, having overcome his early failures. In fact, he became the author of the Gospel that bears his name.

The church received instructions concerning Mark. There is no indication of any prior communication between Paul and the church; thus, probably Tychicus transmitted some oral directives.[4]

The possibility of a future visit to Colossae by Mark is implied in the conditional clause ("if he comes to you"). If that were to occur, the church was to give him a hospitable reception.

Jesus Justus. The given name of this Jew was "Jesus" (*Iēsous*), the Greek equivalent for the Hebrew Joshua. It is the oldest name containing the divine name Yahweh. It therefore means "Yahweh saves" or "Yahweh is salvation." Both Jews of Israel and of the dispersion often gave this name to their male children. He probably changed his name to Justus after his conversion. All that is known of him is found in this verse. He was a Jew, a fellow worker, and a source of comfort to Paul.

Gentile Workers (4:12–14)

Epaphras. The name Epaphras appears three times in the biblical record (1:7; 4:12; Philem. 1:23). Four aspects of his life and ministry are given here. First, he was from the church at Colossae ("who is one of your number"). He may have been the founder of the church; if not, he definitely was its main pastor-teacher (1:7). He traveled to Rome to inquire about Paul and to inform the apostle about the spiritual condition of the Colossian believers (1:8).

Second, Epaphras was a servant of Christ. This complimentary title was used elsewhere only of Timothy (Phil. 1:1). He was a true spiritual slave whose will was totally submissive to the will of Christ.

Third, Epaphras was a prayer warrior. His prayers were intense and persistent ("always"). They involved the effort of his total being. The participle "laboring earnestly" (Greek, *agōnizomenos*) stresses the expenditure of physical, emotional, and mental energy. His prayers were intercessory ("for you") as well. Although Epaphras was himself a prisoner, he was concerned about his spiritual children in Colossae. His prayers were specific and purposeful. He requested that the Colossians might "stand perfect and fully assured in all the will of God." The "stand" refers to their doctrinal integrity and Christian behavior. He did not want them to submit to the deceitful influence of the heretics, especially now that he knew from Paul how dangerous the false teaching really was. He wanted them to have a perfect (Greek, *teleioi*) stand, to become what God had willed for them, to achieve their goals here on earth (1:28). He also wanted their stand to be "fully assured" (Greek, *peplēropho-rēmenoi*). Positionally, they were already complete in Christ (2:10), but they needed to become convinced of their total acceptance in the Savior. Their doctrinal convictions needed to become fully established so they would resist any pressure from false teaching.

Fourth, Epaphras had compassionate concern for the spiritual welfare of believers in his region (4:13). Paul observed this commendable trait and transmitted it to the church ("For I bear him witness"). He had great zeal (Greek, *ekei polun*), a holy jealousy over them.[5] It hurt him to see the believers being misled into error. This burden extended to three groups of Christians: the Colossians, the Laodiceans, and those in Hierapolis. These cities were clustered together geographically and joined together spiritually. What affected one affected the others. It is plausible that Epaphras may have evangelized the entire territory and that he started churches in two of these places (4:15–16).

The church at Laodicea endured this crisis and still was in existence at the end of the first century (Rev. 1:1; 3:14–22). It prospered financially but became spiritually bankrupt. Christ severely warned this church when He sent one of the seven letters to it. Since it is mentioned as one of the seven key churches of Asia, it probably supplanted the church at Colossae in ecclesiastical influence.

This is the only mention of Hierapolis in the New Testament.

Luke. Luke is mentioned only three times in the entire New Testament, each time in Paul's epistles (4:14; 2 Tim. 4:11; Philem. 1:24). However, his life and ministry can be discovered through a correlation of the book of Acts with Paul's epistles.[6]

Luke joined the missionary team of Paul, Silas, and Timothy at Troas and journeyed with them to Philippi (Acts 16:10-39). When the team left for Thessalonica, he remained behind, possibly to oversee the young church and to practice medicine. At the conclusion of his third journey, Paul again traveled into Macedonia, where Luke joined him once more at Philippi (Acts 20:1-6). From that point on, Luke was Paul's constant companion. He went with Paul from Philippi to Troas, Miletus, Tyre, Caesarea, and Jerusalem, where Paul was arrested (Acts 20:6—21:17). When the Romans took Paul from Jerusalem to Caesarea, where he was imprisoned for two years, Luke went also. During this period, Luke gathered information and wrote the third Gospel.

Luke was with Paul during the troubled voyage from Caeserea to Puteoli in Italy (Acts 27:1—28:13). He remained with Paul during the two years of house arrest in Rome (4:14; Acts 28:14-31; Philem. 1:24). At this time, he finished writing the book of Acts.

Paul's Laboring Helpers Mentioned in Colossians		
Epaphras:	1:7; 4:12; Philem. 1:23	Evangelized the Lycus Valley
Tychicus:	4:7, 9	A letter bearer for Paul
Onesimus:	4:9; Philem. 1:1–25	A slave who attached himself to Paul
Aristarchus:	4:10; Acts 19:29	Traveling companion
Mark:	4:10; Acts 15:36–39	Author of the Gospel of Mark
Justus:	4:11	Nothing is known of him
Luke:	4:14	Author of the Gospel of Luke
Demas:	4:14; 2 Tim. 4:10	A helper who later defected
Nympha:	4:15	Hosted a house church
Archippus:	4:17; Philem. 1:2	"A fellow soldier"

It is generally thought that Paul was released from the Roman house arrest; however, he was later seized and brought to a Roman jail for a second time. Since Luke was again with Paul during this second confinement (2 Tim. 4:11), it is safe to conclude that he also traveled with the apostle during the interval between the two Roman imprisonments. Luke, the beloved physician, proved to be a faithful friend.

Demas. Demas is mentioned three times in the New Testament (4:14; 2 Tim. 4:10; Philem. 1:24). In the interval between Paul's two Roman imprisonments, he may have traveled with the apostle, for he was with Paul at the beginning of the second confinement. Unfortunately, a spiritual weakness surfaced in his life; he loved the present world system (2 Tim. 4:10). He thus forsook Paul as the apostle faced martyrdom.

Paul's Readers (4:15–18)

The closing words of Paul's letter to the Colossians contain a salutation, counsel, a prayer request, and a blessing.

At Laodicea (4:15–16)

The brethren. The Colossians served as intermediaries for the apostle Paul. They were to perform a service for him. He asked them to greet the family of God in Laodicea.

Nympha. This is the only mention of Nympha in the Scriptures.[7] Since his name is given, he must have been an influential believer, perhaps the pastor of the congregation that met in his house.

The church. In the first century, believers met in private homes for worship and fellowship (Acts 12:12; 16:40; Rom. 16:5). In cities where there were many Christians, several houses were used as meeting places for smaller groups of the larger congregation (Acts 2:46). The church at Colossae met in the house of Philemon (Philem. 1:2), but this church met in the house of Nympha. This church was located either in Laodicea or Hierapolis—probably the latter, because the former assembly had already been greeted. Separate church buildings did not become a reality until the third century.

The letters. Two letters are mentioned. First, the Letter to the Colossians ("this letter") was to be read in two places—Colossae and Laodicea. Since only the original manuscript existed, the latter had to be read publicly to the entire congregation. And since the letters, written by divinely approved apostles, were inspired and authoritative, they immediately became the basis for faith and practice (2 Tim. 3:16; 2 Pet. 1:20–21). All believers thus needed to know about the doctrinal content of their faith and its implications for their behavior (1 Thess. 5:27; Rev. 1:3).

Paul's letter to the Colossians, although sent to that church, did not become its private possession. The truth of that letter became the doctrinal standard for other churches and believers as well; therefore, it became necessary to circulate the letter. At this time, copies were made so that each church could have at least one.

The public reading of the Old Testament was an essential part of synagogue worship (Luke 4:16–20; Acts 17:2). With this precedent, the reading of the New Testament epistles in the local churches also became a policy as the letters were written and circulated.

Second, there is a controversy about the identity of the "letter that is coming from Laodicea." Some scholars think that it was a letter written by the Laodicean church to Paul, or one written by Paul that has been lost, or the Epistle to the Ephesians. The third view seems to be most plausible. Since Tychicus carried the Ephesian letter to that church, it would be logical to assume that the epistle was passed from church to church in the province of Asia. The book of Revelation was sent to seven churches and was to be read by each, starting with Ephesus and ending with Laodicea (Rev. 1:11). This order followed the sequence of cities on the major road in that region. If Paul's letter to the Ephesians had been circulated in the same fashion, it would have arrived last at Laodicea. Colossae and Laodicea then were to exchange the epistles as the process of circulation continued among the churches.

Archippus (4:17)

Five truths about Archippus's life can be learned from this verse. First, his name means "horse ruler" (Greek, *Archippō*). Paul called him a fellow soldier (Philem. 1:2). He may have been the natural son of Philemon and Apphia (Philem. 1:1–2). Quite possibly, he may have been the pastor of the Colossian church in the absence of Epaphras. This church met in the house of Philemon (Philem. 1:2). Second, Archippus was responsible to the church. Paul gave instructions to the church to speak to Archippus ("say"). The choice of verb shows that the church was to encourage him, not to compel him. Third, Archippus was to be watchful over his ministry. The command "Take heed" denotes scrutiny and vigilance. Fourth, he possessed the ministry (Greek, *tēn diakonian*). This noun can be used either of the office of deacon (1 Tim. 3:8–13) or the general ministry of preaching. Paul identified himself as a minister and claimed that Christ had put him into the ministry (1:23; 1 Tim. 1:12). Fifth, this spiritual ministry came from the Lord and derived its authority from Him ("which you have received in the Lord"). Archippus was ultimately responsible to Christ for his own success or failure.

Closing Remarks (4:18)

Salutation. Paul himself wrote the closing words of his letters (1 Cor. 16:21). He used an amanuensis or secretary to compose the major part of a letter because his eyesight apparently was poor (Rom. 16:22; Gal. 4:15). He always signed the letters so his readers would know they were genuine letters from him (2 Thess. 3:17). He used extremely large letters when he wrote (Gal. 6:11).

Request. Paul asked the Colossian believers to pray for him: "Remember my imprisonment." He did not want to be forgotten in prison. When he wrote, the movement of his hand probably caused the chains to clank.

Henry Alford says this about the closing salutation:

These words extend further than to mere pecuniary support, or even mere prayers: they were ever to keep before [the Colossians] the fact that one who so deeply cared for them, and loved them, and to whom their perils of false doctrine occasioned such anxiety, was a prisoner in chains: and that remembrance was to work and produce its various fruits—of prayer for him, of affectionate remembrance of his wants, of deep regard for his words. When we read of "his chains," we should not forget that they moved over the paper as he wrote. His *right* hand was chained to the soldier that kept him.[8]

Blessing. Paul's closing remarks were direct and simple: "Grace be with you." The heretics elevated legalistic self-effort at the expense of divine grace. People are saved by grace alone, and they should walk by the biblical principles of grace.

STUDY QUESTIONS

1. What are the qualifications for a church representative? How can these qualities be recognized in a believer?

2. How can Christians overcome their early failures in their spiritual lives? Do churches fail to give believers a second chance?

3. How can believers bring comfort and relief to others? How involved should we be in others' lives?

4. What are the marks of a strong prayer life? Do churches spend enough time in corporate prayer?

5. In what ways can laypersons have an effective witness?

6. What is the difference between reading and studying the Bible? What is a good balance?

7. How do believers fail to complete their tasks? How can they break this habit?

SELECTED BIBLIOGRAPHY

Boice, James Montgomery. *Philippians*. Grand Rapids: Zondervan, 1971.

Bruce, F. F. *Philippians*. New International Critical Commentary. Peabody, MA: Hendrickson, 1989.

Carson, Herbert M. *The Epistles of Paul to the Colossians and to Philemon*. Grand Rapids: Eerdmans, 1977.

Harrison, Everett F. *Colossians: Christ All-Sufficient*. Chicago: Moody Press, 1971.

Hendriksen, William. *New Testament Commentary: Exposition of Colossians and Philemon*. Grand Rapids: Baker Book House, 1964.

―――. *New Testament Commentary: Exposition of Philippians*. Grand Rapids: Baker Book House, 1974.

Kent, Homer A., Jr., *Treasures of Wisdom: Studies in Colossians and Philemon*. Grand Rapids: Baker Book House, 1978.

Lightfoot, J. B. *St. Paul's Epistles to the Colossians and to Philemon*. Grand Rapids: Zondervan, 1979.

―――. *Saint Paul's Epistle to the Philippians*. Grand Rapids: Zondervan, 1953.

Martin, Ralph P. *Colossians: The Church's Lord and the Christian's Liberty*. Grand Rapids: Zondervan, 1975.

―――. *The Epistle of Paul to the Philippians*. Grand Rapids: Eerdmans, 1976.

Moule, H. C. G. *Studies in Colossians and Philemon*. Grand Rapids: Kregel, 1977.

Muller, Jac J. *The Epistles of Paul to the Philippians and to Philemon*. Grand Rapids: Eerdmans, 1972.

O'Brian, Peter. *Commentary on Philippians*. Grand Rapids: Eerdmans, 1991.

Pentecost, J. Dwight. *The Joy of Living*. Grand Rapids: Zondervan, 1973.

Robertson, Archibald Thomas. *Word Pictures in the New Testament*. Vol. 4. Nashville: Broadman, 1931.

Silva, Moisés. *Philippians*. Wycliffe Exegetical Commentary. Chicago: Moody Press, 1989.

Simpson, E. K., and Frederick F. Bruce. *Commentary on the Epistles to Ephesians and Colossians*. Grand Rapids: Eerdmans, 1958.

Notes

Chapter 1—Background of Philippians

1. Peter T. O'Brian, *Commentary on Philippians* (Grand Rapids: Eerdmans, 1991), 9-10.

2. Merrill C. Tenney, *New Testament Times* (Grand Rapids: Eerdmans, 1965), 255-56.

3. Probably the reason Luke and Timothy were not seized was because the former was a pure Gentile and the latter was half Greek.

4. In the book of Acts, written by Luke, Luke's presence can be detected in the "we/us" sections of the narrative (cf. Acts 16:10-40).

5. Note the resumption of the "we/us" narrative (Acts 20:5-6) and the continued usage of it throughout the rest of Acts.

6. A better translation for *en holō tō praitōriō* is "among the whole praetorian guard" (soldiers) rather than "in all the palace" (a building).

7. Everett F. Harrison, *Introduction to the New Testament* (Grand Rapids: Eerdmans, 1974), 342.

8. J. B. Lightfoot, *St. Paul's Epistle to the Philippians* (Lynn, MA: Hendrickson, 1981), 67-68.

Chapter 2—Opening Remarks

1. Two early church fathers, Jerome and Augustine, both believed that Paul took his name from Sergius Paulus.

2. J. B. Lightfoot, *St. Paul's Epistle to the Philippians* (Lynn, MA: Hendrickson, 1981), 81.

3. Paul used secretaries in the composition of his other letters (Rom. 16:22; Gal. 6:11; 2 Thess. 3:17).

4. The denominational title *Episcopalian* is the transliteration of this Greek word.

5. The denominational title *Presbyterian* is based on this word.

6. This threefold distinction is made clear in the Greek text: *boske ta arnia mou* (John 21:15); *poimaine ta probata mou* (21:16); and *boske ta probata mou* (21:17).

7. The deity of Jesus Christ is affirmed in this verse by the divine title *Lord* (2:11; 1 Cor. 8:6) and by His union with the Father as the common source of grace and peace.

Chapter 3—The Prayer

1. It is present active indicative. A title for the ordinance of the Lord's Supper, *Eucharist*, is based on the transliteration of this word.

2. The first idea is based on the view that the pronoun *you* is a subjective genitive, whereas the second position considers the pronoun to be an objective genitive.

3. It is a present middle participle.

4. It is a perfect active participle (*pepoithōs*). The perfect tense stresses a present state as a result of a past event.

5. It is an aorist participle (*enarxamenos*).

6. The verb *epitelesei* is a compound word, joining *epi* with *teleō*. The word *telescope* is partially based on this verb.

7. Indicated by the present tense ("have").

8. T. Bently, "Colossians," in *What the Bible Teaches*, eds. T. Wilson and K. Stapley (Kilmarnock, Scotland: John Ritchie, 1983), 201.

9. Indicated by the present active subjunctive.

10. The word "that" introduces a purpose or result of the preceding action. The construction consists of a preposition (*eis*) with an articular infinitive (*to dokimazein*).

11. The verb is a perfect passive participle (*peplērōmenoi*) in a periphrastic construction with "may be" (1:10).

Chapter 4—The Opportunities of Obstacles

1. It is a perfect active indicative of *erchomai*.

2. The next phrase ("and to all the rest") further supports this conclusion.

3. Assuming that no guard was stationed with Paul twice.

4. Markus Bockmuehl, *A Commentary on the Epistle to the Philippians* (London: A. & C. Black, 1997), 80.

Chapter 5—The Blessings of Life and Death

1. Dative, singular, first person personal pronoun.

2. Note the contrast between the tenses of the two Greek infinitives. The first ("to live") is present, whereas the second ("to die") is aorist.

3. The usage of *ei* with the indicative verbal mood introduces a condition true to reality. Although no verb is actually found in this clause, one must be implied.

4. Present active participle.

5. Indicated by the Greek construction: *eis to analusai kai . . . einai*. The purpose preposition *eis* is followed by the article *to*, which joins the two infinitives.

6. It is a present infinitive, whereas the infinitive for departure is aorist.

7. Actually, it is one result with two features. The two nouns, serving as the objects of the preposition, have only one article to designate them: *eis tēn humōn prokopēn kai charan*.

Chapter 6—The Challenge to the Church

1. A report came later, notifying Paul that the church knew about the sickness of Epaphroditus (2:26).

2. The two imperatives are *politeuesthe* (1:27) and *plērōsate* (2:2). The rest of the material is subordinate to these two main verbs.

3. For example, Indianapolis and Minneapolis.

4. Present active indicative.

5. Indicated by the Greek definite article.

6. Aorist active imperative.

7. They are marked by the fourfold usage of "if" (*ei*) and "any" (*tis, ti, tis, tis [tina]*). Grammatically, they are four conditional clauses that assume the reality of the statement.

8. This phrase is emphasized, occurring first in the sentence.

Chapter 7—The Humiliation and Exaltation of Christ

1. The relative clause gives the link between the command (2:5) and the example. Actually, there is no expressed verb in the clause. The past predicate ("was") was supplied to point to Christ's historic incarnation and death.

2. The Jehovah's Witnesses embrace the active position.

3. Albert Barnes, *Barnes' Notes,* 14 vols. (Grand Rapids: Baker, 1983), 12:170-71.

4. Ibid., 171.

5. Theologians identify this truth as the hypostatic union.

6. William Hendriksen, *Philippians, Colossians and Philemon* (Grand Rapids: Baker, 1982), 112.

Chapter 8—The Marks of Humble Service

1. Present middle imperative.

2. J. Dwight Pentecost, *The Joy of Living* (Grand Rapids: Zondervan, 1973), 94.

3. It comes from the verb *kerannumi* ("to mix").

4. It is a perfect passive participle.

Chapter 9—The Three Examples of Humility

1. Indicated by "if" (*ei*) with the present tense.

2. The word *tachometer* is based on this adverb.

3. They are epistolary aorists, viewing the action from the standpoint of the readers. When the church read the letter, Epaphroditus had already been sent.

Chapter 10—The Danger of Legalism

1. Present active imperative.

2. Indicated by the present participle *latreuontes.*

Chapter 11—The Joy of Salvation

1. The verb is a perfect indicative.

2. Frank E. Gaebelein, ed., *The Expositor's Bible Commentary,* 12 vols. (Grand Rapids: Zondervan, 1978), 11:141.

3. James R. White, *The God Who Justifies* (Minneapolis, MN: Bethany House, 2001), 66–67.

4. They are the translation of an articular infinitive, *tou gnōnai.*

5. Perfect passive indicative.

6. Note the present tense of the participles.

Chapter 12—The Joy of Maturity

1. It is a present hortatory subjunctive.

2. Aorist active indicative.

3. Note the two present infinitives: to walk and to be of the same mind.

4. Note the switch from "my" to "us."

5. The pronoun (*hēmōn*) occurs at the very beginning of the sentence.

6. It is a plural noun.

7. R. C. H. Lenski, *The Interpretation of St. Paul's Epistles to the Galatians, Ephesians and Philippians* (Minneapolis, MN: Augsburg, 1961), 861.

8. W. E. Vine, *The Collected Writings of W. E. Vine*, 5 vols. (Nashville: Thomas Nelson, 1996), 2:318.

Chapter 13—The Joy of Peace

1. It is a present verb actually based on a perfect stem.

2. W. Robertson Nicoll, *The Expositor's Greek Testament*, 4 vols. (Grand Rapids: Eerdmans, 1988), 3:466.

3. Present active imperative.

Chapter 14—The Joy of Financial Provision

1. Indicated by the second aorist passive verb.

2. Charles John Ellicott, *Commentary on the Whole Bible*, 8 vols. (Grand Rapids: Zondervan, 1959), 8:88.

3. It is perfect passive indicative.

4. Peter T. O'Brian, *Commentary on Philippians* (Grand Rapids: Eerdmans, 1991), 552.

5. Ibid., 555.

Chapter 15—Background of Colossians

1. T. Bently, *"Colossians,"* in *What the Bible Teaches*, eds. T. Wilson and K. Stapley, (Kilmarnock, Scotland: John Ritchie, 1983), 267.

2. R. C. H. Lenski, *The Interpretation of St. Paul's Epistles to the Colossians, to the Thessalonians, to Timothy, to Titus and to Philemon* (Minneapolis, MN: Augsburg, 1961), 14.

3. Ibid., 266.

4. Ibid., 270.

Chapter 16—The Giving of Thanks

1. Consult the content for Philippians 1:1-3.

2. A causal use of the aorist participle.

3. This is a subjective genitive, meaning that the word in the genitive case ("you") produced the verbal action of the noun preceding it ("faith").

4. It is a present participle used with a perfect sense.

5. It is genitive neuter singular, in grammatical agreement with the gospel.

6. In the verb *epiginōskō*, the prepositional prefix *epi* on the verb stem *ginōsko* intensifies the nature of this knowledge. The title "Gnostic" is based on this verb stem.

7. It is a present middle participle in periphrastic construction with the present indicative of *eimi*.

Chapter 17—The Worthy Walk

1. The first purpose begins with *hina* followed by a subjective purpose clause, whereas the second is introduced by a purpose infinitive *peripatēsai*.

2. The prefix *epi* gives the idea of knowledge upon knowledge.

3. Present middle participle.

4. Homer A. Kent, *Treasures of Wisdom* (Grand Rapids: Baker, 1978), 42.

5. John Eadie, *Commenary on the Epistle to the Colossians* (Grand Rapids: Zondervan, 1957), 36.

Chapter 18—The Exaltation of Christ

1. John Eadie, *Commenary on the Epistle to the Colossians* (Grand Rapids: Zondervan, 1957), 40-41.

2. W. E. Vine, *The Collected Writings of W. E. Vine*, 5 vols. (Nashville: Thomas Nelson, 1996), 2:339–40.

3. Ibid.

4. This is the theological position of the Jehovah's Witnesses, a group that denies both the Trinity and the deity of Christ.

5. W. Robertson Nicoll, *The Expositor's Greek Testament*, 4 vols. (Grand Rapids: Eerdmans, 1988), 3:502.

6. The first verb is in the aorist tense, and the second is in the perfect.

7. The verb is perfect active indicative.

8. R. C. H. Lenski, *The Interpretation of St. Paul's Epistles to the Colossians, to the Thessalonians, to Timothy, to Titus and to Philemon* (Minneapolis, MN: Augsburg, 1961), 58.

Chapter 19—The Work of God and Man

1. Aorist active infinitive.

2. John MacArthur, *The MacArthur New Testament Commentary*, "Colossians & Philemon" (Chicago: Moody, 1992), 61.

3. There are four types of Greek conditional clauses. This is a first-class clause. The same type is used later (3:1).

Chapter 20—The Means of Perfection

1. The English word *stereo*, as in *stereophonic*, is based on this word.

2. Suggested by the perfect passive participle.

3. R. C. H. Lenski, *The Interpretation of St. Paul's Epistles to the Colossians, to the Thessalonians, to Timothy, to Titus and to Philemon* (Minneapolis, MN: Augsburg, 1961), 97.

Chapter 21—The Identification with Christ

1. It occurs before the verb both in the English and Greek texts.

2. Marvin R. Vincent, *Word Studies in the New Testament*, 4 vols. (Peabody, MA: Hendrickson, n.d.), 3:487.

3. This is a periphrastic usage of the perfect passive participle with the present indicative: *este . . . peplērōmenoi.*

4. Vincent, *Word Studies*, 3:490.

Chapter 22—The Contrast in Doctrine

1. They are all nominative singular participles agreeing with the subject of the imperative.

2. The critical Greek text omits the negative.

3. It uses the conditional particle *ei* with the aorist indicative *apethanete*. It is the same type of clause as that in 1:23.

4. William Hendriksen, *Philippians, Colossians and Philemon* (Grand Rapids: Baker, 1982), 112.

Chapter 23—The Change in Behavior

1. Aorist active imperative. It could be ingressive or constative.

2. The term *pornography* is based on this Greek word.

3. Note the usage of the Greek article with the noun.

4. Frank E. Gaebelein, ed., *The Expositor's Bible Commentary*, 12 vols. (Grand Rapids: Zondervan, 1978), 11:212.

5. It is a futuristic present.

6. It is a constative aorist.

7. Aorist middle imperative.

8. Present passive participle.

9. Gaebelein, *Expositor's Bible Commentary*, 11:213.

10. Aorist middle imperative.

11. Perfect passive participle.

12. Charles John Ellicott, *Commentary on the Whole Bible*, 8 vols. (Grand Rapids: Zondervan, 1959), 8:114.

13. Albert Barnes, *Barnes' Notes*, 14 vols. (Grand Rapids: Baker, 1983), 12:278.

14. The relative pronoun "which" (*hē*) is in the feminine gender, agreeing with its antecedent "peace" (*eirēnē*).

15. The phrase "in all wisdom" can go grammatically with either the imperative or the participle.

16. Barnes, *Barnes' Notes*, 11:279–80.

Chapter 24—The Responsibilities of Believers

1. The first identifies the verb in the middle voice; the second in the passive. Both voices in the present tense use the same Greek ending.

2. Present active imperative.

3. Present active imperative.

4. Present active imperative. It is the same verb as that used for the children.

5. Present middle imperative.

6. It is debatable whether this verse (3:25) pertains only to the slave, only to the master, or to both. The general principle applies to both, but its primary application here is to the slave.

7. Author's view.

8. Present active imperative.

9. Charles John Ellicott, *Commentary on the Whole Bible*, 8 vols. (Grand Rapids: Zondervan, 1959), 11:116.

Chapter 25—The Blessing of Friends

1. Four, if the Laodicean letter was not one of these.

2. The term can be understood in either way.

3. This speculation is based on the fact that only the Gospel of Mark contains this account.

4. The verb could be an epistolary aorist.

5. The critical Greek text used "pain" *(ponon)*.

6. Indicated by the "we" and "us" sections in Acts. Luke, the author, inserted himself into the narrative in this way.

7. The UBS Greek text reads "Nympha" (feminine) rather than "Nymphas" (masculine). The subsequent pronoun is also changed from "his" to "her."

8. Henry Alford, *The Greek Testament*, 4 vols. (Chicago: Moody Press, 1958), 3:247.

About the Author

Robert Gromacki is Distinguished Professor Emeritus of Bible and Greek at Cedarville University, where he has taught for more than forty years. Outside of his ministry at Cedarville, he is perhaps best known for his *New Testament Survey*, a major textbook in colleges and seminaries throughout the United States. His other publications include *The Virgin Birth, Salvation Is Forever*, and *The Holy Spirit*, a part of the Swindoll Leadership Library Series. Dr. Gromacki received his Th.M. from Dallas Theological Seminary and his Th.D. from Grace Theological Seminary. For the last several years, Dr. Gromacki has served as pastor of Grace Community Church in Washington Court House, Ohio.

About the General Editors

Mal Couch is founder and president of Tyndale Theological Seminary and Biblical Institute in Fort Worth, Texas. He previously taught at Philadelphia College of the Bible, Moody Bible Institute, and Dallas Theological Seminary. His other publications include *The Hope of Christ's Return: A Premillennial Commentary on 1 and 2 Thessalonians, A Bible Handbook to Revelation*, and *Dictionary of Premillennial Theology*.

Edward Hindson is professor of religion, dean of the Institute of Biblical Studies, and assistant to the chancellor at Liberty University in Lynchburg, Virginia. He has authored more than twenty books, served as coeditor of several Bible projects, and was one of the translators for the New King James Version of the Bible. Dr. Hindson has served as a visiting lecturer at both Oxford University and Harvard Divinity School as well as numerous evangelical seminaries. He has taught over fifty thousand students in the past twenty-five years.